T0339817

THE ROAD TO THE THRONE

THE ROAD TO THE THRONE

HOW LIU BANG
FOUNDED CHINA'S HAN DYNASTY

HUNG HING MING

Algora Publishing
New York

Library of Congress Cataloging-in-Publication Data —

Hung, Hing Ming.
    The road to the throne: how Liu Bang founded China's Han dynasty / Hing Ming
Hung.
       p. cm.
    Includes index.
    ISBN 978-0-87586-837-0 (soft cover: alk. paper) — ISBN 978-0-87586-838-7 (hard
cover: alk. paper) — ISBN 978-0-87586-839-4 (ebook) 1. Han Gaozu, Emperor of China,
247-195 B.C. 2. China—Kings and rulers—Biography. 3. China—History—Han dynasty,
202 B.C.-220 A.D. I. Title.
    DS748.16.H354H86 2011
    931'.04—dc22
                           2011004225

Front cover: Liu Bang, Emperor Gaozu

Printed in the United States

TABLE OF CONTENTS

INTRODUCTION   1

CHAPTER 1: THE BACKGROUND   5

  1. The Period of Warring States (403 BC–221 BC)   5

  2. The Birth of Liu Bang   7

  3. Ying Zheng, King of the State of Qin, Unifies China   7

  4. Under the Rule of the Qin Dynasty   10

  5. The Death of the First Emperor of the Qin Dynasty   12

  6. Liu Bang Kills a Great Serpent and Rises Up in Rebellion 17

CHAPTER 2: THE GREAT UPRISINGS AGAINST THE QIN DYNASTY   21

  7. The Uprising Led by Chen Sheng and Wu Guang   21

  8. The Reinstatement of the States of Zhao and Yan   23

  9. The Reinstatement of the States of Qi and Wei   24

  10. Counterattack by the Army of the Qin Dynasty   24

  11. Liu Bang Revolts in Pei County   25

  12. Xiang Liang and Xiang Yu Rebel in the Area to the East of the
     Yangtze River   27

  13. The Great Changes in the State of Zhao   29

  14. Liu Bang's Military Operations   30

  15. The Death of Chen Sheng, King of Zhang Chu   31

  16. Qin Jia Makes Jing Ju King of the State of Chu   32

  17. Xiang Liang and Xiang Yu Lead their Army to the Area to the West
     of the Yangtze River   35

18. Xiong Xin Is Made King Huai of the State of Chu   37
19. The Setbacks Suffered by the State of Chu and the Death of Xiang Liang   39

CHAPTER 3: THE COMMON EFFORT TO OVERTHROW THE QIN DYNASTY   47

20. The Promise Made by King Huai of the State of Chu   47
21. The Battle of Julu   51
22. Liu Bang's March to the Area of Guanzhong   57
23. Zhang Han Surrenders to Xiang Yu   65
24. Zhao Gao Kills the Second Emperor of the Qin Dynasty and Puts Ying Zi Ying on the Throne of the State of Qin   67
25. Liu Bang Takes the Area of Qin, and Ying Zi Ying, the King of the State of Qin, Surrenders to Liu Bang   68
26. Xiang Yu's March to the Area of Guanzhong   72
27. The Banquet in Hongmen   76
28. The Making of Kings   81
29. Liu Bang's March into Hanzhong   87
30. The Rebellion of the State of Qi and the State of Zhao against Xiang Yu   89
31. Han Xin Is Appointed Commander-in-Chief of the Army of Han   91

CHAPTER 4: THE STRUGGLE BETWEEN LIU BANG AND XIANG YU   99

32. Liu Bang's Actions to Pacify the Area of Guanzhong   99
33. Xiang Yu's Decision to Attack the State of Qi   104
34. Liu Bang's Actions to Conquer the Areas around the Yellow River   106
35. The Battle of Pengcheng   111
36. Liu Bang Meets Qi Ji   114
37. Liu Bang's Strategic Decision in Xiayi   115
38. Wei Bao's Betrayal of Liu Bang   119
39. The Battle to Defeat the King of the State of Wei   120
40. The Battle of Jingxing   124
41. Ying Bu Turns against Xiang Yu   130
42. Chen Ping's Tricks to Drive a Wedge between Xiang Yu and His Devoted Followers   131
43. Ji Xin Dies for Liu Bang and Xingyang Falls   133
44. Li Yi Ji's Advice to Take Chenggao   139
45. Li Yi Ji's Plan to Persuade the King of the State of Qi to Surrender   140
46. Han Xin Defeats the State of Qi   141
47. The Battles of Chenggao   143
48. Bo Ji Becomes Liu Bang's Concubine and Liu Heng Is Born   144
49. The Confrontation between Liu Bang and Xiang Yu in Guangwu Mountain Area   144
50. Xiang Yu Threatens to Cook Liu Bang's Father into Soup   145
51. Han Xin Pacifies the State of Qi   147

52. Han Xin Is Made King of the State of Qi	149
53. The Decisive Battle in Gaixia	153
54. Peace and Order Resumes in the Realm	163

CHAPTER 5: THE FOUNDING OF THE HAN DYNASTY — 167

55. Liu Bang Becomes Emperor of the Han Dynasty	167
56. Happy Family Reunion	169
57. The Three Outstanding Persons of the Han Dynasty	170
58. Tian Heng, the Former King of the State of Qi, and His Five Hundred Followers	170
59. Liu Bang Moves His Capital from Luoyang to Guanzhong	172
60. Zhang Liang Retires from the Scene of State Affairs	174
61. The Rebellion of Zang Tu, the King of the State of Yan	175
62. Lu Wan Is Made King of the State of Yan	176
63. Han Xin's Conspiracy for Rebellion	177
64. The Creation of Marquises	179
65. The Creation of the Second Batch of Marquises	187
66. The Rise of the Huns	192
67. The King of the State of Haan Is Transferred to Defend the Northern Frontier against the Huns	194
68. Haan Xin, the King of the State of Haan, Betrays the Han Dynasty and Defects to the Huns	194
69. Liu Jing's Advice to Improve Relations with the Huns	198
70. The Emperor's Intention to Replace the Crown Prince	199
71. Chen Xi's Rebellion and the End of Han Xin	200
72. The End of Haan Xin, the Former King of the State of Haan	203
73. Kuai Che Is Spared by the Emperor	204
74. The Death of Peng Yue, the King of the State of Liang	205
75. Zhang Liang's Plan to Stabilize the Position of the Crown Prince	207
76. The Rebellion of Ying Bu, the King of the State of Huainan	208
77. The Emperor's Visit to Pei, His Hometown	213
78. Liu Bi Is Made King of the State of Wu	214
79. The Areas of Dai Are Pacified	214
80. Liu Bang's Last Effort to Replace the Crown Prince	214
81. Premier Xiao Is Jailed	216
82. Lu Wan's Rebellion	219
83. The Death of Liu Bang, the Emperor of the Han Dynasty	223

CHAPTER 6: MEMBERS OF THE LÜ FAMILY CONSPIRE TO USURP THE THRONE AND LIU HENG ASCENDS TO THE THRONE OF THE HAN DYNASTY — 227

84. Troubles in the Palace after Liu Bang's Death	227
85. Cao Shen Succeeds Xiao He as Premier of the Han Dynasty	228

86. The Death of Zhang Liang, Marquis of Liu 230

87. Empress Dowager Lü Zhi Takes Power 230

88. The Death of Empress Dowager Lü Zhi 234

89. The Lü Family is Exterminated 235

90. Liu Heng, King of the State of Dai, Ascends the Throne of the Han
    Dynasty 238

Introduction

My goal in writing this book is to tell a story for the American people, the story of a great Chinese emperor from ancient times. Translation is a good way to convey foreign history, but in this case translation alone cannot fulfill the purpose. To round out the history, I have had to select material from a variety of biographies and organize all the different parts, sometimes using a bit of imagination to fill in details of the background and environment that would hold the narrative together; and I have used reasonable inference and drawn attention to some of the interrelations of historical events in order to present the story of this vivid character in all its full color.

Interwoven into the chronological narrative of battles fought and alliances forged, forced, or flouted, we find lessons in diplomacy and gamesmanship, examples of good leadership versus bad, hot-headed fighters versus disciplined warriors who bide their time and win the day, and examples of how to test people's loyalty, gauge a man's weaknesses, win over public opinion, and prevail under the most disadvantageous conditions. In an era we may think was run only by sheer force and autocratic rule, the official record teaches that the greatest achievements were won by the persons who recognized others' talents and accepted advice, who rewarded wise subordinates, and who shared the wealth rather than playing winner-takes-all.

For English-speaking readers who are less familiar with Chinese pronunciation, I should note that different names may seem very similar to each other. However, each vowel is pronounced separately, so that Han and Haan are in fact quite different, and Xiang (pronounced something like "Shi-ang") is distinct from Zhang. Further, family names are followed by given names, and it is no mistake if you come across relatives named Tian Jiao and Tian Jian, or Liu Heng and Liu Hong.

The stories of this period are so popular in China that some of them have been made into dramas, including "Xiao He Runs After Han Xin in the Moonlit Night" and "Xiang Yu Says Farewell to His Concubine Yu Ji," while many set phrases in Chinese are derived from the stories of this period, such as "breaking the cooking utensils and sinking the ships," "banquet in Hongmen," "secretly marching to Chencang," "monkey in a human hat," and "Walking in the dark wearing a beautifully embroidered robe."

Most of the material used in writing *The Road to the Throne* are taken from the "Records of the Grand Historian" (Chinese: 史記 or shiji) by the great Sima Qian (145 BC–85BC) of the Early Han Dynasty, which is not only a great work of history but also a great work of literature. The book launched a system for relating history: by describing historical events through individual biographies of emperors, kings, marquises, generals and officials. The same historical event is reflected in several biographies, so that the descriptions add up to form the full view of an event. Thus in order to get a proper picture of the historical record, I read all the biographies concerned and picked out the related facts, then put them together to tell this story.

Some of the materials are taken from "History of the Former Han Dynasty" (Chinese: 前漢書 or qianhanshu) by Ban Gu (32–92) of the Later Han Dynasty. This book basically follows the system laid down by the Records of the Grand Historian.

"A Comprehensive Mirror for the Aid of Government" (Chinese: 資治通鑑 or zizhitongjian) by Sima Guang (1019–1086) of the Song Dynasty is a Chronicle. I used this book as well, as a thread to link all the materials pulled from different sources.

Portrait of Liu Bang, Emperor Gaozu of the Han Dynasty, (256 BC–195 BC)

Map of China

CHAPTER 1: THE BACKGROUND

1. THE PERIOD OF WARRING STATES (403 BC–221 BC)

During the period of Warring States, over two thousand years ago, China consisted of seven states. They were the State of Qi (now the most part of Shandong Province), the State of Chu (now the areas of Jiangsu Province, Anhui Province, Hubei Province and Hunan Province), the State of Zhao (now the southern part of Hebei Province and northern part of Shanxi Province), the State of Yan (now the northern part of Hebei Province and the west part of Liaoning Province), the State of Wei (now the northern part of Henan Province and southern part of Shanxi Province), the State of Haan (now northwest part of Henan Province and the southern part of Shanxi Province) and the State of Qin (now Shaanxi Province and Sichuan Province and the east part of Gansu Province).

The seven states waged wars against one another. The State of Qin had the topographical advantage. It was composed of two parts: the area of Guanzhong in the north and the area of Ba and Shu in the south. "Guanzhong" means the area within the mountain passes, and indeed Guanzhong was surrounded by high mountains, broken by four passes. Hanguguan Pass was in the east, Wuguan Pass in the south, Xiaoguan Pass in the north and Sanguan Pass in the west. To the east, the area of Guanzhong was protected by the Yellow River as well as the mountains.

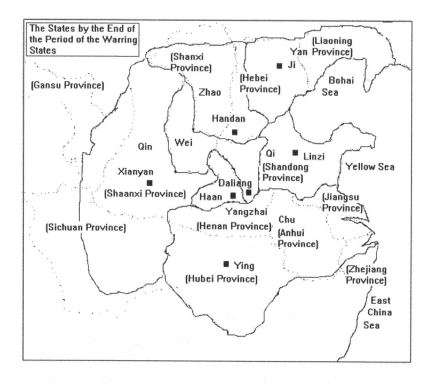

The land of the State of Qin was rich and the people were valiant. Due to new governmental measures taken in 361 BC, agricultural production and military contribution were encouraged. In ten years time, Qin became the strongest of the states. Then the six states in the east allied with each other to deal with the State of Qin; in response, the State of Qin made allies with distant states and attacked the neighboring ones.

In September 260 BC, the army of the State of Qin under the command of General Bai Qi and the army of the State of Zhao under the command of General Zhao Kuo fought a battle in Changping (now to the northwest of Gaoping County of Shanxi Province). The Qin army won a resounding victory over the Zhao army. Zhao Kuo was killed in this battle and 450,000 soldiers of the State of Zhao were captured. The cruel General Bai Qi of the State of Qin issued an order to kill all of the captives, and with several days, all 450,000 Zhao soldiers were indeed killed and buried. From then on, the State of Zhao was no match for the State of Qin. This battle laid a solid foundation for the State of Qin to unify the whole realm of China.

2. THE BIRTH OF LIU BANG

By the end of the period of Warring States, a peasant named Liu Zhi Jia with his wife and two sons lived in Zhongyangli of Fengyi (now Peixian, Jiangsu Province), within the State of Chu. They earned their living by toiling in the fields. One day, the peasant's wife went out of the house. It was spring, and the sun was shining warmly. While she was walking along the edge of a marsh, she felt sleepy, so she lay on the ground and fell into a deep sleep. A moment later, the sky became dark, clouds were gathering, and thunder and lightning filled the sky. Liu Zhi Jia waited for his wife for quite some time and began worrying about her, so he decided to go out to see what had happened. Bringing a bamboo hat, he went out to look for his wife. When he found his sleeping wife by the edge of the marsh, he was astonished. A dragon was floating up and down above her, and sometimes the dragon got very close to her. Despite the deafening thunder and blinding lightning, she was sleeping peacefully with a smile of satisfaction on her face. Some time later, the sky cleared and the sun shone again. His wife woke up. Liu Zhi Jia asked her what had happened. She said, with blushes on her cheeks, that she had met a god in her dream, and the god was very intimate to her. Not long later, she found she was pregnant. Ten months later, in 256 BC, she gave birth to a very healthy baby boy. The peasant named his third son Liu Bang.

Liu Bang grew up and became a tall handsome man with a straight and high nose and a beautiful beard. He was kind-hearted, benevolent, open-minded and magnanimous. He did not like to do farm work but he liked to make friends, and often brought them home to have meals.

3. YING ZHENG, KING OF THE STATE OF QIN, UNIFIES CHINA

Ying Zheng succeeded his father Ying Yi Ren to the throne of the State of Qin in May 247 BC at the age of thirteen. Some years later, he began to expand his reach. In 230 BC, he sent General Nei Shi Teng to attack the State of Haan, the nearest state, and captured Haan An, the king. Now the King of the State of Qin turned the State of Haan into the Prefecture of Yingchuan. In 229 BC, he sent General Wang Jian to attack the State of Zhao, and in 228 BC, General Wang Jian captured Zhao Qian, King of the State of Zhao. Zhao Qian's son Zhao Zi Jia escaped to the area of Dai (now the northern part of Shanxi Province) and claimed himself King of the State of Dai. In

227 BC, the King of the State of Qin sent General Wang Jian to attack the State of Yan. A decisive battle was fought on the West bank of Yishui River within the territory of the State of Yan and the Yan army was defeated. In 226 BC, General Wang Jian and his son Wang Ben took Ji (which is now Beijing), the capital of the State of Yan. The King of the State of Yan escaped to Liaodong (now Liaoyang, Liaoning Province). In 225 BC, King of the State of Qin sent General Wang Ben to attack the State of Wei. The General ordered his soldiers to dig a channel to divert water from the Yellow River to flood the city of Daliang (now Kaifeng, Henan Province), the capital of the State of Wei. Wei Jia, King of the State of Wei, surrendered.

In 224 BC, the King of the State of Qin sent General Wang Jian with a great army of 600,000 men to attack the State of Chu. The Qin army defeated the Chu army in Pingyu (now Pingyu, Henan Province). When General Xiang Yan, the commander-in-chief of the Chu army, saw that he had lost the battle, he drew out his sword and killed himself. The victorious army of the State of Qin occupied cities and towns of the State of Chu. In 223 BC, General Wang Jian captured Fu Chu, the King of the State of Chu, and the territory the State of Chu was dissolved into several prefectures of the State of Qin.

In 222 BC, the King of the State of Qin sent Wang Ben to attack Liaodong; and he captured Ji Xi, the King of the State of Yan. In the same year, Wang Ben marched his army to the State of Dai and captured Zhao Zi Jia, the local king. In 221 BC, Wang Ben with his great army marched from the southern part of the State of Yan into the land of the State of Qi and captured Tian Jian, the king. From then on the six states of China were unified as one.

Since the whole of China was unified as one, the rulers of the State of Qin became the Qin Dynasty: the King of the State of Qin changed his title to Emperor of the Qin Dynasty, taking the name of "First Emperor of the Qin Dynasty." He assigned his successor the designation of "Second Emperor of the Qin Dynasty," and so on, to the Fifth and endless emperors of the Qin Dynasty. By doing so, he hoped that his dynasty would last forever.

He divided the whole realm into 36 prefectures, all of which were under the central government. In order to prevent the people from rebelling against the Qin Dynasty, he ordered that all the weapons from the original six states be collected and he had such weapons smelted into twelve enormous metal figures, each of which weighed 170 tons. He did not allow the people to have any weapons; five households were allowed to share one metal knife for kitchen use.

Portrait of the First Emperor of the Qin Dynasty

He sent General Meng Tian to drive the Huns out of the area of the Great Bend of the Yellow River (in the east part of Ningxia Hui Autonomous Region, and the south part of Inner Mongolia Autonomous Region). In order to prevent the Huns from entering the areas of the Qin Dynasty, he ordered a great wall to be built. Thousands and thousands of people were sent to build this great wall, and many of them died performing this extraordinary task. And many people were sent to build the Epang Palaces and the mausoleum of the First Emperor of the Qin Dynasty. The Chinese people lived in great suffering.

4. UNDER THE RULE OF THE QIN DYNASTY

According to the administrative system of the Qin Dynasty, the whole realm was divided into 36 prefectures. Under a prefecture, there were counties. Each county was divided into several townships. A township was divided into several sub-townships, which were the grassroots units. After the State of Chu had been conquered by the State of Qin, the area of Pei became Pei County in the Prefecture of Sishui. In the east part of Pei County, there was a sub-township named Sishuiting which covered an area of about five square miles. Four officials ran the sub-township. One was in charge the overall work—the chief of the sub-township; two were in charge of public security—catching thieves. One was in charge of clerical work. Liu Bang applied for the job, and after some time practicing, he was appointed as the chief of the sub-township. At that time, he was already 36 years old.

As a junior official from a small place, Liu Bang often went to the county government office to report on his work. There he made friends with Xiao He, who was in charge of secretarial work of the county government office; Cao Shen, who was in charge of the jails of Pei County; Xiahou Ying, who was also a junior official in the county town; and Ren Ao, who was a jail keeper. Every time Liu Bang went to the county town, they got together to drink wine and have a hearty talk. Xiao He took good care of Liu Bang. Whenever Liu Bang was sent out for work in Xianyang, the capital of the Qin Dynasty, Xiao He gave Liu Bang 500 coins, while he only gave 300 coins to others. Whenever the work of the chiefs of the townships and sub-townships was appraised, Xiao He always reported to the governor of Pei County that Liu Bang was the best.

Liu Bang was once appointed to escort some people to Xianyang to work on building the Epang Palace in Epang near Xianyang for the First Emperor of the Qin Dynasty. After he delivered the people to the government authority, he took the opportunity to walk around the capital. While he was taking in the scenery, he saw a great procession coming out of the palace. He stood by the roadside and looked on. The First Emperor of the Qin Dynasty was taking a tour around the capital. Liu Bang looked at the magnificent procession and grand carriages with great admiration. When the procession passed, he said to himself, "A true man should lead a life as great as the life of this emperor."

In the prime of his life, Liu Bang was still single. It seemed that he did not care very much about marriage. It so happened that an old man by the name of Lü Gong from Shanfu County came with his family to visit the governor of Peifeng County, with whom he was good friends. Lü Gong decided to settle down in this county town. In order to celebrate his arrival, the governor of the county held a banquet in the new home of the Lü family. Xiao He was in charge of the banquet. He set the rule that the officials who contributed less than 1,000 coins would have to sit in the outer hall, and those who contributed over 1,000 would be regarded as distinguished guests and would be invited to sit in the inner hall with the host. When the time came, Xiao He's protégé Liu Bang handed him a note on which was written "10,000 coins as gift," but actually he had not brought any money with him. Xiao He had to usher him into the inner hall.

Lü Gong, being a very good fortune-teller, was greatly surprised at Liu Bang's appearance. Lü Gong immediately stood up, went to the door and led Liu Bang to the table of the host and the high-ranking officials. Although Liu Bang was a very low-ranking official, he talked very freely with the host and the officials. He drank freely during the banquet. When the banquet was over and the guests were leaving, Lü Gong eyed Liu Bang, signaling that he wanted him to stay. After all the guests had left, they sat down for some more drinks. Then, Lü Gong said to Liu Bang, "I have done a lot of fortune-telling for many people by reading their faces. But none of them has a face as noble as yours. I hope you will seize your chance and work hard for your bright future. I have a daughter named Lü Zhi. I want to marry her to you so that she can take care of your household." Liu Bang accepted Lü Gong's offer with pleasure. After Liu Bang had left, Lü Gong's wife said angrily, "You always wanted to marry our daughter to a nobleman. The governor, who is a nobleman, once expressed his intention to marry our daughter, but you refused. Now you have promised to marry our daughter to Liu Bang without asking my opinion. Is Liu Bang a nobleman?" Lü Gong said, "A woman such as you will not be able to understand this." So Lü Zhi was married to Liu Bang.

Not long later she gave birth to a baby girl. The girl was named Liu Yuan. Several years later, she gave birth to a baby boy. The boy was named Liu Ying.

Liu Bang worked most of the time away from home and only came back on vacation. Lü Zhi and her two children stayed home to do farm work. One day, while Lü Zhi was working in the fields with her two children, an old man walked past. When he saw that there was a pot of water, he begged Lü Zhi to give him some water, for he was very thirsty. Lü Zhi immediately poured some water in a bowl and gave it to the old man. When the old man was drinking water, he studied Lü Zhi's face. Then he said, "You will be the noblest lady in all the realm." Then she brought the two children in front of the old man and asked him to foretell their fortune. The old man studied the boy's face carefully, and then said to Lü Zhi, "You will be very noble because of this boy." After studying the face of Liu Yuan, the old man said, "This girl will be very noble too." After that, the old man walked on his way.

It happened that Liu Bang was on vacation that day, and went to the fields to look for his wife and the two children. When he arrived, his wife said, "Just now an old man foretold our fortune. He said that all of us three will be very noble persons. You'd better go fast to catch up with the old man so that he can tell your fortune, too." Liu Bang ran quickly and caught up with the old man. After reading Liu Bang's face carefully, the old man said, "Just now I read the face of the son of a lady. He bears a strong resemblance to you. You have an extremely noble appearance. You will enjoy extreme power." Liu Bang bowed to the old man and said, "If I become rich and noble as you have predicted, I will repay your kindness handsomely." The old man walked on and disappeared.

5. THE DEATH OF THE FIRST EMPEROR OF THE QIN DYNASTY

The First Emperor of the Qin Dynasty wanted to live forever. It was said that a potion for immortality could be found in the islands far out at sea. Anyone who took the medicine would become an immortal. The First Emperor of the Qin Dynasty made a long trip from Xianyang to Langya (now Longya Shan, in the south of Shandong Peninsula) which was by the Yellow Sea. He decided to send people to the sea to look for this medicine.

Xu Shi, a local resident of Langya, came to see the First Emperor of the Qin Dynasty. He told the Emperor that there were three islands out there: Penglai Island, Fangzhang Island and Yingzhou Island; and these islands were inhabited by immortals. He promised to go out to sea to search the islands for the potion for immortality. So the First Emperor of the Qin Dynasty sent Xu Shi out to sea, with a fleet headed by Xu Shi, with 3,000 young boys and 3,000 young girls and seeds of grain. On the day when they sailed out of the harbor of Langya, the First Emperor of the Qin Dynasty sat on the Langya Platform (Langya Tai, up the Langya Hill, overlooking the harbor of Langya) to see them off.

It is said that Xu Shi and the 3,000 boys and 3,000 girls sailed to Japan and settled down there.

In 218 BC, the First Emperor of the Qin Dynasty started his second trip to the east. When the procession reached Bolangsha (now southeast of Yuanyang, Henan Province), two men launched a surprise attack with the intention of assassinating the emperor. They lay in ambush by the roadside. When the procession arrived, they saw several identical carriages. They could not decide which one the First Emperor of the Qin Dynasty was in. One of the two men, with unusual strength, threw a sixty kilogram hammer at one of those carriages and hit it dead on. Unfortunately, there was no one but a driver in the carriage. The driver was killed by that heavy hammer. The Emperor gave the order to search for the assassins. But they had run away and disappeared.

In October 211 BC, the First Emperor of the Qin Dynasty went on a tour to the east part of the country. Premier Li Si went with him. Prince Ying Hu Hai, the youngest son of the First Emperor of the Qin Dynasty, went with him. When the procession reached Pingyuan (now Pingyuan, Shandong Province) in July 210 BC, the First Emperor fell ill. He hated any mention of the word "death," so none of his courtiers dared to ask him what should be done if he should die. When his illness worsened and knew he was going to die, he asked Zhao Gao, a eunuch (a castrated manservant) in charge of legal affairs, to write a letter to his eldest son Prince Ying Fu Su, asking the Prince to go back to Xianyang to preside over his funeral.

Prince Ying Fu Su was at that time the supervisor of a great army of 300,000 men under the command of General Meng Tian stationed in the north border around the Great Wall. The letter was sealed and was kept by Zhao Gao. Before an envoy was sent to take the letter to Prince Fu Su, the First Emperor of the Qin Dynasty died in Shaqiu (now Guangzong, Hebei Province). Considering that Shaqiu was far away from Xianyang and it would be a long time before Prince Fu Su could respond, Premier Li Si decided to keep the emperor's death secret to avoid an inevitable battle for the throne between the sons of the First Emperor who were in the capital. Only Premier Li Si, Zhao Gao, Prince Hu Hai and several eunuchs knew that the First Emperor of the Qin Dynasty had died. The procession went on its way.

Now Zhao Gao decided to make use of the letter. Zhao Gao was very experienced in legal affairs and knew very well how to judge cases; he had been promoted by the First Emperor to take charge of legal matters, and he was engaged to teach Prince Hu Hai how to judge cases. In the past he had developed a grudge against Meng Tian and his brother Meng Yi. Now, since the letter was in his hands, he could use it to kill Meng Tian and Meng Yi.

Zhao Gao went to persuade Prince Hu Hai to agree with his scheme. He would write a letter in the name of the First Emperor ordering Ying Fu Su and Meng Tian to kill themselves. In return, Prince Ying Hu Hai would be made the crown prince. Zhao Gao added, "We have to discuss this matter with Premier Li Si. Without his cooperation, we cannot succeed." And he went to talk with Li Si. He said, "Now the First Emperor has written a letter to his eldest son and has decided to give him the seal of the emperor. Prince Hu Hai keeps the letter and the seal. As for who will be the crown prince, you and I have the power to decide. What shall we do?" Li Si said, "How can you say a thing like that! We are only subjects of the emperor. It's not for us to go against his will!" Zhao Gao said, "Do you think you compare with Meng Tian in ability, strategy, contributions, and the trust of Prince Ying Fu Su, the eldest son of the First Emperor?" Li Si knew he did not. Zhao Gao continued, "If Prince Ying Fu Su becomes emperor, he will certainly appoint Meng Tian as the premier. Then you will clearly have to retire and go home. Prince Ying Hu Hai is a kind and sincere person. He may succeed to the throne. Think about it and tell me your decision." Li Si agreed with him. Then they made up an order in the name of the First Emperor of the Qin Dynasty stating that Prince Hu Hai would be made the crown prince. They wrote another letter to Prince Ying Fu Su in the name of the First Emperor, stating that Ying Fu Su had never made any contribution in expanding the territory of the Qin Dynasty but had criticized the First Emperor of the Qin Dynasty in his statements to the emperor and complained that he was not allowed to go back to the capital to be the crown prince. The letter also stated that General Meng Tian had not corrected Prince Fu Su's mistake. It was ordered in the letter that Prince Fu Su and General Meng Tian should kill themselves and the army should be handed over to General Wang Li, General Wang Jian's grandson.

The Mausoleum of the First Emperor of the Qin Dynasty

When Prince Ying Fu Su received the letter, he cried and went to his own room, drew out his sword and was ready to kill himself. General Meng Tian said, "His Majesty is away from the capital on a tour. He has entrusted 300,000 soldiers to me to defend the border. His Majesty appointed you as supervisor of the army. How can you kill yourself on the basis of a letter sent by an envoy? Are you sure that the letter is really written by His Majesty? You'd better make sure by asking His Majesty himself. You have time to be sure that the order was really issued by His Majesty." But the envoy urged them once and again. And Prince Ying Fu Su said, "If the son is ordered by his father to kill himself, he should kill himself immediately." With his own sword, Prince Ying Fu Su killed himself. General Meng Tian refused to commit suicide; he was arrested and put into prison. Prince Ying Hu Hai also gave an order to arrest Meng Yi and threw him into jail. Not long afterward, Meng Tian and Meng Yi were killed. The procession hurriedly made their way back. As soon as they reached Xianyang, the death of the First Emperor of the Qin Dynasty was announced. Crown Prince Ying Hu Hai succeeded to the throne, and he became the Second Emperor of the Qin Dynasty. In September 210 BC, the funeral of the First Emperor of the Qin Dynasty was held. He was buried at the foot of Lishan Mountain in the outskirts of Xianyang.

A Standing Archer from the Terracotta Army

Copper carriage and horses unearthed near the Mausoleum of the First Emperor of the Qin Dynasty

The Terracotta Army of the Qin Dynasty

6. Liu Bang Kills a Great Serpent and Rises Up in Rebellion

Under the severe rule of the Qin Dynasty, people were conscripted to hard labor for the construction of the Great Wall, the building of Epang Palaces, and the tomb for the First Emperor in the Lishan Mountains, or to garrison the frontiers. Every day, people were on the roads making their way to the places they had been sent. They had to reach their destination on time; otherwise, they would be put to death. In 209 BC, the Second Emperor issued an order to all the counties to send people to Lishan Mountain to complete the construction of the First Emperor's mausoleum. The county government of Pei rounded up about a hundred criminals from the jails, and Liu Bang was assigned the task of escorting the convoy to the Lishan Mountains near Xianyang.

On the way, many of the criminals escaped. Several days after the convoy had left Pei County, they reached the bank of a big marsh which was about a hundred miles away from home. A pavilion stood on the top of a hill by the marsh. An old man was selling wine and food in the pavilion. Liu Bang left the criminals outside while he walked into the pavilion and bought two bowls of wine and a dish and sat down beside a table facing west. It was late afternoon. The sun was setting. The sky in the west was red with the sinking sun. Liu Bang could see the rolling hills of Mang-Dang Mountains lying in the northwest against the red sky. Close by, he could see the great marsh with its mud and reflecting waters. There was a road through the marsh leading to the distant Mang-Dang Mountains. Liu Bang fell into deep thought. Nearly thirty of the criminals had escaped during these ten days, and more would escape later. According to the laws of the Qin Dynasty, he would be put to death even if he managed to get the rest of the conscripts to the destination. That is to say, he was facing death not matter what. When he looked up at the distant mountains, an idea came to him, and he made up his mind. After he had made the decision, he felt relieved. He bought more wine and drank slowly until night fell. He rose from the bench and walked out of the pavilion and untied the prisoners, one by one. They looked at him in great surprise. When all the criminals were untied, Liu Bang said, "You are all free now. You may go anywhere you want. But you'd better not go home just now, for you will be caught and killed."

All the prisoners knelt down on their knees and expressed their heartfelt thanks to him. One of them asked, "What will you do? You will be in great danger after you set us free." Liu Bang said, "Don't worry about me. I will go into hiding somewhere." They left. About ten persons remained. Liu Bang asked, "Why don't you go away?" They said, "We will go wherever you go."

Then they walked down the hill into the road through the marsh leading to Mang-Dang Mountains. Liu Bang said to one of his followers, "You go ahead as a vanguard. Keep a distance of half a mile ahead of us. If you find anything strange, come back and report it to me." The man set out immediately. Liu Bang and the rest of the men set out several minutes later. It was a moonless night. The dark sky was dotted with twinkling stars. The vast marsh was silent. Suddenly the person who had gone ahead turned back hurriedly and reported to Liu Bang, "A huge white serpent is lying across the path. We had better turn back and find another way to the mountain." Liu Bang said, "We are warriors. Why should we be afraid of a serpent?" He went forward and saw the serpent. There it was: a huge serpent lying across the road. When Liu Bang was approaching the serpent, it raised its head and opened its mouth threateningly. Its sharp teeth could be seen, and its tongue was flickering in and out of its mouth like lightning. Its eyes were bright in the dark like two lanterns. The serpent moved its head back and forth and was ready to strike at any moment. Liu Bang drew his sword. He jumped to the right side of the road. The serpent flashed to the right and struck fiercely. But with a quick move, Liu Bang jumped to the left and got very close to the body of the big serpent. He raised his sword and with a powerful swing, he struck the middle of the serpent, cutting it in half. Blood spilt out of its body dyeing the green grass red. The head part of the serpent heavily fell to the right side of the road. The tail part moved to the left side of the road, making way for Liu Bang and his party.

Liu Bang's followers were shocked at the sight of the terrible fight between Liu Bang and the huge serpent, but he turned around and said to them, "The serpent is dead. The way is clear. Let us go on our way." They all replied in great respect, "Yes!" The way was clear, and they walked past the dead serpent and went on their way. But after he had gone about three miles, Liu Bang felt so drunk that he lay down and fell into a deep sleep.

Later that night a man went past the place where Liu Bang had killed the serpent. He saw an old woman crying bitterly over a dead serpent. When the man asked her why she was crying so, she answered, "Someone has killed my son." Then the man asked, "Why has your son been killed?" The old woman pointed at the dead serpent and said, "My son was the son of the White Emperor. He turned into a serpent lying on the way. He has just been slain by the son of the Red Emperor." What the old woman said seemed absurd to the man and he thought the old woman was telling a lie. So he raised his hand to strike her. But all of a sudden the old woman disappeared. The man walked on and came upon Liu Bang and his followers. He told them what the old woman had said and how the woman had disappeared.

Liu Bang exclaimed, "Isn't it strange?" But inwardly he was very glad, because now he knew that he would be the son of the Red Emperor. His followers respected him all the more.

Just a year before, a fortuneteller had told the First Emperor of the Qin Dynasty that there was a stream of air arising from somewhere in the southeast of the realm signifying that "the son of heaven" (an emperor) would arise there, so he had made a tour to the Guiji Prefecture (including the area which is now Nanjing in Jiangsu Province) and destroyed the topography there so as to prevent the new emperor from coming into being. Liu Bang suspected that he himself must be the emperor whom the First Emperor of the Qin Dynasty had tried to destroy. So in order to avoid being captured by the officials of the Qin Dynasty, he led his followers to the most remote parts of the Mang-Dang Mountains so that no one could find them.

When the governor of Pei County found out that Liu Bang had freed all the criminals and he himself had also run away, the governor ordered Liu Bang's home to be searched, but no one could find him. He ordered the arrest of Liu Bang's wife Lü Zhi, and had her thrown into jail. She had no money to bribe the jail keepers, so she was treated badly and was often insulted crudely.

Ren Ao, a jail keeper who was a friend of Liu Bang, kept an eye on Lü Zhi although she was not under his charge. One day Ren Ao when went to the jail to see Lü Zhi, he heard her weeping while a jail keeper was mocking her and insulting her gratuitously, with coarse words. Ren Ao was very angry. He rushed up to the jail keeper and struck him hard in the face; they had a terrible fight. The matter was brought before the governor. The governor asked Xiao He to make a judgment on the matter. Xiao He said, "The jail keeper has no right to insult a female prisoner with unfounded and dirty words. He should be punished for this misconduct. Although Ren Ao was wrong to hit the jail keeper, he should be excused for he did this out of justice." The governor agreed with him. Then Xiao He went on, "Lü Zhi is a woman. She just takes care of the housework. She had nothing to do with the incident of Liu Bang's setting free of the criminals. I think you'd better release her. By doing so, you will show your lenience to the people." The governor also agreed with him on this point and Lü Zhi was released from jail.

As soon as Lü Zhi got out, she went looking for her husband, taking her two children with her. She set off on a journey and went past the road in the great marsh where Liu Bang had killed the great serpent and on into the remote area of the Mang-Dang Mountains. About fifteen days later, Lü Zhi with her children arrived at the cave where Liu Bang and his followers were hiding. Liu Bang was greatly surprised and asked, "How did you find me?" She said, "It's easy. Wherever you go, there is a cloud of five colors in the sky over your head. I just followed that cloud of five colors and found you." From then on, many people of Pei County came and joined him. Very soon he had an army of about a hundred men.

7. THE UPRISING LED BY CHEN SHENG AND WU GUANG

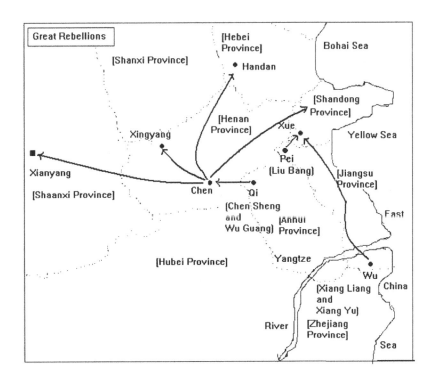

Chen Sheng was a poor peasant in Yangcheng area (now Dengfeng County, Henan Province); Wu Guang was a peasant in Xiayang (now Taikang County, Henan Province). In July 209 BC, nine hundred poor people were conscripted to serve as frontier guards in Yuyang (a place in Miyun near Beijing); nine hundred people were gathered together and stationed in Daze Village (now in Suxian area of Anhui Province), ready to march to Yuyang. Chen Sheng and Wu Guang were among them; they were appointed leaders. They had to get the people to Yuyang at an appointed time. But torrential rains came down and prevented them from leaving. They were badly delayed. No matter how fast the men marched, there was no way now for them to make it to their destination on time.

According to the law of the Qin Dynasty, anyone who missed a deadline would be put to death. What could Chen Sheng and Wu Guang do? They decided to revolt; and one day Chen Sheng and Wu Guang killed the military officers. Then they gathered together the 900 people being sent to garrison the frontiers and said to them, "We have all missed the deadline. According to the law, we should be put to death. Even if we are pardoned, six or seven out of every ten of us will die in the hard conditions along the frontier. Since we are going to die anyway, why don't we rise up against the rulers and die heroically; or even have the chance to become kings or lords or generals through our struggle?"

All the 900 people decided to follow them. Chen Sheng named himself General, and Wu Guang was made Captain. They attacked Daze Village and captured it. Then Chen Sheng led his army to storm Qi, the county town, and took it. Very soon his army grew; now he had an army of more than 10,000 men with cavalry and chariots. Chen Sheng marched his army to Chen (now Huaiyang, Henan Province). A battle was fought outside the city. The Qin army was defeated and Chen Sheng's army occupied the city. Several days later, Chen Sheng claimed himself King of the State of Zhang Chu (meaning the Greater State of Chu), and he made the city of Chen the capital of the State of Zhang Chu.

Zhang Er and Chen Yu were both from Daliang (now Kaifeng of Henan Province). They were devoted friends although Zhang Er was much older than Chen Yu. They were so devoted to each other that one would die for the other. They went to see Chen Sheng. Chen Yu proposed to the King of Zhang Chu, "I know that Your Majesty will raise all the army in the area of Chen and Chu and march westward to take the area of Qin and overthrow the Qin Dynasty. Your Majesty will not be able to take the area to the north of the Yellow River on his own. Zhang Er and I have been to the area of the former State of Zhao, and we know the topography and the people there very well. We offer you our assistance to take that area." Chen Sheng accepted the offer. Then he made arrangements for the march to the west and outlined the battle plans for the areas of the former six states. First Wu Guang was appointed Acting King to supervise all the generals in the westward march to take Xingyang (now Xingyang, Henan Province), a strategic point of military importance. Then he appointed Wu Chen general and appointed Zhang Er and Chen Yu captains. He put 3,000 men under Wu Chen's command, and ordered them to occupy the areas of the former States of Zhao and Yan. He sent Zhou Shi to take the areas of the former States of Qi and Wei. He granted Zhou Wen, a local person of virtue, the seal of general to lead an army to march into the area of Qin.

Zhou Wen marched his army westward, gathering soldiers and horses on the way. When he reached Hanguguan Pass (now in the northeast of Lingbao, Henan Province), his forces had grown into an army of over 300,000 men. They stormed the defenses at the pass and took it. Zhou Wen's army marched quickly into the area of Qin and very soon they reached Xi (to the east of Lintong, Shaanxi Province), threatening Xianyang.

Acting King Wu Guang led his army to attack Xingyang, but could not conquer it because Li You, the son of Premier Li Si of the Qin Dynasty, defended the city staunchly. Wu Guang and his army were stuck there.

8. The Reinstatement of the States of Zhao and Yan

The army under the command of Wu Chen crossed the Yellow River at the port of Baima (now in the northeast of Huaxian, Henan Province); then they marched into the area of the former State of Zhao. Zhang Er and Chen Yu gathered together the local gentry and called on them to rise against the rule of the Qin Dynasty. The local gentry raised armies and joined Wu Chen. Wu Chen's army expanded from 3,000 men into an army of 50,000 men overnight. In a short time Wu Chen took more than thirty cities and marched smoothly into Handan (now Handan, Hebei Province), the capital of the former State of Zhao. Wu Chen declared himself King of the State of Zhao. He made Chen Yu the chief general and Zhang Er the premier of the State of Zhao.

Wu Chen sent General Han Guang to occupy the area of the former State of Yan, and sent Li Liang to occupy the area of Changshan (now Quyang, Hebei Province).

Han Guang with his army fought bravely in the area of the former State of Yan and occupied Ji (now Beijing), the capital of the former State of Yan. Han Guang followed Wu Chen's example and declared himself King of the State of Yan.

9. The Reinstatement of the States of Qi and Wei

Zhou Shi, under the order of Chen Sheng, led an army to take the areas of the former States of Wei and Qi. When he reached Di (now Gaoqing, Shandong Province), they ran into opposition. Tian Dan, a descendant of the former king of the State of Qi, with his cousins Tian Rong and Tian Heng, killed the governor of Di and proclaimed himself King of the State of Qi. He led his army to attack the army commanded by Zhou Shi. Zhou Shi's army was defeated. Then Tian Dan led his army eastward and pacified the area the former State of Qi.

Zhou Shi regrouped his army and turned to the area of the former State of Wei. After some fighting, Zhou Shi put down all resistance in the area of the former State of Wei. He installed Wei Jiu, a descendant of the former King of the State of Wei, on the throne of the State of Wei; and Wei Jiu appointed Zhou Shi premier of the State of Wei.

By September 209 BC, the State of Chu (under King Chen Sheng), the State of Zhao (under King Wu Chen), the State of Wei (under King Wei Jiu), the State of Yan (under King Han Guang) and the State of Qi (under King Tian Dan) had been reinstated; they had broken off the rule of the Qin Dynasty.

10. Counterattack by the Army of the Qin Dynasty

The Second Emperor of the Qin Dynasty was shocked. Zhou Wen's great army of 300,000 men had reached Xi, which was not far from Xianyang. The Second Emperor held court to discuss this matter with his ministers. The Emperor said, "Now the whole realm is in great chaos. Now people everywhere are in rebellion. Zhou Wen is about to attack Xianyang. What shall we do?"

The court was silent for some time, for no one had any idea how to deal with this critical situation. Then Zhang Han, the minister in charge of taxation, stepped forward, bowed to the emperor and said, "Now the enemy is very close to the capital. It is impossible to mobilize the armies in other counties to come to the rescue. But there are many convicts working in the Lishan Mountain. If we set them free and arm them, we can organize an army in a very short time to meet Zhou Wen's army."

"Good idea." The Second Emperor immediately issued an order to pardon all the criminals in the realm and in a short time, an army of several hundred thousand men was mustered. The Second Emperor put this army under Zhang Han's command.

In November 209 BC, Zhang Han led the army to meet Zhou Wen's army at Xi. After a fierce battle, Zhou Wen was defeated. Zhou Wen withdrew through Hanguguan Pass to Caoyang. Zhang Han was in hot pursuit. Another battle was fought, and Zhou Wen was defeated again. He fled to Mianci (now Mianci, Henan Province). Ten days later, Zhang Han caught up with him. Zhou Wen saw that there was no hope to escape. He drew his sword and killed himself.

Zhang Han now directed his victorious army to relieve the siege of Xingyang. Wu Guang, king of the State of Yan, was killed by one of his subordinates. A battle was fought outside the city of Xingyang, and the army sent by Chen Sheng to take Xingyang was totally destroyed.

11. Liu Bang Revolts in Pei County

People of many counties killed their governors in solidarity with Chen Sheng's uprising. The governor of Pei County was afraid that he would meet the same fate. In September 209 BC, the governor of Pei County decided to take the initiative and lead the whole county in rebellion against the Qin Dynasty.

Xiao He and Cao Shen said to the governor, "You are a high-ranking official appointed by the court of the Qin Dynasty. Now you are going to betray the government that has appointed you. What if the people of Pei do not follow you? You'd better call back those who are now in exile and you might gather together several hundred of them. With their help, you might force the people of the county to follow you in the rebellion." The governor agreed with them and said, "Then send someone to look for them and bring them here to assist me."

Xiao He and Cao Shen hurried out of the governor's office to the market place to find Fan Kuai, a butcher and the brother-in-law of Liu Bang. (Fan Kuai was the husband of Lü Xu, younger sister of Liu Bang's wife Lü Zhi). Xiao He said to him, "The governor wants to revolt against the Qin Dynasty; that means betraying his master, and he is afraid that the people of Pei may not follow him. He needs reinforcements to help get the people of Pei to follow him. Since you know the whereabouts of Liu Bang, you should go to find him and ask him to bring all the people under him to hurry back to Pei." Fan Kuai set out for Mang-Dang Mountain immediately. Very soon he found Liu Bang and conveyed to him what Xiao He had said. By then, Liu Bang already had several hundred men. He gathered them together and marched to Pei.

Before Liu Bang reached Pei, the governor changed his mind because he suspected that Xiao He and Cao Shen's plan was a trick. He gave the order to shut the city gates and to arrest Xiao He and Cao Shen and kill them. Xiao He and Cao Shen escaped by getting out over the city wall in baskets held with ropes; and they joined Liu Bang. Liu Bang wrote letters which read, "Respected elders of the city of Pei, people of the whole realm have suffered from the cruel rule of the Qin Dynasty for a long time. Lords and heroes of the realm have risen in rebellion against the rule of the Qin Dynasty. If you defend the city for the governor appointed by the court of the Qin Dynasty, the lords and heroes of the realm will attack this city. If the city falls, you will all be slaughtered. If you kill the governor and select a capable person to govern the city so as to respond to the lords and heroes in rebellion against the Qin Dynasty, your families can be preserved intact. Otherwise, all of you will be killed. I hope this can be avoided." The letters were wrapped around arrows and shot into the city. People read the letters and decided to take action. They killed the governor and then opened the city gates to let in Liu Bang and his followers.

The people of Pei wanted to make Liu Bang the governor of Pei. Liu Bang said, "Now the whole realm is in great disorder. New lords have risen all over the realm. It is essential to select a competent person to be the general to lead the people; otherwise we will suffer massive casualties. You'd better select a more qualified man to lead the people of Pei." Xiao He and Cao Shen were just civil servants and knew that they did not have the ability to lead the people, so they strongly recommended Liu Bang. But Liu Bang still did not accept the position. So they agreed to decide the matter by divination. It was shown by the divination that Liu Bang was the best choice. Thus the people of Pei made Liu Bang The Duke of Pei.

A ceremony was held to commemorate Huangdi, the great emperor of ancient times. They had many big drums made for the ceremony, and they killed oxen and goats and spilled the blood on the drums. All the flags and banners were red, representing the color of the son of the Red Emperor who had killed the son of the White Emperor.

Xiao He, Cao Shen, Fan Kuai, Xiahou Ying and Ren Ao joined Liu Bang. A man named Lu Wan also joined Liu Bang and became the captain of his bodyguards. Lu Wan was born on the same day in the same month and the same year and in the same village as Liu Bang. They had been playmates in their childhood and were close friends in their youth. Another local person of Pei, named Zhou Bo, also joined Liu Bang. He was from a poor family. He made a living by making reed mattresses. Sometimes he would play the flute in funeral ceremonies so as to earn some money. He was good at martial arts and was a very strong archer. A man named Yong Chi also joined Liu Bang. He was a native of Pei, from a rich and powerful family. He did not like Liu Bang; they had had some conflicts in their youth and he still held a grudge.

Xiao He and Cao Shen recruited 3,000 men in the area of Pei. Liu Bang appointed Xiao He in charge of the general affairs of the army. Xiahou Ying became the driver of Liu Bang's carriage and was appointed commander of the troops of chariots. Liu Bang divided the 3,000 men into several groups and put them under the command of Cao Shen, Fan Kuai, Zhou Bo and Yong Chi. With this army, Liu Bang attacked Huling and Fangyu (both now in the southwest of Shandong Province), but could not take them. Then he withdrew to Feng (now Feng County of Jiangsu Province). Liu Bang was 48 years old that year.

12. Xiang Liang and Xiang Yu Rebel in the Area to the East of the Yangtze River

Xiang Liang, a son of the famous General Xiang Yan of the former State of Chu, and his brother's son Xiang Yu lived in Wu (in the southern part of Jiangsu Province). Xiang Yu was eight feet tall and strongly built. He had double pupils in his eyes. He was very powerful. He could lift up a big brass tripod with one hand. When he was young, he did not like to learn how to read and write. His uncle taught him how to use the sword. But very soon Xiang Yu ran out of patience with that, too. His uncle was angry.

Xiang Yu said, "I can write my name, so it is no use learning reading and writing any more. Using a sword, I can only fight against one or two persons. I want to learn something with which I can fight against 10,000 enemies." Ah, his uncle was glad to hear that. So he taught Xiang Yu the art of war.

The First Emperor of the Qin Dynasty made on a tour to east China, and his procession went past Guiji (now Suzhou City, Jiangsu Province) to the Zhe River (now Qiantang River, Zhejiang Province). When the procession of the First Emperor of the Qin Dynasty went by, Xiang Yu and his uncle Xiang Liang stood by the roadside and looked on. Xiang Yu said, "I will take his place." His uncle clapped his hands over Xiang Yu's mouth.

In September 209 BC, when the news that Chen Sheng and Wu Guang had held an uprising against the Qin Dynasty reached the area of Wu, the Governor of Guiji Prefecture wanted to respond to the rebellion. He said to Xiang Liang, "The people of the area to the west of the Yangtze River have all risen against the Qin Dynasty. It is time to overthrow the rule of the Qin Dynasty. As the saying goes, the one who strikes first will gain the initiative. The one who strikes later can only react to the situation. I want to raise an army. You and Huan Chu will take command of this army."

At that time, Huan Chu was in hiding in the area of the marshes. Nobody but Xiang Yu knew where he was. Xiang Liang told the governor that Xiang Yu was the only person who could find Huan Chu and that he would call Xiang Yu to see the governor. Then he went out of the office and told Xiang Yu what to do. He had Xiang Yu wait outside the office and loosen his sword in its sheath. Then he went into the office and said to the governor, "Xiang Yu has come. He may be called in to take your order to find Huan Chu." The governor said, "Let him come in."

Xiang Liang went out to summon Xiang Yu. As soon as Xiang Yu went into the office, Xiang Liang shouted, "Act now!" Xiang Yu drew out his sword, and with one stroke of his sword he cut off the governor's head. Xiang Liang picked up the official seal of the governor and fastened it to his belt. With the head of the governor in his hand, Xiang Liang shouted to the other officials, "Surrender now!" All the officials were in a panic. Some officials and guards resisted; Xiang Yu fought them and killed nearly a hundred of them. The rest prostrated themselves on the ground in submission.

Xiang Liang gathered together the gentry of Guiji and told them that he had decided to rebel against the Qin Dynasty. They all expressed their support for him. Then an army of 8,000 men was organized. Xing Liang and Xiang Yu led this army to occupy the rest of Wu Prefecture.

13. The Great Changes in the State of Zhao

Wu Chen, the King of the State of Zhao, sent Li Liang to take the area of Changshan (an area around Shijiazhuang of Hebei Province). Li Liang with 5,000 soldiers soon took the area of Changshan and returned to Handan to report his victory to the King of the State of Zhao. In November 209 BC, the King of the State of Zhao sent him to take the area of Taiyuan (now the area of Shanxi province). But when the army under Li Liang marched to Jingxing (now Jingxing, southwest of Hebei Province), it could not go on any further because the Qin army blocked the way. He turned back to Handan to ask for more troops. When he was near the capital, he saw a great procession with a hundred horsemen and many banners. Li Liang thought it was the procession of the King of the State of Zhao, so he prostrated himself by the roadside and touched his head to the ground until the procession passed. In fact it was not the king, but the king's elder sister inside the main carriage. Li Liang felt greatly humiliated. He sent an officer under him with a party of soldiers to kill the king's sister.

Li Liang went on with his main force to move quickly to start a surprise attack on Handan. The army in Handan was not vigilant; Li Liang took the city easily. He rushed into the palace and killed Wu Chen. A friend of Zhang Er got news of Li Liang's rebellion, and rushed to inform Zhang Er and Chen Yu of the news. They immediately escaped the city in fear for their lives. Then they gathered 50,000 scattered soldiers.

One local person came to see Zhang Er and Chen Yu. He said, "You two are only guests in the State of Zhao. The people here will not obey you. The best thing to do is to find a descendant of the former King of the State of Zhao and put him on the throne. Then the people of the State of Zhao will follow your instructions." Zhang Er and Chen Yu agreed with him. They sent out officers to look for the descendant of the King of the State of Zhao. At last they found Zhao Xie and he was made King of the State of Zhao.

Since Handan was still in the hands of Li Liang, Zhang Er and Chen Yu escorted the King of the State of Zhao to Xindu (now Xingtai, Hebei Province), where they settled down.

14. Liu Bang's Military Operations

After Liu Bang's attempt to take Huling and his withdrawal back to Feng, Ping, the supervisor of the Qin Army in Sishui Prefecture (including the northern part of Jiangsu Province and the northern part of Anhui Province) led his army to lay siege to Feng. This was in September 208 BC. Liu Bang gave the order to shut all the gates and not to do battle to the Qin army. Ping shouted to Liu Bang and his men, "You rebels, you are so bold as to rebel against the court. Surrender now and you may save your necks. If you don't, when the city falls, all of you will be put to death."

Two days later, Liu Bang led his army out of the city. The soldiers under the command of Cao Shen, Fan Kuai, Xiahou Ying, Yong Chi and Zhou Bo were lined up in battle formation. The two armies met and the battle began. After a terrible fight, the Qin army was defeated and Ping ran back to Huling. Liu Bang ordered Xiao He and Xiahou Ying to chase Ping to Huling. Xiao He shouted to Ping, who was standing at the watchtower atop the city wall, "Now the people of the whole realm have risen against the rule of the Qin Dynasty. The Qin Dynasty is doomed to fall. We have surrounded the city. You have nowhere to go. The best choice for you is to surrender." Seeing that he could not escape, Ping surrendered and put the city of Huling in the hands of Liu Bang.

Then Liu Bang ordered Yong Chi to defend the city of Feng with some troops, and he himself led the main force to Xue (now Weishan, Shandong Province) to attack Zhuang, the Governor of Sishui Prefecture appointed by the court of the Qin Dynasty. Zhuang was defeated and ran away to Qi, but was caught and killed by an officer under Liu Bang. Then Liu Bang led his army to Kangfu (south of Jining, Shandong Province) and stationed his army in the area of Fangyu (south of Jining, Shandong Province).

At that time, Zhou Shi came with an army to attack Feng under the order of the King of the State of Wei. Zhou Shi sent an envoy to the city of Feng. The envoy said to Yong Chi, "The city of Feng formerly belonged to the State of Wei. Now the State of Wei has been reinstated and most of the cities of the former State of Wei have been recovered by the State of Wei.

You'd better surrender Feng to us and you'd better come over to us. If you surrender, we will make you governor of Feng and the Lord of Feng. If not, we will attack the city. If the city falls into our hands, we will kill everyone in the city."

Yong Chi thought for some time and decided to turn over and hold the city of Feng for the State of Wei. Very soon, the news was reported to Liu Bang. Liu Bang was shocked, and led the main force back to Feng. Yong Chi was on the top of the city wall. Liu Bang shouted from below: "I have been very kind to you and have entrusted the city of Feng to you. Why have you betrayed me?" Yong Chi said, "What do you think you are? You are not a nobleman. You are not qualified to be The Duke of Pei. You were a humble junior official from a peasant's family. I feel ashamed to be your subordinate. Now I have been appointed Governor of Feng and made Lord of Feng by the King of the State of Wei. I am defending this city for the King of the State of Wei, not for you."

Liu Bang could not tolerate such insults. He was in a great rage and ordered his army to attack the city. But Yong Chi had mobilized the people of Feng. Many people went up to the top of the city wall to help Yong Chi's army defend the city. When Liu Bang's soldiers got close, volleys of arrows and stones rained down. They could not get to the foot of the city wall. Liu Bang had to give up the attack and withdraw to Pei. Liu Bang hated Yong Chi and the people of Feng for their betrayal. But for now he had to suppress his anger and wait for another chance.

15. The Death of Chen Sheng, King of Zhang Chu

Having eliminated the army of Zhang Chu which had laid siege to Xingyang, Zhang Han sent an envoy to report his victories to the Second Emperor of the Qin Dynasty. The Second Emperor was overjoyed and sent Generals Sima Xin and Dong Yi with 10,000 men to reinforce Zhan Han's army. The reinforced Qin army under the command of Zhang Han swept east, destroying many armies in rebellion against the Qin Dynasty. In December 208 BC, the Qin army reached the City of Chen, the capital of Zhang Chu. At that time, only General Zhang He and his army remained in Chen. King Chen Sheng ordered General Zhang He to lead his army out of the city to resist the Qin army. King Chen Sheng himself supervised the army at the top of the city wall. A battle was fought, and the army under Zhang He was defeated; Zhang He was killed in that battle. Chen Sheng had no more army to defend the city and had to leave the City of Chen for Ruyin (now Fuyang, Anhui Province), then for Chengfu (now Guoyang, Anhui Province). On the way to Chengfu, Chen Sheng's driver Zhuang Jia killed him. Zhuang Jia surrendered to Zhang Han — with Chen Sheng's head. Lü Chen, one of Chen Sheng's generals, led an army to storm the City of Chen and took it. Zhuang Jia was caught and executed for his crime of murdering the King of Zhang Chu. Lü Chen collected the remains of Chen Sheng and buried it in the Mang-Dang Mountains.

16. Qin Jia Makes Jing Ju King of the State of Chu

Qin Jia was originally a general under Chen Sheng. When Chen Sheng was defeated and left the city of Chen, no one was aware of the whereabouts of him. So Qin Jia made Jing Ju, a descendant of the royal family of the former State of Chu, the acting king of the State of Chu. Qin Jia and Jing Ju stationed their army in Liu (25 kilometers south of Pei Xian, Jiangsu Province). When Liu Bang got the news that Qin Jia and Jing Ju had stationed their army in Liu, he decided to go there to ask them for help to take back the city of Feng. When his army of about 3,000 men was marching towards Liu, the vanguard came to Liu Bang and reported, "There is a contingent of armed men marching towards us."

Liu Bang galloped forward and saw a group of armed men headed by a tall, slim man. Liu Bang and the man greeted each other. After the formalities, they introduced themselves. The man said, "My surname is Zhang, given name Liang. I am going to Liu to see Qin Jia and Jing Ju." Liu Bang said, "My surname is Liu, given name Bang. I am from Pei. I am also going to see Qin Jia and Jing Ju. Since we are going to the same place, let's go together." On the way they talked freely and heartily as if they had known each other for a long time.

Zhang Liang was a descendant of an eminent noble family of the former State of Haan. His grandfather Kai Di had served as premier for three generations of the Kings of the State of Haan, and his father Ping served as premier for two generations of the Kings of the same state. Twenty years after Zhang Liang's father died, the State of Qin conquered the State of Haan. At that time Zhang Liang had not become an official of the State of Haan. Three hundred members of his clan, including his younger brother, were killed by the Qin soldiers. He was determined to revenge the State of Haan. He spent all the money he had to search for a brave man to assist him in killing the First Emperor of the Qin Dynasty. At last, he found a brave man of unusual strength. He had an iron hammer of sixty kilograms made. In 218 BC, the First Emperor of the Qin Dynasty made a tour to the east. Zhang Liang got the information that the First Emperor would pass Bolangsha (now Yuanyang County, Henan Province). So Zhang Liang and the man lay in ambush by the roadside. When they saw that the carriages of the First Emperor's procession were passing by, they were surprised to see that there were more than ten carriages which were exactly the same. They could not make out which one the First Emperor of the Qin Dynasty was sitting in. So the man threw the heavy hammer with all his might at the one which they supposed must be the carriage of the First Emperor. The carriage was totally destroyed. Then they ran as fast as they could into the forest behind the place where they had hid themselves and disappeared.

Unfortunately, the hammer had hit a decoy carriage. The First Emperor of the Qin Dynasty was in a great rage and gave orders to search for the assassins all over the realm. Zhang Liang's original surname was Ji. In order to avoid being caught, he changed his surname into Zhang and went into hiding in Xiapi (now Suining, Jiangsu Province).

One day, Zhang Liang was taking a walk near a bridge. An old man in poor clothes walked by and kicked his shoes down the bank of the river near the bridge. The old man said to Zhang Liang, "Young man, go down and get my shoes back for me." Zhang Liang was angered by the rude manner of the old man and wanted to refuse. But he saw that the man was really very old indeed, and he suppressed his anger. He went down the bank, picked up the shoes and went up to the old man sitting on a stone by the bridge. The old man said, "Put the shoes on for me." Zhang Liang knelt down and put on the shoes for the old man. The old man smiled and walked away. Zhang Liang watched the old man walk away in great surprise. The old man walked about half a kilometer and then turned back. He said to Zhang Liang, "You are a promising young man and worthy to be taught. Five days from now, meet me here at dawn." Zhang Liang knelt down and said, "Yes, I will." Five days later Zhang Liang went there in the early morning. But the old man was already there. The old man said angrily, "Why are you late? When you have made an appointment with an old man, you must be on time. Meet me here five days from now. You must come here early." Five days later, Zhang

Liang got up early and when he got there, the roosters began to crow, but the old man was already there. The old man said angrily again, "You are late again. Why? Meet me here five days from now." Five days later, Zhang Liang went there before midnight. Some time later, the old man arrived. The old man said with satisfaction, "You are on time today." Then the old man produced a book and said, "Read this book and you will be the military adviser to an emperor. Ten years from now, there will be great turmoil all over the realm. You may use what you learn from this book to assist the true emperor. Thirteen years from now, come to see me in Gucheng Hill in Jibei. You will see a yellow stone at the foot of that hill. It will be me." He gave the book to Zhang Liang and left without saying anything more.

In the morning Zhang Liang looked at the book and found that it was "On the Art of War by Jiang Tai Gong". Jiang Tai Gong was regarded the greatest militarist in Chinese history. He helped King Wu of Zhou to establish the Zhou Dynasty which lasted for eight hundred years (1122 BC–256 BC).

Zhang Liang liked the book very much; he read it every day and learned it by heart. Zhang Liang had a strong sense of justice and was always ready to help others. Xiang Bo, a relative of Xiang Liang and Xiang Yu, once killed a local bully and fled from home to Xiapi. Zhang Liang hid Xiang Bo in his home. Ten years later, Chen Sheng rose up in Daze in rebellion against the rule of the Qin Dynasty. In response to Chen Sheng's uprising, Zhang Liang organized an army of more than a hundred young men in Xiapi. When Chen Sheng died and Qin Jia made Jing Ju King of the State of Chu, Zhang Liang wanted to join Qin Jia and Jing Ju. So he led this group of young men to Liu. On the way, he met Liu Bang. He talked with Liu Bang and found that he was a broadminded man and would become a true master. Zhang Liang changed his mind. Instead of joining Qin Jia and Jing Ju, he put himself and his men under the command of Liu Bang. Liu Bang appointed Zhang Liang as military adviser.

Liu Bang reached Liu and was received by Qin Jia and Jing Ju. He said to them, "I have come for help. The city of Feng surely belongs to the State of Chu and I have appointed Yong Chi to defend that city. But Zhou Shi of the State of Wei has incited the defection of Yong Chi and Yong Chi has turned over to the State of Wei and is now holding the city of Feng for the State of Wei. Can you lend me some troops to help me get back the city of Feng?" Qin Jia said, "I agree with you in that the city of Feng belongs to the State of

Chu and would most like to assist you to recover the city of Feng. But now the situation is critical. We must deal with the Qin army before we can lend you any troops."

At that time Zhang Han was leading his army in pursuit of Chen Sheng's other generals. He sent General Yi to pacify the area of the State of Chu. General Yi's army swept from the south, destroyed the city of Xiang (now north to Suixi County of Anhui province) and killed all the people in that city. Then they reached the east to Dang (now northeast to Yongcheng, Henan Province). Qin Jia and Liu Bang led their army to the west of the city of Xiao (now Xiao Xian, Anhui Province) to meet the Qin army in battle. The armies of Qin Jia and Liu Bang could not overcome the enemy. They had to retreat back to Liu.

In February 208 BC, Liu Bang led his army of 3,000 men to attack Dang. He laid siege to the city. Three days later Liu Bang gave the order to attack. Cao Shen, Fan Kuai and Zhou Bo led the soldiers under their command in battle formations to advance to the city wall and they began to storm the city. Soldiers put ladders against the city wall and climbed up very quickly. Very soon they took the city. Six thousand Qin soldiers surrendered. Liu Bang incorporated the soldiers who had surrendered into his own forces. Now Liu Bang's army grew into an army of 9,000 men. Carrying on the momentum of victory, Liu Bang marched his army to Xiayi (now Dangshan, Anhui Province). Zhou Bo led his soldiers to storm the city. It was Zhou Bo who first gained the city wall. Then the army under Liu Bang took the city of Xiayi. Cao Shen led his soldiers in pursuit of the defeated Qin army to Yu (a county west to Dangshan). After the victory of Xiayi, Liu Bang led his army back to the area of Feng.

17. Xiang Liang and Xiang Yu Lead their Army to the Area to the West of the Yangtze River

In January 208 BC, Zhao Ping, a general sent by Chen Sheng to take the area of Guangling (now Yangzhou, Jiangsu Province), got the news that Chen Sheng had been defeated and the Qin Army was coming, so he sailed across the Yangtze River to see Xiang Liang. He said to Xiang Liang, "The areas to the east of the Yangtze River have been pacified. The situation in the areas to the west of the Yangtze River is very critical. You should immediately lead your army to the west to attack the Qin Army." Then Xiang

Liang, Xiang Yu and the 8,000 men sailed across the Yangtze River. At that time Xiang Yu was twenty-four years old.

Having crossed the Yangtze River, the army under Xiang Liang and Xiang Yu marched westward. On the way Xiang Liang was informed that Chen Ying had taken Dongyang (now northwest to Tianchang, Anhui Province). He immediately sent an envoy with a letter to Chen Ying asking him whether he would like to joint force with him and fight against the Qin Army together. When Chen Ying received the letter from Xiang Liang, he said to the officers of the army, "The Xiangs have been generals of the State of Chu for several generations. They have made great contributions for the State of Chu. If we join Xiang Liang, our cause will surely be successful." All the officers agreed with him. Then Chen Ying with his 20,000 followers joined Xiang Liang.

Xiang Liang's army continued its march to the west. When Xiang Liang and his men were crossing the Huai River (in the mid-west part of Jiangsu Province), Ying Bu and his men joined Xiang Liang's army. Ying Bu was from Liucheng (now Liu'an, Anhui Province). When he was young, a fortuneteller had said to him, "You will be punished as a criminal, but later you will be a king." When he grew up, Ying Bu was in fact punished for breaking a law, and on his face a tattoo was made to signify that he was a criminal. Others were sorry for him, but he smiled and said, "The fortuneteller said that I would be punished as a criminal before I could be a king. Now the first part of the prediction has come true." He was sentenced to hard labor in the Lishan Mountains (in Xi'an, Shaanxi Province) to work in the construction site of the tomb for the First Emperor of the Qin Dynasty. There were about a 100,000 convicts working there. He made friends with many of them. Then he and many criminals escaped and became robbers along the Yangtze River. When Chen Sheng and Wu Guang rose in rebellion against the Qin Dynasty, he gathered an army of more than 1,000 men. When he got the news that Xiang Liang had revolted in Guiji, he led his army to the east to Guiji to join Xiang Liang because Ying Bu knew that Xiang Liang was the son of the famous General Xiang Yan. He was very glad to meet Xiang Liang by chance by the side of the Huai River.

At the same time, General Pu also led an army to join Xiang Liang by the side of the Huai River.

Xiang Liang's army grew into an army of 60,000 men. Then the army was stationed in Xiapi. At that time, Qin Jia had made Jing Ju Acting King of the State of Chu because Chen Sheng had been defeated and nobody knew where Chen Sheng was. Qin Jia and Jing Ju stationed their army in Pengcheng (now Xuzhou City, Jiangsu Province) to resist Xiang Liang's army. Xiang Liang said to his officers, "It was Chen Sheng who first rose against the Qin Dynasty. Everybody knows that he is the King of the State of Chu. The military situation is now unfavorable. We do not know the whereabouts of Chen Sheng. Now Qin Jia has betrayed Chen Sheng and made Jing Ju King of the State of Chu. He must be punished for it." So Xiang Liang commanded his army to attack Qin Jia and Jing Jus' army. After several battles, Qin Jia and Jing Ju were killed.

18. Xiong Xin Is Made King Huai of the State of Chu

Then news came that Zhang Han had defeated Chen Sheng's army and that when Chen Sheng had retreated to Chengfu, he was killed by his carriage driver. Then Xiang Liang called all the generals under him to Xue to hold a military conference. When Liu Bang learned that Xiang Liang and Xiang Yu had reached Xue with a great army, he decided to go to see them.

In April 208 BC, with a hundred horsemen, Liu Bang rode to Xue. When he arrived, Xiang Liang warmly welcomed him. Xiang Yu was not there because he had been sent by Xiang Liang to take the city of Xiangcheng. After the formalities, they sat down. Liu Bang said, "I would most willingly join force with you in the common cause against the rule of the Qin Dynasty. But for now, I have a request. The city of Feng was originally in my hands. I entrusted the task of defending the city to Yong Chi. Then Zhou Shi came with an army to take the city of Feng for the State of Wei. He claimed that the city of Feng originally belonged to the State of Wei. He succeeded in persuading Yong Chi to hand the city of Feng to the State of Wei and to defend it for the State of Wei. Now I want to get this city back. Will you assign some troops to assist me to get it back from the State of Wei?"

Xiang Liang said, "The city of Feng really belongs to the State of Chu. I firmly support your action to get it back. I will assign 5,000 soldiers with ten high ranking military officers to help you get back the city." Liu Bang stood up and bowed to Xiang Liang and took his leave. In May 208 BC, with the reinforcements, Liu Bang came to the foot of the city wall of Feng. Yong Chi stood at the top of the city wall. Liu Bang shouted to him, "Surrender now and I will spare you. Otherwise, when the city falls, I will kill you."

Yong Chi shouted back, "No, I will not surrender. I will not be your subordinate even if I should die." Liu Bang was in such a fury that he gave the order to storm the city. The army under Yong Chi could not withstand the attack by the army under Liu Bang, and very soon the city fell.

Yong Chi fled to the State of Wei. Liu Bang left some troops to defend the city, and he himself led the main force to join Xiang Liang. By that time, Xiang Yu had been away to Xiangcheng for about a month. Xiang Yu led his army to Xiangcheng. He ordered his army to storm the city. But the defenders of the city fought bravely and repulsed the attack. The following day, Xiang Yu launched another attack, and the city fell. Xiang Yu was so angry with the people of that city, that he gave the order to kill everyone in the city, no matter old or young, man or woman. When he left, not a living soul remained in the city. A month later, he led his army back to Xue and Liu Bang and Xiang Yu met with each other for the first time.

Fan Zeng, an old man of over seventy, was a resourceful man and astute. He said to Xiang Liang, "There is a reason that led to the death of Chen Sheng. When the State of Qin conquered the other six states, the State of Chu was the most pitiful. King Huai of the State of Chu was kidnapped into the State of Qin and never returned. To this day the people of Chu have great pity for him. So as the saying goes: The people of Chu hate the Qin Dynasty so much that people of just three households of Chu will suffice to overthrow the rule of the Qin Dynasty. When Chen Sheng first rose against the rule of the Qin Dynasty, he did not reinstate the State of Chu by putting the descendant of King Huai of the State of Chu on the throne. Instead, he made himself the King of the State of Chu. That is the reason why Chen Sheng did not last long. Now you have started an uprising in the area to the east of the Yangtze River but the generals who rebelled in the Chu area have all submitted to your authority. The reason is, your ancestors served as generals for the State of Chu for several generations, and you have the ability to put the descendant of King Huai of the State of Chu on the throne and reinstate the State of Chu." Xiang Liang accepted his suggestion and sent out people to look for the descendant of King Huai of the State of Chu. At last they found Xiong Xin, the grandson of King Huai of the State of Chu, in a village, where he was serving as a shepherd, tending sheep for others. In June 208 BC, Xiong Xin was made King Huai of the State of Chu. Chen Ying was appointed premier of the State of Chu. The capital was Xuyi (now Xuyi in Jiangsu Province).

When Zhang Liang saw that Xiang Liang had made Xiong Xin King of the State of Chu, he went to see Xiang Liang. He said, "You have put the descendant of the former King of the State of Chu on the throne of the State of Chu. Now out of the former six states, five have been reinstated. They are the States of Chu, Qi, Zhao, Yan and Wei. Only the State of Haan has not yet been reinstated. I think you have the ability to reinstate the State of Haan by putting the descendant of the former King of the State of Haan on the throne of the State of Haan. If you help to reinstate the State of Haan, the King of Haan will be grateful to you and will most willingly obey your orders." Xiang Liang said, "I would most certainly be pleased to reinstate the State of Haan. Do you know any descendant of the former King of the State of Haan who is worthy to be put on the throne?" Zhang Liang replied, "Prince Haan Cheng is a worthy man. He can be put on the throne of the State of Haan." Then Xiang Liang sent Zhang Liang to seek Haan Cheng. Very soon Zhang Liang found Haan Cheng and brought him back to see Xiang Liang. Xiang Liang made Haan Cheng King of the State of Haan, and made Zhang Liang the premier of the State of Haan. Xiang Liang gave Haan Cheng an army of 1,000 men to recover the area of the State of Haan.

Before Zhang Liang left for his mission, he went to see Liu Bang. Liu Bang said, "We have co-operated very closely and pleasantly. I will miss you." Zhang Liang said, "You have always accepted my suggestions readily. You are always my true master. I am now leaving to assist the King of the State of Haan to recover the area of the State of Haan. I will be away for a while. But I will come back to you when my mission is completed." They said goodbye to each other and then Zhang Liang and the King of the State of Haan with the army of 1,000 men marched westward to the area of the former State of Haan.

19. The Setbacks Suffered by the State of Chu and the Death of Xiang Liang

Since Zhang Han had defeated Chen Sheng, he directed his army to attack Linji (now to the southwest of Changyuan of Henan Province, to the north of the Yellow River) where the King of the State of Wei was. The situation was critical. Wei Jiu, King of the State of Wei, sent Zhou Shi to the State of Qi to ask for help. Tian Dan, King of the State of Qi, with Tian Rong, immediately led an army to rescue the King of the State of Wei. One night, Zhang Han's army moved very quickly and silently to the camps of the army of the State of Qi and started a surprise attack. Tian Dan, the King of the State of Qi, was killed and his army scattered. Zhou Shi of the State of Wei was also killed in this battle.

Then Zhang Han laid siege to Linji. Wei Jiu, the King of the State of Wei, sent an envoy to see Zhang Han with a letter. The letter read, "You have come for me only. The people of the city are innocent. Please spare my people after I die." Zhang Han sent back the envoy with his promise that he would not harm the people of the city after Wei Jiu died. When Wei Jiu got Zhang Han's promise, he walked calmly up the stairs to the top of the city wall. Then he set fire on himself and was burned to death. Linji fell into the hands of Zhang Han. Wei Jiu's younger brother Wei Bao fled to the State of Chu. King Huai of the State of Chu gave Wei Bao several thousand men to recover the area of the former State of Wei.

When the people of the State of Qi got the news that Tian Dan, the king of the State of Qi, had been killed in the area of Linji, they put Tian Jia on the throne of the State of Qi. Tian Jia was the younger brother of the last king of the State of Qi before the State of Qin conquered the State of Qi. Tian Jiao was made premier and Tian Jian was made chief general. Tian Rong gathered together the scattered soldiers of the State of Qi who had come to rescue the King of the State of Wei, and retreated to Dong'e (now Dong'e, Shandong Province). But Zhang Han pursued Tian Rong to Dong'e and laid siege to the city.

At that time, Xiang Liang was leading the armies under the command of Liu Bang and Xiang Yu in the attack of the city of Kangfu (now to the south of Jining, Shandong Province). When Xiang Liang got the news that Tian Rong was surrounded by the Qin Army under the command of Zhang Han and that Tian Rong was in great danger, he gave up the attack of Kangfu and led his army to Dong'e to rescue Tian Rong. Xiang Liang's army moved quickly and very soon they reached the area of Dong'e. Xiang Liang arranged his army into battle array. Xiang Yu was in charge of the middle formation. Liu Bang was in charge of the left and Ying Bu was in charge of the right. Zhang Han immediately responded to the action taken by Xiang Liang. He left some troops to maintain the siege. Then he arranged the rest of his troops in battle formation to deal with the Chu army. Xiang Liang gave the order to attack the enemy, and the Chu soldiers fell upon the Qin army. Xiang Yu galloped quickly to the battle formation of the Qin army and found Zhang Han. They fought fiercely. At the same time, the soldiers under the command of Cao Shen, Zhou Bo and Fan Kuai fell upon the Qin army and destroyed their battle formation. The detachment of battle chariots under the command of Xiahou Ying drove quickly into the Qin army and the Qin soldiers fell back. After several exchanges, Zhang Han found that he was not a match for Xiang Yu, and he turned round and waved to the Qin soldiers in siege of the city of Dong'e to retreat. The Qin army collapsed.

At this time, the army of the State of Qi under the command of Tian Rong came out of the city and joined in attacking the defeated Qin army. The Qin troops were in great disorder and scattered in all directions. Zhang Han led the remaining soldiers to retreat westward.

Tian Rong called back all his soldiers who were ready to pursue the Qin army. He led his soldiers back to the State of Qi. Before Tian Rong with his army reached the State of Qi, Tian Jia knew that he was no match for Tian Rong, so he fled to the State of Chu. Tian Jiao, the premier, ran away to the State of Zhao. Tian Jian was already in the State of Zhao asking for help, so he stayed there. Tian Rong put Tian Shi, Tian Dan's son, on the throne of the State of Qi. Tian Rong became the premier, and Tian Heng became the chief commander of the army of the State of Qi.

Having defeated Zhang Han's army in Dong'e, Xiang Liang directed his army in hot pursuit of the defeated Qin army. Xiang Liang sent an envoy to the State of Qi to urge Tian Rong to send an army to join in the fight against Zhang Han and his army. Tian Rong sent an envoy to see King Huai of the State of Chu. The envoy of the State of Qi said, "The State of Qi is willing to send an army to fight against Zhang Han and his army. The condition is that the State of Chu shall kill Tian Jia and the State of Zhao shall kill Tian Jiao and Tian Jian. Otherwise, the State of Qi will not send any army." King Huai of the State of Chu said, "Tian Jia has been a king as I am now. He has been driven out of the State of Qi. He has no other way out but has come to the State of Chu for refuge. It is unjust to kill Tian Jia in such a circumstance." Tian Rong also sent an envoy to the State of Zhao to ask the King of the State of Zhao to kill Tian Jiao and Tian Jian, but the King of the State of Zhao refused to do so. The envoy of the State of Qi said, "When a man is bitten by a poisonous snake by the hand, he should immediately cut his hand off. If he is bitten by a poisonous snake on the foot, he should immediately cut his foot off. That is the only way to save his life. Now the relation between you and Tian Jiao and Tian Jian is not at all as close as the relation between the man and his hands and feet. Why don't you kill them for the interest of the State of Zhao? If the Qin army is revitalized and comes to attack you, you will be destroyed." But no matter how hard the envoy of the State of Qi tried, the King of the State of Zhao refused to kill Tan Jiao and Tian Jian. So the State of Qi did not send any army to assist Xiang Liang.

Since the State of Qi would not send any army to assist him, Xiang Liang had to rely on his own forces in pursuit of Zhang Han and his army. He sent Xiang Yu and Liu Bang to attack Chengyang (now a place to the north of Heze, Shandong Province). They attacked the city and took it. In the battle in Dong'e and the battle in Chengyang, Xiang Yu and Liu Bang fought side by side, and they became very good friends. After the battle of Chengyang, Xiang Yu said to Liu Bang, "I see that you are a kind and trustworthy person. We have fought side by side like two brothers. Shall we become sworn brothers?" Liu Bang said, "That's a good idea." They held a ceremony and pledged to be devoted to each other. Since Liu Bang was older than Xiang Yu, Liu Bang became the elder brother and Xiang Yu the younger brother. Then Liu Bang and Xiang Yu moved their army from Chengyang to Puyang (now Puyang City of Henan Province). In the east of Puyang they fought against the army commanded by Zhang Han. Again Zhang Han was defeated. Then he regrouped the scattered soldiers and the Qin army became strong again. Zhang Han led the Qin army to withdraw into the city of Puyang. The city of Puyang was protected by the Yellow River in the north. Zhang Han ordered the soldiers to dig a canal to the south of the city to lead water round the city so as to prevent the Chu army from attacking the city. The Chu army had to give up the attempt of taking the city of Puyang. Xiang Yu and Liu Bang maneuvered the Chu army southward to attack Dingtao (now Dingtao in the west part of Shandong Province), but the Chu army could not take it.

Then Xiang Yu and Liu Bang moved their troops westward to Yongqiu (now Qixian of Henan Province). The defender of Yongqiu was Li You, the son of Premier Li Si of the Qin Dynasty. When the Chu army reached Yongqiu, Li You led his army out of the city and arranged his army in battle formations. He himself was in charge of the middle formation. Liu Bang and Xiang Yu led their army to the battlefield and the battle began. The Chu soldiers fought bravely and the Qin army collapsed. Xiang Yu rode straight at Li You and killed him with a stroke of his sword. Seeing that their chief commander had been killed, the Qin soldiers ran for their life in all directions. Liu Bang and Xiang Yu won a great victory. Then under the order of Xiang Liang, Liu Bang and Xiang Yu led their army to Waihuang (now north of Minquan, Henan Province) and lay siege to that city.

Xiang Liang marched his army from Dong'e to Dingtao. The general of the Qin army in Dingtao led his troops to cope with the Chu army. After a battle, the Chu army defeated the Qin army. The Qin Army retreated into the city. Xiang Liang laid siege to it. Since then the Qin army shut all the gates of Dingtao and would not come out for a decisive battle. At that time, Zhang Han and his troops stayed in the city of Puyang and would not come out to fight. Since Liu Bang and Xiang Yu had won a great victory in Yongqiu and killed Li You, and Xiang Liang himself won a victory outside Dingtao, Xiang Liang became very conceited and arrogant. He thought that Zhang Han had been defeated and did not have the strength to fight him. He thought that the Qin Army would be easy to deal with. The Chu army's vigilance against the Qin army was relaxed. Xiang Liang held banquets frequently to celebrate his victories.

Song Yi, a general under Xiang Liang, was worried because he had found out that Qin army reinforcements had arrived secretly and thus the Qin army might launch a surprise attack any time. But Xiang Liang ignored this fact and still believed that Zhang Han did not have the strength to carry out an attack on him. Song Yi went to see Xiang Liang. He said, "After a victory, the general who underestimates the force of his enemy and the soldiers who become relaxed will surely be defeated. Now, as I see it, the soldiers have become relaxed after these victorious battles. More and more Qin soldiers have been sent to reinforce Zhang Han's army. This is very dangerous."

But Xiang Liang would not listen to him. Xiang Liang said to Song Yi, "I need to send an envoy to the State of Qi to persuade the King of the State of Qi to send troops to cooperate in the action against the Qin army under Zhang Han. You are the best candidate for this mission. Get ready and go tomorrow." Song Yi had to leave; he left Dingtao for the State of Qi.

On his way Song Yi came across Xian, an envoy sent by the King of the State of Qi to Xiang Liang. Song Yi asked him, "Are you going to see Xiang Liang?" Xian said, "Yes." Song Yi said, "I have sufficient reason to believe that Xiang Liang will soon be defeated. If you travel slowly, you may avoid the disaster. If you go quickly, you will be caught in it." Xian was surprised and asked Song Yi, "On what grounds have you come to this conclusion?" Song Yi said, "Xiang Liang has won successive victories and has become

very proud. He thinks that Zhang Han has no strength to carry out any attack on him. His soldiers have let down their guard. It would be difficult for
them to fight another battle. I have found out that reinforcements of the Qin
army have secretly arrived. The Qin army may launch a surprise attack any
time. I tried to persuade Xiang Liang to be on his guard, but he would not
listen to me. Instead, he has sent me away as an envoy to your state. I predict
that the Qin army's surprise attack will take place within the next few days
and Xiang Liang will be defeated."

In Puyang, Zhang Han was secretly preparing a surprise attack on the
Chu army. The second Emperor of the Qin Dynasty had sent reinforcements
to him, and Zhang Han's army was strong enough to fight with the main
force of the Chu army. One day in September 208 BC, Zhang Han led his
army out of Puyang. Each of his soldiers kept a stick clamped in his mouth
so that no sound would be made during the march. After one day and one
night's march, the Qin army reached the camps of the Chu army under Xiang
Liang outside the city of Dingtao at dawn. Their action had not been discov-
ered because the Chu army had let down their guard and no scouts had been
sent out by Xiang Liang to watch the activities of the Qin army. The Qin
soldiers burst into the camps of the Chu army and set fire to the tents of the
Chu army. They fell upon the sleeping Chu soldiers with uproarious war
cries, killing everyone they saw. The camps of the Chu army were in great
confusion. The desperate cries of the Chu soldiers in great panic mingled
with the war cries of the Qin soldiers shook the sky. Many Chu soldiers
were killed while sleeping. Some woke up but were killed before they could
put up a fight. Many Chu soldiers woke up and ran out of their tents without armor and weapons. They ran in all directions. Xiang Liang woke up
and went out of his tent with a sword in his hand to see what had happened.
Zhang Han rode at him and killed him with his spear. Very few Chu soldiers
escaped. It was a tremendous disaster for the State of Chu.

Xiang Yu and Liu Bang were on their way to Chenliu (now Chenliu,
Henan Province) after several unsuccessful attacks on Waihuang (a place
near Minquan, Henan Province) when some soldiers who had escaped from
Dingtao caught up with them and reported to them the disaster in the
camps of the Chu army outside Dingtao. When Xiang Yu learned that his
uncle had been killed by Zhang Han, he was so sad that he cried bitterly.
Then he raised his head to heaven and said in tears, "Zhang Han, you have

killed my uncle. You are my sworn enemy. I will not live under the same sky with you. I swear I will kill you and avenge my uncle with your head."

Liu Bang was sad too, but he tried his best to comfort Xiang Yu. "We are sworn brothers. Your uncle is also my uncle. We are determined to avenge him. But for now, the most important thing is to make a decision on our next move. Under the present situation, we have to give up our plan to attack Chenliu. Since the main force of the Chu army under your uncle has been defeated, the morale of our army will be greatly affected. It would be better to move our army back to the east. General Lü Chen is nearby. Let's join forces with him and retreat together." Xiang Yu agreed with him. They immediately maneuvered their army east to Pengcheng (now Xuzhou, Jiangsu Province) with General Lü Chen. General Lü Chen's army was stationed in the east of Pengcheng. Xiang Yu's army was stationed in the west of Pengcheng. Liu Bang's army was stationed in Dang (now northeast to Yongcheng, Henan Province). A young man named Guan Ying, who was a peddler of silk, joined Liu Bang's army. Liu Bang appointed him commander of his guards.

King Huai of the State of Chu found that Xuyi was not a safe place to stay because Zhang Han might attack it at any time. He decided to move to Pengcheng. With all the ministers, King Huai of the State of Chu arrived in Pengcheng. The first measure he took was to merge the army under Xiang Yu and the army under General Lü Chen in one and put this army directly under his own command. He appointed Liu Bang governor of Dang Prefecture, in command of all the armies in Dang. He granted the title of Lord of Wu An to Liu Bang, and the title of Lord of Chang An to Xiang Yu. He appointed Lü Chen minister in charge of civil affairs, and Lü Qing, Lü Chen's father, prime minister.

20. THE PROMISE MADE BY KING HUAI OF THE STATE OF CHU

Since Xiang Liang's army had been defeated, Zhang Han thought that the remaining armies of the State of Chu were not a threat to him anymore. He directed his army across the Yellow River and marched north to attack the State of Zhao.

At that time, Xian, the envoy of the State of Qi, was in the State of Chu. He said to King Huai of the State of Chu, "On my way to Dingtao to see Xiang Liang as an envoy of the King of the State of Qi, I met Song Yi. He predicted that Xiang Liang would be defeated. Several days later Xiang Liang was indeed defeated. Song Yi has great military talent if he could see the signs of defeat before the battle took place." When Song Yi came back from his mission to the State of Qi, King Huai of the State of Chu received him and talked about with him military affairs. Song Yi answered the King's questions fluently and made many sound suggestions. King Huai of the State of Chu had a very good impression of Song Yi.

King Huai of the State of Chu decided to send an army to Guanzhong (the Qin areas within the passes of Hanguguan, Wuguan, Xiaoguan and Sanguan) to overthrow the rule of the Qin Dynasty. In order to select a general who had the ability to lead this army into Guanzhong, he held court to discuss this matter. When all the military officers and civil officials had come, King Huai of the State of Chu said, "We must send an army to march into Guanzhong and root out the Qin Dynasty. We need a capable general to lead this army. Now I solemnly make the following promise: the general who is the first to march into Guanzhong and put down that area will be made king of Guanzhong. Will anyone of you take up this task?" Liu Bang responded, "I will." Xiang Yu said, "I will go, too." The other generals were silent. They did not want to go into Guanzhong because the Qin army was very strong.

King Chen Sheng and Xiang Liang had been defeated by the Qin army under the command of Zhang Han. It would not be an easy task to march into Guanzhong. So King Huai of the State of Chu said, "We appreciate that the Lord of Wu An and the Lord of Chang An have expressed their willingness to march into Guanzhong. But we need only one general to lead the army. We will send the Lord of Wu An. The Lord of Chang An may stay behind, ready for other needs that may arise." Xiang Yu was agitated and said in a tone of determination, "I have a profound hatred of the Qin Dynasty. The Qin army has killed my uncle Xiang Liang. I will march into Guanzhong with the Lord of Wu An to overthrow the rule of the Qin Dynasty." Seeing that Xiang Yu was determined to go with Liu Bang into Guanzhong, King Huai of the State of Chu said to Xiang Yu, "We give you our consent that you may go with Lord of Wu An to Guanzhong. Now go and prepare for the march." Liu Bang and Xiang Yu and some of the other generals left.

Some old generals stayed behind. One of them said to King Huai of the State of Chu, "Xing Yu is not the right person to lead the army to march into Guanzhong. Although he is brave, he is brutal. When he took the city of Xiangcheng, he had all the people there slaughtered. When he left, not a living soul remained in that city. Previously, King Chen Sheng and Xiang Liang achieved great success and occupied many cities and vast lands, but in the end both of them met with failure and were killed. It would be better for us to send a kindhearted and capable person to lead an army to march westward in the name of justice. He should tell the people in the Qin area that he has come to release them from the cruel rule of the Qin Dynasty. The people of Qin have suffered from their rulers for a long time. If this person enters the area without harming the people there, he will succeed in taking that area peacefully. We must not send a cruel person such as Xiang Yu to Guanzhong. The Lord of Wu An has always been kindhearted and lenient. He is the only right person to be sent." So King Huai of the State of Chu made up his mind to send Liu Bang instead of Xing Yu to march into Guanzhong.

But he found that it was extremely difficult to persuade Xiang Yu to stay behind. Just as he was wondering what to do, an official rushed in and reported, "An envoy sent by the King of the State of Zhao has come to beg for an urgent audience." King Huai of the State of Chu said, "Let him in." The envoy came in and presented a letter written by Zhao Xie, King of the State of Zhao. The letter read, "Zhang Han has led a great army to attack our state. Our army has suffered great set back. We have retreated into the city of Julu. The Qin army has laid siege to the city. The city may fall at any time. Please send an army to rescue us as soon as possible."

The envoy explained to King Huai of the State of Chu how the situation in the State of Zhao had unfolded: having defeated the Chu army under the command of Xiang Liang outside Dingtao, Zhang Han with his victorious army crossed the Yellow River and marched into the State of Zhao; the Qin army defeated the army of the State of Zhao and took Handan, the capital of the State of Zhao; Zhang Han forced all the people in Handan to move to Henei (now Wuzhi, Henan Province) and then he ordered the Qin army to destroy the city of Handan; when the Qin army left for the north, the city was totally in ruin; the King of the State of Zhao, and Zhang Er, the premier of the State of Zhao, retreated into the city of Julu (now Julu, Hebei Province); the Qin army under the command of Zhang Han surrounded the city of Julu. Chen Yu, the chief general of the State of Zhao, gathered all the scattered Zhao soldiers together, and he got about 30,000 men; he stationed his army to the north of the city of Julu; Zhang Han stationed his army in Jiyuan to the south of city of Julu; a road with walls on both sides had been built to ensure the transportation of food to the Qin army laying siege to Julu; the King of the State of Zhao had sent several envoys to King Huai of the State of Chu, to the King of the State of Qi and the King of the State of Yan asking for help.

King Huai of the State of Chu immediately summoned all the generals and ministers to discuss this matter. He showed the letter of the King of the State of Zhao to them. Xiang Yu stood up and said, "I swear I will kill Zhang Han to revenge my uncle. I am willing to lead an army to rescue the King of the State of Zhao." Then King Huai of the State of Chu declared his decision, "We have decided to send an army to rescue the King of the State of Zhao. We hereby appoint Song Yi commander-in-chief, the Lord of Chang An second chief commander and Fan Zeng the third commander. All the generals of the State of Chu will be under the command of Song Yi. The Lord of Wu An will lead the army under his command to march into Guanzhong in accordance with the original plan."

In the second September of 208 BC (that year was a leap year and thus it had two Septembers), Liu Bang left Pengcheng and rode back to Dang where his army was stationed. Then he started his march to Guanzhong with his army. This was the first time that Liu Bang alone led an army to penetrate deep into the hostile land of Qin. He knew that it would be a very difficult and dangerous task but he was confident that he could accomplish it.

On the way he gathered the scattered soldiers under Chen Sheng and those under Xiang Liang. In October 208 BC, Liu Bang's army reached Chengwu (now Chengwu, Shandong Province). The commanding general of the Qin army stationed in Chengwu was Wang Li. When Liu Bang led his army to the city of Chengwu, General Wang Li led his army out of the city and arranged his army in battle array to the south of the city to prevent the advance of Liu Bang's army. The officers and men of Liu Bang's army fought bravely and defeated the Qin army. General Wang Li led his defeated army to retreat northward and joined Zhang Han who was leading his army to destroy the State of Zhao.

In December 208 BC, Liu Bang's army marched north to Chengyang (now a place to the north of Heze, Shandong Province). An army of the Qin Dynasty stationed in Gangli, a county near Chengyang. Liu Bang's army attacked the Qin army in their camps and defeated them.

The envoy sent by the King of the State of Zhao reached the State of Qi and was received by Tian Shi, the King of the State of Qi, and Tian Rong, the premier of the State of Qi. The envoy presented the letter written by the King of the State of Zhao to the King of the State of Qi. After reading the letter, the King of the State of Qi passed the letter to Tian Rong. Then Tian Rong said to the envoy angrily, "Tian Jiao and Tian Jian are still in the State of Zhao. We once asked the King of the State of Zhao to kill them, but he refused to do so. We warned him that if he did not kill Tian Jiao and Tian Jian, he would have to bear the consequence himself. Now he has got what he deserves. We will not send any troops to rescue him." The envoy had to go back in great frustration. Tian Du, a general of the army of the State of Qi, resented the attitude of Tian Rong. He led the troops under him to march out of the State of Qi to rescue the King of the State of Zhao against the will of Tian Rong.

The envoy sent by the King of the State of Zhao to the State of Yan reached Ji, the capital of the State of Yan, and was received by Han Guang, the King of the State of Yan. The King of the State of Yan sent General Zang Tu with an army to rescue the King of the State of Zhao.

21. The Battle of Julu

In the second September of 208 BC, Song Yi with his army started from Pengcheng and marched north to rescue the King of the State of Zhao in Julu. They marched northward to Baima (now a place within the area of Huaxian, Henan Province), where the whole army crossed the Yellow River. Then the army continued its march to Anyang (now Anyang, Hebei Province). When the army reached Anyang, Song Yi gave the order to stop marching and pitch camps there. Song Yi's army stayed in Anyang without moving a step forward. One day in October 208 BC, Xiang Yu went to see Song Yi and said to him, "The Qin army has besieged the King of the State of Zhao in the city of Julu. The city may fall at any moment. We should march north quickly and cross the Zhang River. If the Chu army attacks the Qin army from outside and the Zhao army from inside of the city, then the Qin army will surely be defeated."

But Song Yi said, "That is not correct. Now the Qin Army is fiercely attacking the State of Zhao. If the Qin army wins, then the Qin soldiers will be very tired. Then we have a better chance to attack the Qin army. On the other hand, if the Zhao army defeats the Qin army, then I will lead my army westward in marching formation accompanied by drums. The Qin Dynasty will surely fall. So it is better to let the Qin army and the Zhao army fight each other first. I am not as good as you in actual combat face to face with the enemy. But when it comes to devising strategies and making plans, you are not as good as I." Then Song Yi issued an order to the whole army. It read, "Anyone who is as fierce as a tiger, as cruel as a wolf and as greedy as a bear but does not obey orders shall be put to death."

Song Yi sent his son Song Xiang to the State of Qi to take the position of a high-ranking official. Song Yi saw his son off in Wuyan (now Dongping, Shandong Province) where a grand banquet was given. This was during the winter and there was rain. The soldiers of the State of Chu were suffering from cold and hunger. Xiang Yu turned to his fellow generals and said, "The officers and men of our army are all determined to fight with the Qin army. There is a famine this year. The soldiers only have beans mixed with vegetables for food. There is no surplus food in the army. But Song Yi gave a grand banquet to see his son off with good food and wine. He would not order the army to cross the Zhang River. If we cross the river, we may forage in the State of Zhao and attack the Qin army together with the army of the State of Zhao and the armies from other states. Instead, he said that he would wait until the Qin army and the Zhao army finish fighting and then take action after he sees which army has won the battle. The strong army of the Qin Dynasty is attacking the newly established Zhao army. It is clear that the Qin army will defeat the Zhao army. When the army of the State of Zhao is put to rout, the army of the Qin Dynasty will not be weakened. The State of Chu has just suffered great setback. King Huai of the State of Chu is worried about the situation. He has put all the army he can raise under Song Yi's command. The survival of the State of Chu may depend on the outcome of this battle. Now Song Yi is not taking care of his soldiers but is only attending to his own private matters. He is not a man to whom the survival of the state can be entrusted."

One morning in November 208 BC, when the Chu army had stayed in Anyang for 46 days, Xiang Yu went into Song Yi's tent, killed Song Yi and then went out of the tent with Song Yi's head in one hand and his sword in the other. He gathered the officers and men together and said, "Song Yi has conspired with the State of Qi to betray the State of Chu. King Huai of the State of Chu gave me a secret order to kill him." At that time, all the officers and men were awed by what he had done and nobody said anything against him. They said that it was the Xiangs that had re-established the State of Chu and that what he had done was just, suppressing a traitorous act, so they made him acting commander-in-chief.

Then Xiang Yu sent a party of soldiers to catch Song Yi's son. They caught up with him within the territory of the State of Qi and killed him. Xiang Yu sent Huan Chu back to Pengcheng to tell King Huai of the State of Chu what had happened. Then King Huai of the State of Chu officially appointed Xiang Yu commander-in-chief of the army of the State of Chu to rescue the State of Zhao.

The Qin army under Zhang Han was attacking the city of Julu fiercely. Zhang Han ordered General Wang Li to lead the Qin army of 100,000 men under him to lay siege to Julu. Zhang Han stationed the Qin army of 200,000 men in a place named Jiyuan to the south of Julu. Since Zhang Han had built a walled road leading to Julu to protect the transportation of food to General Wang Li, who was the commanding general in charge of attacking the city of Julu, the Qin army had sufficient food, so their attack became more and more fierce. There were just a few troops of the State of Zhao inside the city of Julu and they did not have enough food. Zhang Er sent several messengers to Chen Yu asking him to fight hard to rescue them. But Chen Yu considered that he had too few troops and he would not be able to defeat such a strong army. So he did not dare to fight his way through to rescue them. Later on, Zhang Er was so enraged at Chen Yu that he sent Zhang Yan and Chen Ze to reprimand Chen Yu. Zhang Yan conveyed the words of Zhang Er to Chen Yu, "You and I are friends sworn to share life and death. Now the King and I may die any time. You have an army of tens of thousands of men. But you are not willing to come to our rescue. Since we are friends sworn to death and you should keep your promise, why don't you attack the Qin army and fight and die in battle? If you fight with the Qin army, you still have a ten or twenty percent chance of survival." Chen Yu said to Zhang Yan and Chen Ze, "I think, even if we fight our way forward, we cannot rescue the King. But there is a risk that the whole army will be destroyed. The reason why I do not want to die together with the King and Zhang Er is that I may take revenge for them on the Qin army. It is no use dying together. If I attack the strong Qin army with this small number of troops, it would be like putting meat into the mouth of a hungry tiger."

But Zhang Yan and Chen Ze insisted that Chen Yu should engage the Qin army in spite of the fact that there would be no hope of Chen Yu coming back alive. Zhang Yan said, "The situation is critical. Julu may fall at any time. You must fulfill your promise with Zhang Er by fighting to the death. You should not consider what would happen after you die." Chen Yu said, "It is no use dying in such a way. If you want to have a try, you may go." Chen Yu had to give them 5,000 men to give it a try. But as soon as they met the Qin army in battle, all of them were killed in action.

At that time, the army of the State of Qi under General Tian Du and the army of the State of Yan under General Zang Tu arrived to help the State of Zhao. They saw that the Qin army was so strong that they did not dare to go into battle. So they just pitched camp beside the camp of Chen Yu's army. Zhang Au, Zhang Er's son, also came from the State of Dai with an army of

10,000 men to rescue the King of the State of Zhao and his father. He also pitched camp beside the camp of Chen Yu's army. Tian An, the grandson of Tian Jian, the former king of the State of Qi before the State of Qi was conquered by the State of Qin, came from Jibei (now Tai'an, Shandong Province) to rescue the King of the State of Zhao.

Since Xiang Yu had killed Song Yi, he had become the most powerful man all over the State of Chu. In December 208 BC, he sent Ying Bu and General Pu with 20,000 men as vanguards. They crossed the Zhang River and then marched quickly to relieve the city of Julu. They went into battle as soon as they arrived. When Wang Li saw that the Chu army was marching towards Julu, he sent a detachment to check the advance of the Chu army. The two armies confronted each other. Ying Bu gave the order to his officers and men to engage the enemy. Then he urged his horse to gallop forward and took the lead in the assault. His soldiers followed him and charged the enemy. The Qin army was defeated and retreated back to join the main force. Then Ying Bu and General Pu commanded their army to attack the walled road on which Zhang Han transported food to the Qin army under General Wang Li's command. The Qin soldiers could not resist the attack by the Chu army, and they ran away.

The Chu soldiers destroyed the walled road and no more food could be transported to the Qin army under General Wang Li, and several days later, the Qin soldiers began to starve. The Chu army had achieved a victory. But the Chu army was greatly outnumbered by the Qin army. Zhang Han ordered his army to stage a counterattack; in the counterattack they drove the Chu army back and were able to rebuild the wall-road. The food supply was resumed and the Qin army under Wang Li prospered. So Ying Bu and General Pu had to pitch camp and wait for the main force to come.

Chen Yu sent a messenger to Xiang Yu asking for more troops. In January 207 BC, Xiang Yu with his army crossed the Zhang River. After they all reached the northern bank of the river, Xiang Yu ordered that all the ships be sunk to the bottom of the river and all the cooking utensils be destroyed. He also ordered that every soldier should carry enough solid food for three days. After the orders of Xiang Yu had been carried out, before the army started to march, Xiang Yu said to all his officers and men, "The ships have all been sunk and the cooking utensils have all been destroyed. We will have to fight to the death. We will not return without victory!" Then the whole army was set on a forced march with the determination that they would fight to win victory; otherwise they would die in battle. There was no way to turn back without victory. They went past the ruins of Handan and continued their march to the area of Julu, covering a distance of eighty kilometers in one day and one night. It was about midnight when they reached Julu. Ying Bu and General Pu joined Xiang Yu and reported to him about their action. After a short discussion, Xiang Yu decided to surround the Qin army under the command of Wang Li.

Morning came. The sun rose. The Chu army was drawn up in calm and confident array with Xiang Yu in command of the middle formation, Ying Bu in command of the right and General Pu in command of the left. Wang Li immediately made his arrangement. He sent a strong army out of the camp in battle array face to face with the Chu army. Xiang Yu issued the order to assault. The two armies joined and the battle began. The battle went on fiercely. The spirit of the Chu soldiers was keen. They fell upon the Qin soldiers with uproarious war cries that shook the sky. They were irresistible. They made their way forward fiercely, killing every Qin soldier on their way. Some Chu soldiers fell in battle, but others pressed on. Although the Chu army was inferior in number, each Chu soldier could take on nine or ten Qin soldiers. The soldiers of the armies of the other states were so shocked at the sight of the fierce fighting that they all stayed inside the walls of their camps and just looked on. They did not dare to go out to join in the battle. The fighting went on from morning till sunset, when the two sides withdrew for the night. The Chu soldiers were very tired. They did not bother to pitch camp. They just spent the night in the open. The next morning, the Chu soldiers got up and were ready for battle again.

Zhang Han had commanded his army from Jiyuan to reinforce the Qin army under Wang Li. Xiang Yu personally led an army to stop the advance of the Qin army commanded by Zhang Han. A fierce battle was fought. Zhang Han had to withdraw back to Jiyuan. The walled road was totally destroyed. Under Wang Li there was no hope for the Qin army to get any support from Zhang Han and there was no hope for them to get any further food supplies wither. Nine battles were fought. General Su Jiao of the Qin army was killed. Wang Li saw that his last moment had come. Leaving General She Xian to guard the camp, he rode out for a decisive battle. He met Xiang Yu in the battlefield. After several bouts, he was hit by Xiang Yu and fell from his horse. The Chu soldiers rushed up and captured him. When the Qin soldiers saw that their chief commander was captured, they threw down their weapons and surrendered. General She Xian saw that the Qin army had lost the battle but he would not surrender. Then he set fire to the tents inside the camp and to himself. The fire rose very high and burned up everything in the camp, and burned General She Xian to death.

There was no more fighting in the battlefield. There were no more war cries. The air fell silent. The sun was setting. The sky in the west was as red as blood. Xiang Yu had won the day. Finally, all the wagons and carts of the Chu army were lined up to form the walls of a campsite. Two wagons were erected in the middle of the wall with their shafts up to form the gate of the campsite. Then Xiang Yu led his army into this campsite.

The generals of the armies of the other states who had just looked on within the walls of their camps saw that the battle was over and that Xiang Yu had won a glorious victory, without their assistance. They were ashamed. They all rode out to the campsite of the Chu army. When they reached the gate made of the shafts of two wagons, they got down off their horses and crawled on all fours into the campsite, prostrating themselves at Xiang Yu's feet with great shame. They all expressed their respect for this great general and said that they would put themselves and their armies under Xiang Yu's command. Xiang Yu became the commander-in-chief of the united army of the States of Chu, Qi, Yan, Zhao and Dai.

The siege of Julu was raised. The King of the State of Zhao and Zhang Er came out of the city to the campsite of the Chu army. Xiang Yu received them. They expressed their hearty thanks to Xiang Yu and the generals of other states for their effort to save them from destruction.

When Zhang Er met Chen Yu, they had a fierce quarrel. Zhang Er blamed Chen Yu for not fighting hard enough to rescue them. Then Zhang Er asked, "I sent Zhang Yan and Chen Ze to ask for your help. Where are they now?" Chen Yu said, "Zhang Yan and Chen Ze insisted that I should die in fighting with the Qin army to show my devotion to our friendship. I disagreed with them. They said that they would have a try themselves. So I assigned them 5,000 men to go and fight the Qin army. They attacked the Qin army, but all of them died in action." Zhang Er said, "I don't believe it. It is you who killed them." Chen Yu said angrily, "I didn't know that you hated me so much. Will you be satisfied if I turn in my general's seal?" In saying that, he took out his general seal and pushed it in front of Zhang Er. Zhang Er was so surprised that he did not know what to say. He would have refused to accept it, but Chen Yu stood up and went to use the toilet. A man sitting beside Zhang Er said, "You will regret if you give up the chance to get what you can get. Now that General Chen Yu has given you his general seal, you should take it; otherwise, you will regret." Zhang Er followed his advice and took the seal. With that seal, he took all the troops under the command of Chen Yu. When Chen Yu came back, he found that Zhang Er had pocketed his seal and would not give it back to him.

Zhang Er escorted the King of the State of Zhao to Xindu (now Xingtao, Hebei Province). Then he returned with all the army under him to Julu to join Xiang Yu in the confrontation with the Qin Army under Zhang Han. Chen Yu left with several hundred followers to a place near the Yellow River, fishing and hunting for a living. From then on, the two men who had sworn to be friends unto death drifted apart and became mortal enemies.

22. Liu Bang's March to the Area of Guanzhong

While Xiang Yu was fighting his battles in Julu, Liu Bang was on his way marching to the areas of Guanzhong. In February 207 BC, Liu Bang met Peng Yue in the area of Changyi (now in the west of Jinxiang in the west part of Shangdong Province).

Peng Yue was a native of Changyi. He made a living by fishing in the marshes in the area of Juye (now Juye, Shandong Province). When Chen Sheng rose in rebellion against the rule of the Qin Dynasty, someone said to Peng Yue, "Now heroes of the realm have all risen against the rule of the Qin Dynasty. You may follow their example and rise up as well." Peng Yue said, "Now the two dragons are fighting fiercely. We may wait for a while to see the outcome." A year later, about a hundred young men among the marshes got together and organized themselves into an army. They went to see Peng Yue. They asked him to be their leader. Peng Yue refused, but they insisted; then he agreed. Then Peng Yue ordered, "We shall gather together at sunrise tomorrow morning. Anyone who is late will be put to death."

The next day, about ten men were late. They arrived after sunrise. The latest one arrived at noon. When the army had been lined up, Peng Yue said, "I am already old. You all made me the leader of this army. I gave the order yesterday that we should gather together at sunrise this morning. But many of you were late. According to military law, all who were late should suffer the death penalty. But I will not kill all of them. I order that the one who arrived here the latest be executed." And he ordered the squad leader to carry out the execution. The young men burst into laughter. They said, "Why are you so serious? We will not be late from now on." But Peng Yue said resolutely to the squad leader, "Carry out my order, now!" The squad leader took the man to a space of open ground and beheaded him. All the rest were shocked at the terrible execution. Now they understood military obedience; now they were obedient to Peng Yue. Then Peng Yue led this army into battle. In time, his army expanded into more than 1,000 men.

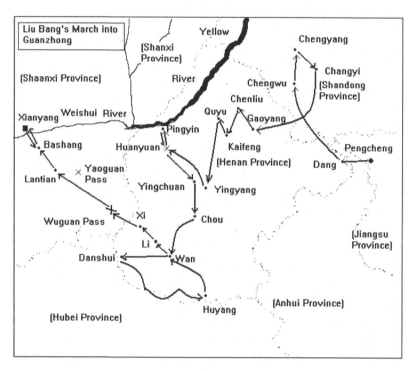

Liu Bang had a conference with Peng Yue. Liu Bang decided to attack the city of Changyi. Peng Yue offered his assistance in the attack of the city. The army under Liu Bang and the army under Peng Yue marched to the city of Changyi. They began to attack the city. But arrows and missiles rained down from the top of the city wall, and the soldiers under Liu Bang and Peng Yue could not get close to the city wall. They had to give up the attack and withdraw. Liu Bang said to Peng Yue, "I will continue my way to the west. Are you going with me?" Peng Yue said, "I would like to do the same. But all the officers and men of my army are local to this place. They would not leave their homeland. I will stay here to lead them in the struggle against the rule of the Qin Dynasty. I am sure I will have an opportunity to render my service to you later." So they parted. Liu Bang continued his march to the west with his army. Peng Yue led his army back to the marshes of Juye.

Liu Bang maneuvered his army west. When his army passed Gaoyang (now a place near Chenliu of Henan Province), a Confucian scholar by the name of Li Yi Ji asked to see Liu Bang. It happened that one of the officers of the cavalry of Liu Bang's army was from the place where Li Yi Ji lived. Li Yi Ji said to him, "I have seen many generals of different states. They all seem to be good for nothing. They do not listen to words with foresight. I hear that although The Duke of Pei is rude, he is easy to approach. He has great ambition. This is the man whom I really want to follow. Will you introduce me to him? When you see him, you may introduce me like this: 'In my home place, there is an old Confucian scholar by the name of Li Yi Ji. He is over sixty, and eight feet tall. The people of my home place all say that he is an insane scholar, but he says he is not mad.'" The officer said, "The Duke of Pei does not like Confucian scholars. If a Confucian scholar with a hat went to see him, he would take off the scholar's hat and piss in it. When he talks with other people, he curses loudly. So it is better not to mention that you are a Confucian scholar." Li Yi Ji said, "Just tell the Duke of Pei that I am a Confucian scholar."

The officer conveyed Li Yi Ji's words to Liu Bang, and Liu Bang sent a messenger to summon Li Yi Ji. When Li Yi Ji entered the house where Liu Bang was staying, Liu Bang was sitting on the edge of his bed, bare footed, with two young females kneeling, washing his feet. Li Yi Ji went to him. He just made a bow but did not kneel down. He said, "Are you helping the Qin Dynasty to oppress the other states or helping the other states to overthrow the rule of the Qin Dynasty?" Liu Bang cursed loudly, "You pedantic Confucian scholar. People all over the realm have suffered from the cruel rule of the Qin Dynasty for a long time. The people of all other states have risen in revolt against the Qin Dynasty. I will certainly not help the Qin Dynasty to oppress the people of the other states!" Li Yi Ji said, "If you have gathered so many people around you in order to overthrow the rule of the Qin Dynasty, you should not be so impolite when you receive an old man like me." At these words, Liu Bang immediately stopped the foot-washing and got dressed neatly. Then he invited Li Yi Ji to take a seat and apologized for his rudeness.

Li Yi Ji talked about the diplomatic relations of the united front of the six states against the State of Qin and the policy adopted by the State of Qin to break the united front during the period of Warring States. Liu Bang was very glad to hear what Li Yi Ji had to say. He asked Li Yi Ji, "What strategy should I adopt?" Li Yi Ji said, "Now you have an army of only 10,000 men. This army is made up of disparate soldiers you have gathered on your way. Now, with this army you are going to take the heavily defended area of Qin. This is practically like putting yourself into the mouth of a tiger. Chenliu is a strategic point. It is a traffic center from which you can go anywhere. A lot of food is stored in the city of Chenliu. I am well acquainted with the governor of Chenliu. If you officially appoint me as your envoy, I will try my best to persuade him to surrender. If he refuses to surrender, you will take the city by force. Then I will help attack the city from within." Liu Bang took his advice and appointed him as an envoy to go first, and then Liu Bang's army followed.

Liu Bang unleashed a surprise attack and successfully took the city of Chenliu (now Chenliu, Henan Province) with the help of Li Yi Ji. In appreciation he granted Li Yi Ji the title of the Lord of Guangye and entrusted to him the responsibility of diplomatic envoy to handle the relations among different states.

Li Yi Ji's younger brother Li Shang had gathered together several thousand young men in the area of Chenliu. When Liu Bang conquered Chenliu, Li Shang led his army of 4,000 men to join Liu Bang. Liu Bang appointed him general to command this army.

In March 207 BC, Liu Bang moved his army southwest to attack the city of Kaifeng (now a place to the southwest of Chenliu, Henan Province). Liu Bang assigned the task of attacking the north gate to Fan Kuai and the task of attacking the east gate to Cao Shen. They led their troops to the gates to challenge the Qin army to battle. Zhao Ben, the commander of the Qin army defending Kaifeng, ordered his troops to go out of the gates to meet Liu Bang's army. Liu Bang's army started a fierce attack to the Qin army. Fan Kuai took the lead of the attack. Guan Ying, who had joined Liu Bang's army in Dang, fought bravely and killed many Qin soldiers. Jin She, an officer under Cao Shen, killed a Qin general and many Qin soldiers. Zhao Ben saw that his troops could not resist the assault by Liu Bang's army. He ordered all the remaining troops to retreat into the city and seal all the gates.

Liu Bang laid siege to the city and challenged the Qin army to battle, but Zhao Ben refused to go out to fight.

A scout came hurriedly to report to Liu Bang that General Yang Xiong of the Qin army was marching his army from Baima to relieve the City of Kaifeng. Liu Bang immediately raised the siege of Kaifeng and moved his army eastward to intercept Yang Xiong's army. A battle was fought in the area west of Baima. But Yang Xiong forced his way to the east of Quyu (northeast of what is now Zhongmou, Henan Province) where he arranged his army into battle formation. Liu Bang led his army in pursuit of the Qin army. When he saw that Yang Xiong had arranged his army in battle array, he ordered his army to fan out for the battle. Cao Shen, Fan Kuai and Xiahou Ying led the army to attack. A fierce battle began. In the heat of the fray, an army of about 1,000 men arrived and joined in the attack on the Qin army. The Qin army broke formation and the Qin soldiers fled in disorder. Many Qin soldiers were captured. Yang Xiong escaped to Xingyang. Liu Bang won a great victory.

When the battle was over, the leader of the army which had recently arrived rode up to Liu Bang, got off his horse and knelt down in front of Liu Bang. When the man looked up, Liu Bang was surprised to see that it was Zhang Liang. Liu Bang went forward to help him up and said in great affection, "It's you, Zhang Liang! How have you been since we parted?" Zhang Liang said, "After I left Xue with the King of the State of Haan and 1,000 soldiers, we went back to the area of the former State of Haan. We took several cities, but very soon they were retaken by the Qin army. So we had to move to Yingchuan area and we carried out guerrilla warfare there. When I got the news that you had arrived in this area, I decided to join you again. I am very glad that I could see you here." The two friends talked for a long time.

Not long later, news came that the Second Emperor of the Qin Dynasty was very angry with Yang Xiong for his defeat; he sent an envoy to Xingyang to execute Yang Xiong as a warning to other generals of the Qin army.

In April 207 BC, with the help of Zhang Liang, Liu Bang moved his army south to occupy the area of Yingchuan (now the area from the south of Xinzheng to the Ying River, Henan Province) and several cities. When Liu Bang was ready to continue his march west, news came that General Sima Wang of the State of Zhao had taken Henei (now Wuzhi, Henan Province) and was moving west, planning to cross the Yellow River. He intended to march into the areas of Guanzhong. Liu Bang conferred on this matter with

Zhang Liang. Zhang Liang said, "I think that Sima Wang will most probably cross the Yellow River in the area of Pingyin, because Pingyin is the ferry crossing point; there the Yellow River is comparatively narrow. We should occupy that place to prevent Sima Wang from crossing the Yellow River and marching into Guanzhong. But we have to pass Luoyang before we can get to Pingyin. Luoyang is a big city and heavily defended by the Qin army. There are many Qin troops stationed in the areas south of Luoyang. We must try our best to avoid fighting on our way. We'd better go through Huanyuan Mountain where there are no Qin troops; Huanyuan is such a dangerous and difficult mountain that the Qin generals consider it a natural barrier and they do not station any troops to defend it." Liu Bang accepted his advice and led his army in the march to Pingyin (on the southern bank of the Yellow River near Mengjin, Henan Province). On their way, they passed Huanyuan Mountain (between Dengfeng and Goushi, Henan Province). The winding road was narrow with ninety-two twists and turns with a precipice on one side. Liu Bang's army crossed this mountain with great difficulty. When they came out on the other side, they found that they had reached the area of Luoyang. Liu Bang's army marched quickly north. In the north of Shi Village (in the area of Yanshi, Henan Province), to the east of Luoyang, some Qin troops were lined up in battle formation. Liu Bang's army broke them up and defeated the Qin army. Then they marched to Pingyin and occupied that place. When Sima Wang saw that the ferry crossing port had been occupied by Liu Bang and there was no hope for him to cross the Yellow River, he turned back to Henei with his army.

In June 207 BC, Liu Bang and his army returned from Pingyin to Yingchuan (now the area near Yuzhou, Henan Province) through the same route. When he reached Yingchuan, he held a meeting with the King of the State of Haan and Zhang Liang. Liu Bang said to the King of the State of Haan, "I will go south and will march into Guangzhong through Wuguan Pass. I hope Zhang Liang will go with me to assist me on the way. Will Your Excellency let him go with me?" The King of the State of Haan agreed. Liu Bang thanked him and proposed that the King of the State of Haan should stay behind in Yangzhai and take care of the cities they had occupied. The King of the State of Haan heartily agreed to that. Then the King of the State of Haan called in a general. He said, "Haan Xin, you may lead 1,000 soldiers to accompany the Duke of Pei in the march into Guanzhong." General Haan Xin said, "Yes!" Haan Xin was eight feet tall. He was a descendant of King

Shang of the former State of Haan before the State of Haan was conquered by the State of Qin.

Having taken his leave of the King of the State of Haan, Liu Bang, accompanied by Zhang Liang, went on his way south with his army. When Liu Bang and his army reached the area of Nanyang Prefecture (the area around Nanyang City, Henan Province), Yi, the commander of the Qin army in this area and the governor of Nanyang Prefecture, led an army to intercept the advancing army of Liu Bang in Chou (now a place near Yexian, Henan Province). They fought to the east of the city of Chou. The Qin army was crushed and Yi led his defeated army to Wuyang (now Fangcheng, Henan Province). Liu Bang's army pursued the Qin army to Wuyang. Another battle was fought to the east of that city. The Qin army was defeated again. Yi retreated to the city of Wan (now Nanyang City, Henan Province) leaving many horses behind, which Liu Bang was glad to add to his cavalry.

Liu Bang reached the city of Wan. The city walls were very strong and Qin soldiers were standing in combat readiness along the top. Liu Bang pondered his options. If he tried to storm the city, his army would suffer many casualties; if he laid siege, he would be delayed in his march to the areas of Guanzhong. So he simply ordered his army to go around the city of Wan and leave it unconquered and continue their march west.

Yi was standing at the top of the city wall, ready to resist the inevitable assault. He was very nervous. But when he saw that Liu Bang's army circumvent the city and continue their way west, he was relieved. After Liu Bang's army had marched for fifteen kilometers, Zhang Liang rode up to Liu Bang and said to him, "I know that you are eager to reach Guanzhong. But the Qin troops are still many and they have occupied strategic points. If we leave the city of Wan untaken, then the Qin army of Wan will attack us from behind; and there are strong Qin troops ahead of us. We will be in a very dangerous situation." Liu Bang recognized the danger and when night fell, he led his army back to Wan by another path, with all flags furled and no sound to be made. They arrived at the outside of the city of Wan before dawn and surrounded the city in three rings. Yi was still sleeping when a soldier dashed in and reported that Liu Bang's army had come back and had surrounded the city. Yi hurried to the top of the city wall and saw that indeed, Liu Bang's army was ready to storm them. When Yi saw that he could not resist the attack, he drew out his sword, put it to his own throat and was ready to kill himself.

Chen Hui, an official under the governor, rushed forward and took away the sword from Yi's hand. Chen Hui said, "Death is not the only solution. The situation is not as desperate as you think. There is still hope. If you agree, I will go out to negotiate with Liu Bang on your behalf." Yi agreed and ordered the soldiers to let Chen Hui down the city wall with a rope. Chen Hui said to the soldiers surrounding the city, "Take me to the Duke of Pei. I have important things to tell him." Chen Hui was taken to Liu Bang's tent.

Liu Bang received him and asked, "What do you want to tell me?" Chen Hui said, "As far as I know, King Huai of the State of Chu has made the promise that the general who first enters the areas of Guanzhong will be made King of Guanzhong. Now you are stuck in front of the strong city of Wan. Wan is the capital of a big prefecture. There are many cities and counties under the jurisdiction of Nanyang Prefecture. This prefecture is a land of abundance and it has a large population. If the officials of these cities think that they will all be killed if they surrender, they will be resolute in defending their cities. If you attack the heavily fortified city of Wan, your army will suffer great losses. It will take you a long time to capture the city and you will be greatly delayed in marching into Guanzhong; you will lose the chance to be made King. Yet if you do not take the city of Wan and only go around it, the strong army of Wan will be a threat to your rear. My suggestion is to allow the Governor of Nanyang Prefecture to surrender and make him a marquis. Let him remain governor of Wan. You may take his army with you to march west. Then the generals defending the cities ahead will gladly open the gates of their cities to welcome you. Then you may march forward without any resistance."

Liu Bang was impressed. "I agree! Go back and tell him that I have accepted his surrender and will make him a marquis." In July 207 BC, Yi, the Governor of Nanyang Prefecture, opened the city gate and welcomed Liu Bang into the city. Liu Bang made him the Marquis of Yin. Chen Hui was handsomely rewarded and promoted to a high position.

Liu Bang put the troops of Wan in the van of his army and marched west. All the cities ahead were taken without a fight. When his army was marching along the road to Danshui (now Danshui in the southwest part of Henan Province), an army of about 3,000 men lined the roadside. The commander of this army was Wang Ling, who was from Pei, the same home place of Liu Bang. He and Liu Bang had been good friends in their youth. Liu Bang had treated him as his elder brother. When Liu Bang revolted in Pei,

Wang Ling had not wanted to be a subordinate of Liu Bang. He left Pei and went to the area of Nanyang Prefecture where he organized an army and carried out military operations. When he found out that Liu Bang was leading an army to march into Guanzhong, he decided to meet him on the way. When he saw Liu Bang, he rode up to him and saluted him on horseback. Liu Bang was surprised to see Wang Ling there and said, "Is that you, Wang Ling? Why are you here?" Wang Ling said, "Since I left Pei, I have organized an army and have fought against the Qin army in this place." Liu Bang asked, "Are you going to join me to march into Guanzhong?" Wang Ling said, "I am afraid not. I prefer to go on with my fighting in the Nanyang area." Liu Bang said, "I hope we will meet again." Liu Bang went on his way and Wang Ling stayed behind.

Liu Bang's army swung southeastward to Huyang (now Huyang, Henan Province), where Liu Bang met with Mei Xuan, a general sent by Wu Rui, Lord of Po (the ruler of the barbarian areas to the south of the Yangtze River). They marched together northward, passed the city of Wan again and took Li (to the northwest of Nanyang, Henan Province). Then Liu Bang's army marched westward and took Xi (now Xixia, Henan Province). By the end of July 207 BC, Liu Bang was marching towards Wuguan Pass. He was sure to be the first general to enter the areas of Guanzhong.

23. Zhang Han Surrenders to Xiang Yu

After the battle of Julu, the army of the State of Chu under Xiang Yu wiped out the army of the Qin Dynasty under General Wang Li. In February 207 BC, the Qin army under Zhang Han was stationed in Jiyuan (a place to the south of Julu). The united army of the States of Chu, Zhao, Qi, Yan and Dai under Xiang Yu was stationed in Zhangnan (also a place near Julu). The two armies were confronting each other in a stalemate. The army under Xiang Yu pressed on. The Qin army under Zhang Han retreated several times. At last Zhang Han led his army across the Zhang River and retreated to Yinxu (now Xiaotun Village of Anyang, Henan Province). The Second Emperor of the Qin Dynasty sent an envoy to reprimand Zhang Han. Zhang Han was afraid, so in April 207 BC, he sent Shima Xin back to Xianyang to explain to the Second Emperor the unfavorable situation they were in and to ask for reinforcements. When Shima Xin arrived in Xianyang, he immediately went to the gate of the palace asking for an audience. But at that time, all the power of the Qin Dynasty was in the hands of Zhao Gao, the premier. Zhao Gao would not receive Sima Xin. It was clear that Zhao Gao did not trust him. Shima Xin was afraid and decided to go back to his army. He was sure that Zhao Gao would send troops to catch him, so he did not go back the same way he had come but took another route. As Sima Xin had expected, Zhao Gao sent a party of soldiers to run after him along the way from which he had come, but the soldiers did not find him.

When Shima Xin reached his army, he reported to Zhang Han, "Now the power of the Qin Dynasty is in Zhao Gao's hands. I think he means us harm. If we win, Zhao Gao will be jealous of our success. If we lose, we cannot escape death. We are in a tight spot." Zhang Han said, "You're right. We are in a very difficult situation. We must try to find a way out."

While Zhang Han was thinking hard and trying to find a solution, he received a letter from Chen Yu, the former commander-in-chief of the army of the State of Zhao. In the letter, Chen Yu said that General Bai Qi and General Meng Tian had made great contributions to the State of Qin, but they had both ended up in tragedy: Bai Qi was ordered to kill himself by the King of the State of Qin; Meng Tian was killed by the Second Emperor of the Qin Dynasty. He told Zhang Han that the Qin Dynasty was doomed to fall and that Zhang Han could not survive after the Qin Dynasty had fallen. He pointed out that the only solution for Zhang Han was to turn to the side of the people and unite with the forces of the other states to overthrow the rule of the Qin Dynasty.

Zhang Han made up his mind, but he did not know the intention of Xiang Yu. In June 207 BC, Zhang Han secretly sent Shi Cheng, an officer under him, as his envoy to see Xiang Yu to negotiate a truce agreement. But Xiang Yu turned down his suggestion, for he still hated Zhang Han.

In July 207 BC, Xiang Yu sent General Pu with an army to march southward. This army crossed the Zhang River from the port of Sanhu (now to the southwest of Cixian County, Hebei province). General Pu stationed his army on the southern bank of the Zhang River. A battle was fought and the Qin army was defeated. Then Xiang Yu moved all his army from Julu southward to attack the Qin army on the Yushui River and won a great victory over the Qin army.

Zhang Han sent Sima Xin as his envoy to see Xiang Yu. Sima Xin had been a friend of Xiang Liang. When Sima Xin was a prison officer in Yucyang (to the north of Lintong, Shaanxi Province), he had saved Xiang Liang from trouble. When Sima Xin arrived at the camp of the united army, Xiang Yu received him with due courtesy. Sima Xin succeeded in persuading Xiang Yu to accept Zhang Han's suggestion of a truce agreement. Then Xiang Yu called his officers together to discuss this matter. He said to them, "Zhang Han has sent an envoy to suggest a truce. Our food supply is short, so I intend to accept his suggestion. What do you think about it?" All the officers agreed with Xiang Yu.

Xiang Yu and Zhang Han met in Yinxu (now a place near Anyang City, Henan Province) on the south bank of Hengshui River. After they signed the treaty, Zhang Han told Xiang Yu with tears what Zhao Gao, the premier of the Qin Dynasty, had done to him. Xiang Yu was sympathetic, and made him King of Yong (the west part of the areas of Guanzhong). He kept Zhang Han in the army of the State of Chu. Xiang Yu appointed Sima Xin commander-in-chief of the Qin army of 200,000 men originally under the command of Zhang Han. Xiang Yu put this Qin army in the van of his whole army. His main force of the united army was made up of 400,000 men from the States of Chu, Zhao, Yan, Qi and Dai. Xiang Yu led this great army of 600,000 men on the march towards Guangzhong.

At that time, Wei Bao had taken more than twenty cities of the former State of Wei. Xiang Yu made him King of the State of Wei. Wei Bao was very grateful to Xiang Yu, so he led his picked troops to join Xiang Yu in the march to Guanzhong.

24. ZHAO GAO KILLS THE SECOND EMPEROR OF THE QIN DYNASTY AND PUTS YING ZI YING ON THE THRONE OF THE STATE OF QIN

After Zhang Han surrendered to Xiang Yu, the situation was very unfavorable to the Qin Dynasty. By the end of July 207 BC, Liu Bang's army was very close to Wuguan Pass and Xiang Yu was leading a great army on the march towards Guanzhong. Zhao Gao was afraid that the Second Emperor of the Qin Dynasty would hold him responsible for the failure and punish him. He made up his mind to depose the Second Emperor of the Qin Dynasty, for that was the only way to avoid punishment. But he was not sure whether the ministers would follow him in this action.

He thought of a way to test the ministers' attitude. One day in August 207 BC, when the Second Emperor was holding court, with the ministers lined up on both sides, Zhao Gao entered the chamber with a deer.

He bowed to the emperor and said, "I have brought this horse to present to Your Majesty." The Second Emperor laughed loudly and said, "You are mistaken, Premier. That is not a horse. It is a deer. You are taking a deer for a horse." Zhao Gao said, "It is a horse!" The Second Emperor asked the ministers on both sides, "Is this a horse or a deer?" Some kept silent. Some said, "It is a horse." Very few said, "It is a deer." Zhao Gao identified those who said that it was a deer and later found some fault with them and had them put to death. The ministers were all afraid of Zhao Gao and became obedient to him.

The situation became worse and worse. The Second Emperor sent an envoy to condemn Zhao Gao for his incompetence in suppressing the rebellions. Zhao Gao was afraid. He decided to step up his plan. He conspired with his son-in-law Yan Yue, the commander of the garrison of Xianyang, and his younger brother Zhao Cheng, the commander of the garrison of the palace. Yan Yue led 1,000 soldiers into Wangyi Palace on the pretext that thieves had stolen into the grounds and buildings. And then Yan Yue and Zhao Cheng forced the Second Emperor of the Qin Dynasty to kill himself.

Zhao Gao put Ying Zi Ying, the son of the elder brother of the Second Emperor, on the throne of the Qin Dynasty. On the day when Ying Zi Ying was to go to the Ancestral Temple to receive the seal of the King of the State of Qin, Zhao Gao went to the palace to make sure Ying Zi Ying was going to go. Ying Zi Ying drove a dagger into Zhao Gao's heart and killed him. Ying Zi Ying ascended the throne of the State of Qin.

25. Liu Bang Takes the Area of Qin, and Ying Zi Ying, the King of the State of Qin, Surrenders to Liu Bang

In August 207 BC, Liu Bang took Wuguan Pass by storm and succeeded in entering the areas of Guanzhong. Liu Bang issued an order to his army to prohibit any looting of the people of Qin. His army marched with great discipline and the people of Qin liked Liu Bang and welcomed his army.

Ying Zi Ying, King of the State of Qin, sent generals with a great army to Yaoguan Pass (to the northwest of Shangzhou, Shaanxi Province) to resist his advance. Liu Bang wanted to send 20,000 men to attack the Qin army stationed in Yaoguan Pass. But Zhang Liang said, "The Qin army is still strong. We cannot easily take it. I hear that the commanding general of the Qin army guarding Yaoguan Pass is the son of a butcher. As a rule, such people are greedy. We can buy him over with money. You might just stay inside the camp. You can send several thousand men with a lot of flags and banners to the mountains around the pass so that our enemy will think that we have a large contingent of troops there. And you can send Li Yi Ji and Lu Jia with gold to the Qin army to bribe the commanding general." Liu Bang agreed with his plan.

Liu Bang sent several thousand soldiers to the mountains near Yaoguan Pass with a lot of red flags and banners. When they arrived there, they put up the flags. The commanding general was shocked to see such a display in the mountains near the pass and he thought the army under Liu Bang must be very strong. Then a soldier reported to him that two envoys sent by Liu Bang had come to the gate of the pass and requested to see him.

He invited the envoys into his tent. Li Yi Ji presented the gold to the commanding general of the Qin army, saying, "This is a gift from the Duke of Pei." The commanding general had never seen so much gold in his life. He asked Li Yi Ji, "Why has the Duke of Pei given me so much gold?" Li Yi Ji said, "The Duke of Pei knows that you are a valorous general and he admires you. He wants to be allies with you. The situation has become unfavorable to the Qin Dynasty. It will fall very soon. Can you go on when the Qin Dynasty falls?" The commanding general thought for a moment and said, "I intend to unite with the Duke of Pei and march together to the west to take Xianyang. Will you convey my suggestion to the Duke of Pei and ask him to give his consent to the plan?" Li Yi Ji and Lu Jia agreed and left.

Li Yi Ji and Lu Jia returned to the camp and reported to Liu Bang that the commanding general of the Qin army now intended to unite with him and march to the west to take Xianyang. Liu Bang was very glad and was about to give his consent, but Zhang Liang pointed out, "Now only the commanding general wants to come over, but I am afraid that the officers and men under his command will not follow him. If the officers and men do not follow him, the situation will become dangerous. We'd better attack the Qin army by surprise now that the commanding general is no longer vigilant against us." Liu Bang saw the merit in that analysis and led the army to take a detour around the Yaoguan Pass and attacked the Qin army from behind the pass. Liu Bang's army won a resounding victory over the Qin army and chased the defeated Qin army to the south of Lantian (now Lantian, Shaanxi Province). Another battle was fought in Lantian, where the Qin army was totally defeated. From then on, the State of Qin had no real army to resist the advance of Liu Bang.

In October 207 BC, Liu Bang reached Bashang (now Baqiao near Xi'an, Shaanxi Province) which was very close to Xianyang. At night, a spectacular vision appeared in the southwest sky. Five stars, actually Mercury, Venus, Mars, Jupiter and Saturn, lined up in a straight line. The astronomers predicted that "the virtuous man would prosper, and the virtueless man would suffer disaster."

Liu Bang sent an envoy to Xianyang to see Ying Zi Ying, the King of the State of Qin, with a letter demanding his surrender. Ying Zi Ying had been on the throne for only 46 days. When he received the letter, he realized that he could do nothing to save the State of Qin, so he decided to surrender to Liu Bang. He fastened a white rope round his own neck, meaning that he deserved to be hanged. Then he went to Zhidao Pavilion, which was just a hundred feet west of Bashang, in a carriage lined with white curtains, drawn by a white horse. When he arrived at Zhidao Pavilion, he climbed out of the carriage and stood by the side of the pavilion holding the jade seal of the emperor of the Qin Dynasty in his hands, waiting for Liu Bang to accept his surrender.

Some generals under Liu Bang suggested to him that Ying Zi Ying should be put to death. Liu Bang said, "At the outset, King Huai of the State of Chu sent me to take the areas of Guanzhong because he thought that I was lenient by nature. Now Ying Zi Ying has surrendered. It will bring bad luck to us if we kill someone who has surrendered." Then he went to Ying Zi Ying, took the jade seal of the emperor of the Qin Dynasty, accepted the surrender of Ying Zi Ying and handed him over to the charge of the officers of justice.

Liu Bang marched his army from Bashang to Xianyang. He ordered his army to pitch camps outside the city. Then he entered the city with his generals and a few troops. The generals under him all went to the warehouses of the Qin government to take the gold and silver and cloth and silk to share among themselves. But Xiao He went to the offices of the premier and ministers of the Qin Dynasty and collected all the maps and books and kept them in a safe place. With these maps and books, Xiao He helped Liu Bang get to know the strategic points and the population distribution all over the realm.

When Liu Bang entered the palace with several close friends, he was charmed by the splendid halls and chambers. Several thousand beautiful women and innumerable treasures were kept in the palace. He wanted to stay in the palace to savor some of these treats. He lingered in the chambers of the palace and would not leave.

At that moment, Fan Kuai entered and said, "Do you want to own the whole realm or just to be a rich man?" Liu Bang said, "I want to own the whole realm." Then Fan Kuai said, "Today, I followed you into this palace and saw the beautifully decorated halls and chambers, numerous jewels, jade carvings and all kinds of treasures, and the beautiful women kept in the imperial harem. It is all these luxurious things that led to the downfall of the Qin Dynasty. You don't need these things. You'd better get back to Bashang instead of staying in the palace." Liu Bang would not listen to him.

Fan Kuai went out and came across Zhang Liang. He told Zhang Liang what he had said to Liu Bang and asked him to persuade Liu Bang to leave the palace. Zhang Liang nodded and went into the chamber. He said to Liu Bang, "The Emperor of the Qin Dynasty oppressed the people cruelly and he himself led a luxurious life. This is the reason for the destruction of the Qin Dynasty. You have come all the way here expressly to overthrow the tyrannical rule of the Qin Dynasty. Since your goal is to get rid of the cruel rule of the Qin Dynasty, you should lead a simple life to show your sympathy for the poor people. Now you have just entered the capital of the Qin Dynasty and you have begun to enjoy the luxuries of the Qin Dynasty; you are actually toying with evil as bad as that which the rulers of the Qin Dynasty have committed. There is a saying which goes: medicine, though bitter to the mouth, helps cure the disease; honest advice, though unpleasant to the ear, induces good conduct. I hope you will listen to Fan Kuai's advice." Liu Bang accepted their advice and turned back to Bashang with his army.

In November, Liu Bang called all the elders and gentry in the Qin area together and said to them, "You have all suffered from the harsh laws of the Qin Dynasty for a long time. I made an agreement with all the generals of all the states that the general who first reached the areas within Guanzhong would be the king of Guanzhong. Since I am the general who was the first to reach Guanzhong, I should be made king of Guanzhong. Now I will enact three chapters of law: he who kills a person will be killed; he who has wounded another person will be given punishment equal to the harm he has done to the other person; he who has stolen from another will be given punishment equal to what he has stolen. All the laws enacted by the Qin Dynasty will become void. Apart from this, everything remains the same as before. I have come here only to do away everything that is harmful to you. We will not do anything harmful to you. So you all may be at ease. My army and I have returned to Bashang to wait for all the other generals to come and I will maintain peace with these three chapters of law."

Then the three chapters of law were promulgated through various levels of the original officials. The people of Qin were all happy, and they brought gifts such as cows, sheep, and wine to Liu Bang's army. But Liu Bang did not accept the gifts and persuaded them to take them back, saying, "We have sufficient food stored. We are not in short supply. We don't want to harm the people." When the people heard this, they became even happier. Their only worry was that Liu Bang could not become king of the areas of Guanzhong.

26. XIANG YU'S MARCH TO THE AREA OF GUANZHONG

Since Xiang Yu had put down any resistance in the areas to the north of the Yellow River, he now led the armies of all the states in the march to the areas of Guanzhong. During the reign of the First Emperor of the Qin Dynasty and the Second Emperor of the Qin Dynasty, people of the former other six states had been sent to do hard labor or had served in the Qin areas, and they had been treated very badly by the Qin soldiers. Now many of them had become officers and men in the armies against the rule of the Qin Dynasty, and they had a chance to take revenge. They treated the Qin soldiers who had changed sides like slaves and often insulted them. The Qin soldiers were unhappy about that. They talked secretly among themselves. "We have all been deceived by General Zhang Han and have surrendered to the generals of the other states. If we can successfully enter the areas of Guanzhong and defeat the Qin army, that will be all right. But if we cannot enter the pass, we will have to retreat eastward with the soldiers of the other states. Then our fathers and mothers, wives and children will be put to death by the government of the Qin Dynasty for our surrender. What shall we do?" The generals learned of their concerns and reported to Xiang Yu. Xiang Yu called Ying Bu and General Pu together and said to them, "There are many Qin soldiers in our army. They are unhappy about Zhang Han's decision to surrender. If the Qin soldiers do not follow our orders when we reach Hanguguan Pass, then the situation will be very dangerous. We'd better kill all these Qin soldiers and only spare Zhang Han, Shima Xin and Dong Yi, and march to Hanguguan Pass with these three men." And one night in September 207 BC, the Chu army hit the sleeping Qin soldiers with a surprise attack at midnight, disarmed them, and then killed all of them, 200,000 in total, by burying them alive in a place to the south of the city of Xin'an (now Xin'an, Henan Province). Then Xiang Yu and his great army marched towards Hanguguan Pass.

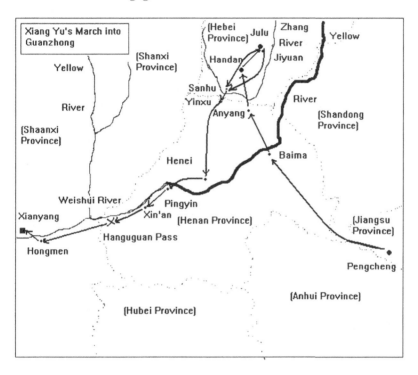

As Xiang Yu's great army of 400,000 men was approaching Hanguguan Pass, someone suggested to Liu Bang, "The Qin area is the richest place all over China. This area has the topographical advantages. I have heard that Xiang Yu has made Zhang Han King of Yong area. If he comes, you will not be made king of Guanzhong. You'd better immediately send an army to guard Hanguguan Pass to keep Xiang Yu's army out. You might recruit the local people so that you may strengthen your army." Liu Bang took his advice and sent an army to guard Hanguguan Pass.

When Xiang Yu reached Hanguguan Pass, the gate was shut tightly. Xiang Yu rode to the foot of the gate of the pass and shouted, "I am Xiang

Yu. Open the gate now." The officer defending the pass shouted back, "I have orders from the Duke of Pei not to let anyone into the pass. You'd better turn back." Xiang Yu was enraged. He ordered Ying Bu, "Take the pass for me, now!" Ying Bu led his soldiers to storm the pass. The soldiers under Ying Bu put ladders against the wall of the fortifications guarding the pass and climbed up quickly. Although the defending soldiers fought bravely, they could not resist the fierce attack of the assaulting soldiers. Very soon the pass was taken by Xiang Yu's army. Xiang Yu and the united army of the states went through that pass into the areas of Guanzhaong.

In December, Xiang Yu reached Xi (a place to the east of Xianyang). He ordered his army to camp in a place named Hongmen, which had been the campsite of the garrison army of the Qin Dynasty. That night, a man came to the gate of the camp of Hongmen, claiming that he had important information to tell Xiang Yu. He was brought to Xiang Yu's tent. The man said to Xiang Yu, "I am an envoy sent by General Cao Wu Shang of Liu Bang's army. He has sent me to tell you: Liu Bang wants to be king of Guanzhong, and he has appointed Ying Zi Ying, the former King of the State of Qin, as the premier, and he has taken all the treasures in the palaces for his own." When Xiang Yu got the message, he was furious. Then he ordered, "Tomorrow morning, provide good food for the soldiers. We will crush Liu Bang's army tomorrow!" At that time, Xiang Yu's great army of 400,000 men was stationed in Hongmen of Xinfeng (Xinfeng Town, Shaanxi Province). Liu Bang's army of only 100,000 men was stationed in Bashang. Hongmen and Bashang were just thirty kilometers way. Fan Zeng said to Xiang Yu, "When Liu Bang was at his home in Pei, he was a greedy man. He liked money and beautiful girls, but since he reached the areas of Guanzhong, he has not taken any valuable things. He has not slept with any of the beauties in the palaces. From this we can see that he has grand ambitions. A fortuneteller told me that he could see clouds of five color figures of dragons and tigers above Liu Bang's head. This time when we attack him we must make sure that he is killed and not let him escape."

When Xiang Bo, Xiang Yu's uncle, got the order, he immediately thought of Zhang Liang, who was now in Liu Bang's army. Ten years ago, Xiang Bo had killed a local bully and ran away from home. He had found refuge in Zhang Liang's home in Xiapi. It was Zhang Liang who had saved his life. Now Zhang Liang was in great danger. It was his turn to save him from destruction. So he mounted his horse, rode out of the camp and galloped to the camp of Liu Bang's army in Bashang. He stopped at the gate of the camp and told the guards that he had something urgent to tell Zhang Liang. He was shown to Zhang Liang's tent. As soon as he saw Zhang Liang, he said, "Get away now, before it is too late!" Zhang Liang asked in great surprise, "What has happened?" Xiang Bo said, "Xiang Yu has issued an order to attack the Duke of Pei's army tomorrow morning. You must leave now." But Zhang Liang said, "The King of Haan has asked me to escort the Duke of Pei to the areas of Guanzhong. Now the Duke of Pei is in great danger. If I run away without telling him, it would be an immoral act on my part. We must inform him of the danger. You sit here for a moment. I will go to his tent and warn him of the danger." Zhang Liang went to Liu Bang's tent. Zhang Ling said, "Tomorrow Xiang Yu will attack our camp!" Liu Bang said in great surprise, "There is no hatred between Xiang Yu and me. Why should he attack me?" Zhang Liang asked, "Who advised you to guard Hanguguan Pass?" Liu Bang answered, "A scholar name Zousheng came to give me that advice. He said that I must guard the Pass to prevent others from coming into the area of Guangzhong so that I could be sure to be the king of the Qin area. Was that a wrong move?" Zhang Liang asked, "Do you think that your army can withstand an attack by the army commanded by Xiang Yu?" Liu Bang said, "I am afraid not." Zhang Liang went on, "There are only 100,000 men in our army. But there are 400,000 men in Xiang Yu's army. It is impossible for our army to resist Xiang Yu's army. Xiang Bo has come to ask me to run away to avoid being killed. But I will not desert you. I must inform you of the danger." "What shall we do?" Liu Bang asked. Zhang Liang said, "You'd better ask Xiang Bo to tell Xiang Yu that you did not intend to prevent Xiang Yu from entering the Qin area, and that you sent an army to guard the pass only to keep out of the bandits. This will help to clarify the misunderstanding. Xiang Bo is Xiang Yu's uncle. Perhaps he may persuade Xiang Yu to give up the attack." Liu Bang asked, "Are you a good friend of his?" Zhang Liang said, "During the reign of the Qin Dynasty, we were already friends. He once killed somebody and came to me for help. I hid him up and helped him escape. Now there is danger, and he has come to warn me of the danger." Liu Bang asked, "Who is senior, you or he?" Zhang Liang said, "He is older than me." Liu Bang said, "Please ask him in and I will treat him as my elder brother." Zhang Liang went out and invited Xiang Bo into Liu Bang's tent. Liu Bang presented a cup of wine to him and proposed a toast to Xiang Bo's health. Then Liu Bang said, "When I entered the areas of Guanzhong,

I did not dare to touch anything. I have pacified all the officials and people in the Qin area. I have sealed all the treasure houses for General Xiang Yu. I sent troops to guard Hanguguan Pass only to prevent bandits from going through the pass. I have been longing for General Xiang Yu to come. I do not dare to betray him. Please tell General Xiang Yu that I will not forget his kindness to me." Xiang Bo promised to do so and said, "You must go to see General Xiang Yu first thing tomorrow morning and apologize to him personally." Liu Bang said that he would go early the next morning. Xiang Bo rode back to his army and reported to Xiang Yu what Liu Bang had said. Then Xiang Bo said, "If the Duke of Pei had not taken the passes first, could you have entered the region so easily? The Duke of Pei has made great contributions, but you are going to attack him. That is not a righteous thing to do. I think we'd better treat him kindly instead." Xiang Yu agreed.

27. THE BANQUET IN HONGMEN

The gate of Hongmen

The site of Hongmen. The vault shape tent is the place where the banquet took place.

Early the next morning, Liu Bang set out in a carriage drawn by two horses. Xiahou Ying was his driver. Zhang Liang,

Fan Kuai, Jin Jiang, and Ji Xin with a hundred men on horses followed. They rode along the main road to Hongmen to see Xiang Yu. When they reached the gate of the camp of Xiang Yu's army, Liu Bang got out of the carriage and his followers dismounted from their horses. Zhang Liang asked the guards of the camp to inform Xiang Yu that Liu Bang had come to visit him. Liu Bang and Zhang Ling were shown to Xiang Yu's tent and the others stayed inside the camp by the gate.

Liu Bang and Zhang Ling went into the tent. Xiang Yu was sitting on a chair with Xiang Bo and Fan Zeng standing on both sides. Liu Bang made a bow to Xiang Yu. Xiang Yu just made a little move on the chair to show his welcome to the guests. Liu Bang apologized to Xiang Yu by saying, "You and I have been fighting side by side against the Qin army. You fought in the areas to the north of the Yellow River, and I fought in the areas to the south of the Yellow River. I did not expect that I could reach the areas of Guan-zhong first and overthrow the rule of the Qin Dynasty. I am very happy to meet you here again. But some ill-intended person has passed false informa-tion to cause misunderstanding between you and me." Xiang Yu said, "It is Cao Wu Shang of your army who gave the information. Otherwise, I would not have prepared the action against you."

Xiang Yu (on the right) and Liu Bang (on the left) at the banquet

Then Xiang Yu invited Liu Bang into a big tent where a banquet was spread. Xiang Yu and Xiang Bo sat on the west side of the tent. Fan Zeng sat on the north side. Liu Bang sat on the south side and Zhang Liang sat on the east side. In front of each one, there was a table on which wonderful food and wine were laid out. There was an open space in the middle of the tent. During the banquet, Fan Zeng eyed Xiang Yu several times and held up his jade three times to urge Xiang Yu to kill Liu Bang. But Xiang Yu ignored his signals. Fan Zeng got up and went out of the tent and called Xiang Zhuang and said to him, "Xiang Yu is not hardhearted enough to kill Liu Bang. You go in and propose a toast to the health of Liu Bang, and then you may offer to perform a sword dance and seize the opportunity to strike Liu Bang in his seat and kill him. If we do not kill him now, we'll all be his prisoners in the future."

Xiang Zhuang went into the tent and proposed a toast to Liu Bang's health. Then he said, "There is no entertainment in the army. I would like to present a sword dance to entertain you." Xiang Yu said, "Good." Xiang Zhuang drew out his sword and began his sword dance. He was moving closer and closer to Liu Bang during the sword dance. It was clear what was coming. Then Xiang Bo also drew his sword and joined in the sword dance. He protected Liu Bang with his own body so that Xiang Zhuang did not have a chance to hit Liu Bang. Zhang Liang went out of the tent and went to the gate of the camp where Fan Kuai was standing. Fan Kuai asked, "What is going on in there?" Zhang Liang said, "Now Xiang Zhuang is performing a sword dance. His intention is to kill the Duke of Pei." Fan Kuai said, "Now the situation is critical. I'll go in to share life and death with the Duke of Pei." With his sword in his right hand and his shield in his left hand, he went to the opening of the tent. The guards would not let him in. He shoved the guards with his shield and several fell down. Then he went through the curtain of the opening into the tent and stood facing westward. When Xiang Zhuang saw Fan Kuai, he immediately stopped his sword dance and left the tent. Fan Kuai stared at Xiang Yu with angry eyes. He was so angry that his hair stood up and his eyes were widely open. Xiang Yu immediately put his hand on the handle of his sword and asked, "Who is he?" Zhang Liang said, "General Fan Kuai under the Duke of Pei." Xiang Yu said, "What a warrior he is! Give him two cups of wine!" The wine was served to him. He knelt down to express his thanks to Xiang Yu. Then he stood up and took the cups of wine and drank it up. Xiang Yu said, "Give him a big piece of the hind of a pig." A big piece of raw pork was served. Fan Kuai put his shield on the ground, and then put the pork on his shield. He drew out his sword and cut up the pork and picked up the cut pieces with his sword and ate the meat. Xiang Yu said, "What a warrior! Can you still drink some more wine?" Fan Kuai said, "I am not afraid of death. Why should I be afraid of drinking some more wine? The Emperors of the Qin Dynasty ruled over the people cruelly. They killed many people and punished people cruelly. People all over the realm rose against the rule of the Qin Dynasty. King Huai of the State of Chu has promised that the general who first destroys the rule of the Qin Dynasty and first reaches Xianyang will be made king of the areas of Guanzhong. Now the Duke of Pei is the general who first destroyed the rule of the Qin Dynasty and reached Xianyang first. He did not touch anything in Xianyang. He returned to Bashang to wait for your coming. He has worked hard and made great contributions. You have not granted him any title for his outstanding service and never said a kind word for his contributions. Instead, you listened to the false accusation made by some person and prepared to kill a man who has rendered such great service. What you planned to do is what the Emperors of the Qin Dynasty have done, and that is what led to the fall of the Qin Dynasty. If I were you, I would not have done that." Xiang Yu did not make a response to this but just said, "General Fan, take your seat." Fan Kuai took a seat beside Zhang Liang.

A moment later, Liu Bang got up and said that he wanted to go to the toilet. On his way out of the tent, he called Fan Kuai and Zhang Liang to go with him. When they were outside of the tent, Liu Bang said, "We are leaving but we have not yet said good-bye to Xiang Yu. What shall we do?" Fan Kuai said, "The man who aims to fulfill a great enterprise does not care for trivial matters. He attends to important matters but disregards formalities. Xiang Yu and Fan Zeng intend to kill us. Why should we say good-bye to them?" Then Liu Bang made up his mind to leave without saying good-bye to Xiang Yu. He asked Zhang Liang to stay behind. Zhang Liang asked, "Have you brought any gifts to present to Xiang Yu and Fan Zeng?" Liu Bang said, "I have brought a pair of round pieces of white jade to present to Xiang Yu and a jade cup to Fan Zeng. I cannot present these gifts to them personally. Will you present these gifts to them for me?" Zhang Liang said, "I will." Liu Bang said to Zhang Liang, "We will go down the hill to a small path along Lishan Mountain. It is only six miles away from here to our army if we go this way. When you think that I have reached our army, you may go in and tell them that I have left." Then they left and Zhang Liang stayed behind. Liu Bang and his men left their horses and the carriage in Hongmen. Only Liu Bang rode a horse. Fan Kuai, Xiahou Ying, Jin Jiang and Ji Xin were going on foot with their swords and shields in their hands. They went by a path at the foot of Lishan Mountain, and then to a side road in Ziyang, and hurried secretly back to Bashang. As soon as he reached the camp of his army, Liu Bang immediately ordered Cao Wu Shang to be arrested and put to death.

Xiang Zhuang (on the right) was trying to kill Liu Bang. Xiang Bo (on the left) was trying to protect Liu Bang. Fan Zeng (sitting in the middle) plotted the scheme.

When Zhang Liang estimated that Liu Bang had safely reached his army, he went into the tent and apologized for Liu Bang by saying, "The Duke of Pei cannot drink much wine but he does not want to refuse to drink your toasts. So he has asked me to present this pair of round pieces of white jade to you and this jade cup to Fan Zeng." "Where is the Duke of Pei now?" Xiang Yu asked. Zhang Liang said, "He knows that you intend to turn on him. So he has left. He is now in his army." Xiang Yu accepted the pair of round pieces of white jade and put them on the small table in front of him. Fan Zeng put the jade cup on the ground, drew out his sword and cut it to pieces. He said with a long sigh, "How foolish you are to have let Liu Bang go. It is Liu Bang who will take away all your power. We will all be his prisoners someday!"

Xiahou Ying, Zhang Liang, Liu Bang, Fan Kuai, Cao Wu Shang (left to right)

28. The Making of Kings

Several days later, Xiang Yu marched his army westward to Xianyang. He had Ying Zi Ying, the former King of the State of Qin, executed. He ordered his army to burn all the palaces of the State of Qin. The fire lasted for three months. He let his soldiers loot the people of Qin. The people of Qin suffered terribly. He went back eastward with all the treasures and beautiful women taken from the Qin palaces. The people of the Qin areas were all disappointed. An official by the name of Han Sheng said to Xiang Yu, "The area of Guanzhong is protected by mountains and the Yellow River around it. It is difficult for the people outside to enter this area. The land of this area is rich. You may establish your capital here and rule all over China." But Xiang Yu would not stay in the area of Guanzhong because all the palaces had been burned down to the ground. He really wanted to go back to the east where he was from. He said, "If I don't go back home when I have become rich and honored, it would be like walking in the dark night wearing beautifully embroidered clothes. Nobody will know that I have become rich and honored." Han Sheng went out and said to others, "I have heard that the Chu people are only monkeys in human hats. Now I know it is true." When his words were reported to Xiang Yu, Xiang Yu had him cooked alive in a big pot.

Xiang Yu sent an envoy back to Pengcheng (now Xuzhou) to ask King Huai of the State of Chu's instruction as to what should be done next. King Huai of the State of Chu instructed that everything should be handled according to his promise that the general who first took Xianyang would be made king of Guanzhong. When Xiang Yu got the instruction, he was furious. He said to the generals, "King Huai of the State of Chu was made king by my uncle Xiang Liang and me. He has not made any contribution in the wars against the Qin Dynasty. Why should he have the power to make such a promise? When people first rose against the rule of the Qin Dynasty three years ago, we made the descendants of the kings of the six states kings of different states just for the purpose of overthrowing the rule of the Qin Dynasty. But we did the fighting and we have experienced all kinds of hardships. It is you and I who have done our best to defeat the Qin army and overthrow the rule of the Qin Dynasty. Since King Huai of the State of Chu has not made the slightest contribution to the wars, we should divide his lands and make ourselves kings in those areas." The generals who had followed him into Guanzhong all agreed.

Xiang Yu had no intention of letting Liu Bang be king of Guanzhong as King Huai of the State of Chu had promised. But Liu Bang really was the first general who had conquered the area of Guanzhong. So Xiang Yu called Fan Zeng to his tent to discuss the matter. Fan Zeng said, "We must not make Liu Bang King of Guanzhong. He would be a great threat to you if he were made King of Guanzhong. We should send him to a remote place so that he will not come out to contend for the power with you. We had better make him king of Ba and Shu. These areas are blocked by great mountains. If he goes there, it will be very difficult for him to come out. And we may make Zhang Han, Sima Xin and Dong Yi kings of the Qin area to block Liu Bang from coming out of the areas of Ba and Shu. That area is called Shu Han, and belongs to the area of Guangzhong." Xiang Yu thought that sounded like a good idea. So it was decided that Liu Bang should be made King of Ba and Shu (now the area of Sichuan Province).

When news came that Xiang Yu would make Liu Bang King of Ba and Shu instead of King of Guanzhong, Liu Bang was so furious that he gave orders to attack Xiang Yu. Fan Kuai, Zhou Bo and Guan Ying all tried to stop him, but he would not listen to them. Then Xiao He came. Xiao He said, "Although the areas of Ba and Shu are bad places, it would better be the king of those areas than be killed." Liu Bang asked, "Why do you say that?" Xiao He said, "Xiang Yu has 400,000 men under his command. You have just less than 100,000. If you lead your army to attack Xiang Yu, you will surely be defeated and killed by him. If you are not made king of Guanzhong as prom-ised by King Huai of the State of Chu, but only made King of Han, you will be under only one man, that is Xiang Yu; but you will have the sympathy of all the people of the whole realm, and gain the support from them. There is a teaching in the Book of Zhou, 'If the heavens grant you something and you refuse to take it, you will suffer from the consequences of your act of not taking it.' The name of Han is a blessed name, because the Galaxy in the sky is called 'Tian Han' meaning the Heavenly River of Han. In the past, King Jie of the Xia Dynasty was a very cruel ruler. Tang of the Tribe of Shang was a very strong leader of the people. He was determined to overthrow the cruel rule of King Jie of the Xia Dynasty. In order to see whether the minority nationalities would still submit to the order of King Jie of the Xia Dynasty, he stopped paying tribute to King Jie. King Jie was angry and ordered the minority nationalities to attack the Tribe of Shang. Tang of the Tribe of Shang found that the minority nationalities still submitted to King Jie. He immediately apologized to King Jie and resumed paying tribute. He waited patiently till the time when the minority nationalities could not stand the cruel rule of King Jie of the Xia Dynasty and would not obey his orders any more. Then Tang of the Tribe of Shang raised a great army and defeated King Jie and overthrew the Xia Dynasty and established the Shang Dynasty. I hope that you will accept the title of King of Han and go to the area of Ba and Shu. You may cultivate the people there and solicit the service of virtu-ous and capable persons in those areas. Then you may use these areas as the starting point to take the areas of Guanzhong and conquer the whole realm." Liu Bang was persuaded and gave up the idea of attacking Xiang Yu.

Liu Bang gave Zhang Liang quantities of gold for his contribution in the march into Guangzhong. Zhang Liang passed all of it to Xiang Bo because Xiang Bo had saved Liu Bang from destruction in Hongmen.

Portrait of King Xiang Yu

Liu Bang was unhappy with being made King of Ba and Shu instead of King of Guanzhong. He wanted the area of Hanzhong (now the southwest part of Shaanxi Province) because that area was a small part of Guanzhong. He discussed this matter with Zhang Liang. Then Zhang Liang went to see Xiang Bo with precious gifts. Xiang Bo agreed to help Liu Bang to get the area of Hanzhong. He went to see Xiang Yu. He said, "Liu Bang was the general who first conquered the area of Guanzhong. He deserves the title of King of Guangzhong. Now there is no hope for him to get that title. I think it would be better for you to give him at least a small part of Guanzhong so as to show your kindness. Hanzhong is the utmost southwest part of Guanzhong. It is a remote place and very inconvenient in traffic. If you give him that area, Liu Bang would be satisfied with it." After some consideration, Xiang Yu at last agreed to give the area of Hanzhong to Liu Bang and grant him the title of King of the State of Han. Liu Bang accepted that title. In that capacity, he made Cao Shen Marquis of Jiancheng, Fan Kuai Marquis of Linwu, and Zhou Bo Marquis of Weiwu in recognition of their contributions in the defeat of the Qin army and their assistance in taking Guanzhong.

In January 206 BC, Xiang Yu made King Huai of the State of Chu Acting Emperor. He moved the Acting Emperor to the areas to the south of the Yangtze River. The capital was Chen (now Chenzhou, Hunan province). In February, he made himself the Conqueror, Great King of the State of Western Chu. He ruled over nine prefectures in the Chu and Liang areas. His capital was Pengcheng. He made Liu Bang King of the State of Han, ruling over Ba and Shu areas and Hanzhong Prefecture, with the capital in Nanzheng (now Nanzheng, Shaanxi Province). In order to block the way from which Liu Bang would come out of Hanzhong, Xiang Yu divided the area of Guanzhong into three states. He made Zhang Han, the Qin general who had surrendered to him, King of the State of Yong, ruling over an area west to Xianyang with the capital in Feiqiu (now a place near Xingping, Shaanxi Province). He made Sima Xin, another Qin general who had surrendered, King of the State of Sai, ruling over an area from Xianyang east to the Yellow River with the capital in Yueyang (now to the north of Lintong, Shaanxi Province). He made Dong Yi, another Qin general who had surrendered, King of the State of Zhai ruling over Shang Prefecture (northern part of Shaanxi Province) with the capital in Gaonu (now a place near Yan'an, Shaanxi Province).

Since Xiang Yu wanted to rule over the former Liang area himself, he changed Wei Bao, King of the State of Wei, into King of the State of Western

Wei, ruling over Hedong (now the area of Shanxi Province) with the capital in Pingyang (now a place near Linfen City, Shanxi Province). He made Shen Yang, a general under Zhang Er, who had first taken Henan Prefecture, King of the State of Henan with the capital in Luoyang (now Luoyang, Henan Province). Haan Cheng, King of the State of Haan, remained King of the State of Haan with the capital in Yangzhai (now Yuzhou, Henan Province). He made Sima Wang King of the State of Yin, ruling Henei Prefecture with the capital in Zhaoge (now Qixian, Henan Province). He moved Zhao Xie, King of the State of Zhao, to Dai Prefecture as King of the State of Dai. He made Zhang Er, the former premier of the State of Zhao, King of the State of Changshan, ruling over the area of the former State of Zhao with the capital in Xiangguo (now Xingtai, Hebei Province). He made Ying Bu King of the State of Jiujiang with the capital in Liucheng (now Liu'an, Anhui Province). Wu Rui, a king in the southern part of China, led the kings of the small states in that part of China assisting Xiang Yu in the fighting and had followed him to the area of Guanzhong. So Xiang Yu made him King of the State of Hengshan with the capital in Zhu (now Huanggang, Hubei Province). Gong Ao, the premier to King Huai of the State of Chu, had pacified Nanjun Prefecture and had rendered great services. So Xiang Yu made him King of the State of Linjiang with the capital in Jiangling (now Jiangling, Hubei Province). Haan Guang, King of the State of Yan, was moved to Liaodong as King of the State of Liaodong with the capital in Wuzhong (now Jixian, Tianjin Municipality). Zang Tu, a general of the former State of Yan, had followed Xiang Yu to relieve the State of Zhao and had marched into the area of Guanzhong with Xiang Yu. Xiang Yu made him King of the State of Yan with the capital in Ji (now a place in the southwest part of Beijing). Tian Shi, King of the State of Qi, was moved to Jiaodong as King of the State of Jiaodong with the capital in Jimo (now a place in Pingdu, Shandong Province). Tian Du, a former general of the State of Qi, had participated in relieving the State of Zhao and had marched into the area of Guanzhong with Xiang Yu. So Xiang Yu made him King of the State of Qi with the capital in Linzi (now Linzi, Shandong Province). Tian An, a former general of the State of Qi, had taken several cities of Jibei Prefecture when Xiang Yu was crossing the Yellow River, then he had put his army under the command of Xiang Yu. So Xiang Yu made him King of the State of Jibei with the capital in Boyang (now a place near Tai'an, Shandong Province).

Tian Rong was not granted any title because he had refused to cooperate with Xiang Liang and had refused to lead his army to join with Xiang
Yu's army in fighting against the Qin army. Chen Yu was not granted any
title either, because after the battle of Julu, he had a quarrel with Zhang Er
and then left his general seal to Zhang Er and gone away. But many people
sympathized with him and said to Xiang Yu, "Chen Yu and Zhang Er have
rendered equal contributions to the State of Zhao. Now Zhang Er has been
made King of the State Changshan, Chen Yu should be granted some title."
So Xiang Yu reluctantly made him Marquis of Nanpi (now Nanpi, Hebei
Province).

29. LIU BANG'S MARCH INTO HANZHONG

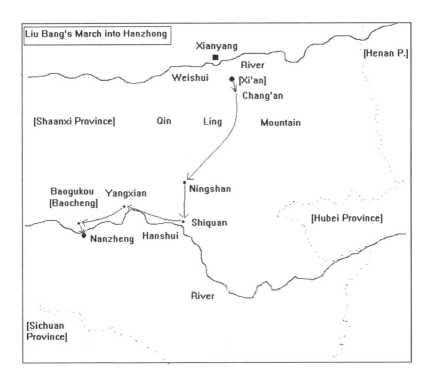

In April 206 BC, all the generals began to leave for the states of which
they had been made kings. When Xiang Yu led his army out of Hanguguan
Pass, he sent some envoys ahead to Pengcheng to force the Acting Emperor

(King Huai of the State of Chu) to leave Pengcheng for a remote area in the south. When the Acting Emperor left Pengcheng, most of his ministers did not follow him.

Xiang Yu allowed Liu Bang to take only 30,000 soldiers to go to Hanzhong with him to make sure that Liu Bang would not turn back on his way to Hanzhong. Over 10,000 men from the armies of the State of Chu and other states voluntarily followed Liu Bang to Hanzhong. When Liu Bang left Bashang, the people saw him off with tears in their eyes. They knew that Liu Bang was a kindhearted person and they really wanted him to be king of Guanzhong.

Between the plains of Weishui River Basin and the Hanshui River Basin, there lay a great mountain called Qin Ling. This great mountain was impassable. In order to conquer the area of Hanzhong and the areas of Ba and Shu, the former kings of the State of Qin had had three mountain roads built from north to south. The first one passed through the east part of Qin Ling Mountain, the second one passed through the middle part and the third one passed through the west part. Liu Bang accompanied by Zhang Liang, and his army took the eastern road. They upheld the red banners with the character of "Han" on them and marched into the great mountain from the south of Chang'an (now Chang'an County, Shaanxi Province). They marched south along the mountain road. They passed Ningshan, Shiquan and Yangxian. They covered a distance of 450 kilometers and at last reached the Hanshui River Basin where Nanzheng was situated. They did not go to Nanzheng directly but turned westward along the north bank of the Hanshui River. Then they reached Baogukou (the entrance of Baogu Valley, now Baocheng, Shaanxi Province) where the south end of the plank road built along the face of the cliff was situated. This was the second mountain road built by the former kings of the State of Qin. It was a road built entirely of wooden planks by the edge of the rocky mountain along the rapids of Baoshui River and Xieshui River with the north end in Xiegukou (the entrance of Xiegu Valley, now southwest to Meixian of Baoji, Shaanxi Province). At 210 kilometers long, it was the shortest road among the three. The road was 4.5 meters wide, enough for wagons and carriages.

Zhang Liang studied the plank road for some time, and then quietly said to Liu Bank, "I suggest that Your Majesty have this plank road burned up." Liu Bang was surprised and said, "This is the shortest road for me to return to Guanzhong. Why should I have it burned?" Zhang Liang said, "By doing so, Your Majesty shows all the other kings and Xiang Yu that Your Majesty has no intention of returning to the east; that will ease Xiang Yu's suspicion of your ambition to engage in a power struggle with him." Liu Bang saw what he meant and agreed with his idea. Then Zhang Liang said, "I have to go back to assist King of the State of Haan. I have to say goodbye to Your Majesty now. I will burn the plank road on my way back." Then Zhang Liang and his party of soldiers got on the plank road and left. Liu Bang and his army turn south to Nanzheng. After Zhang Liang and his soldiers had gone through a section of the plank road, they set fire to that section. In this way, when they reached Xiegukou, the north end of the plank road, the whole plank road of 210 kilometers had been burned away. When the news that Zhang Liang had burned the Bao-Xie plank road reached Zhang Han, the King of the State of Yong, he was greatly relieved because now he did not need to worry about Liu Bang anymore. When Xiang Yu made Zhang Han King of the State of Yong, Xiang Yu had assigned him the main task of preventing Liu Bang from coming back to Guanzhong.

When Liu Bang and his men reached Nanzheng, the capital of the State of Han, they settled down there. Liu Bang appointed Xiao He premier. Cao Shen, Fan Kuai, Xiahou Ying, Zhou Bo, Lu Wan and Guan Ying were promoted to generals.

30. The Rebellion of the State of Qi and the State of Zhao against Xiang Yu

When Tian Rong found out that Xiang Yu had made the decision to move Tian Shi, King of the State of Qi, to Jiaodong (the eastern part of Shangdong Province) as King of the State of Jiaodong, and had made Tian Du King of the State of Qi, he was very angry. He refused to let Tian Shi move to Jiaodong and decided to rebel against Xiang Yu. He sent an army to prevent Tian Du from getting to Linzi to take the throne of the State of Qi. Tian Du had to go to the State of Chu for refuge. Tian Rong asked Tian Shi to stay in Linzi as King of the State of Qi instead of going to Jimo as King of Jiaodong. But Tian Shi's ministers said to him, "Xiang Yu is a powerful and cruel man. He has made you King of the State of Jiaodong. You'd better go to Jiaodong to take the throne there. Otherwise, you will be in great trouble." So Tian Shi secretly left Linzi and went to Jimo to be King of the State of Jiaodong. Now Tian Rong was even more angry. In June, he chased Tian Shi to Jimo and killed him there. Then he directed his army northward to attack Tian An, the King of the State of Jibei. A battle was fought outside Boyang (a place near Tai'an, Shandong Province), the capital of the State of Jibei. Tian An was killed and Tian Rong took the State of Jibei. He unified the three states in the Qi area as the State of Qi and declared himself King of the State of Qi.

At that time, Peng Yue was in Juye (now Juye, Shandong Province) with an army of 10,000 men. He was not under the command of any king. So Tian Rong, King of the State of Qi, gave him a general seal and sent him to attack the State of Chu. Xiang Yu Sent Xia Gong Jiao with an army to prevent the advance of Peng Yue but Peng Yue won.

Zhang Er went to Xiangguo (now Xingtai, Hebei Province) to take the throne of the State of Changshan. Chen Yu did not take this kindly. He said, "Zhang Er and I have made equal contributions. He has been made king but I have been made marquis. Xiang Yu is unfair." He secretly sent Zhang Tong and Xia Yue to pass his words to Tian Rong, King of the State of Qi: "Xiang Yu is unfair in making kings of different states. He made the generals who followed him to Guanzhong kings of good places and moved the original kings to bad places. Now the King of the State of Zhao has been moved to Dai, an area in the north. I think this is unfair. I hear that you have stood up against such injustices. Will you lend me some troops with which I can attack Zhang Er and put Zhao Xie back on the throne of the State of Zhao? When the State of Zhao is reinstated, it will provide natural protection for the State of Qi."

Tian Rong agreed and sent some troops to Chen Yu. Chen Yu also raised an army from the three counties under his jurisdiction. With this army and the army sent by Tian Rong he attacked Zhang Er and defeated him. Zhang Er had to run away. Chen Yu escorted Zhao Xie from the State of Dai to Handan to resume the throne of the State of Zhao. In order to repay Chen Yu's kindness, the King of the State of Zhao made Chen Yu King of the State of Dai; however, Chen Yu did not go to the State of Dai to take his throne. Instead, he stayed in the State of Zhao to assist the newly reinstated king of the State of Zhao, and sent Xia Yue as the premier of the State of Dai to attend to state affairs there.

Once Zhang Er was defeated and had fled, he could not decide whom to turn to: should he go to Xiang Yu or to Liu Bang? He consulted Gan Gong, an astrologer. Zhang Er said, "I am an old friend of Liu Bang. But Xiang Yu is powerful and it is he who has made me King of the State of Changshan.

So I want to go to him." Gan Gong said, "When Liu Bang went into the area of Qin, five stars, that is, Mercury, Venus, Mars, Jupiter and Saturn, were in a straight line in the southwest night sky. It is predicted that the person who first reached the area of Qin will have the control over the whole realm. Although the State of Western Chu is powerful now, it will be conquered by the State of Han." So Zhang Er decided to go to the State of Han.

Xiang Yu had not allowed King of the State of Haan to go back to the State of Haan because Zhang Liang went with Liu Bang to the area of Guan-zhong, and Haan Cheng, the King of the State of Haan, had not made any contribution in the wars again the rule of the Qin Dynasty. He took the King of the State of Haan to Pengcheng and then deposed him. Sometime later, Haan Cheng was killed.

Zang Tu, King of the State of Yan made by Xiang Yu, led an army to Ji, the capital of the State of Yan, to force Han Guang, the former King of the State of Yan, to go to Liaodong to be King of the State of Liaodong. Han Guang refused to go. Then Zang Tu ordered his army to attack the city. Han Guang ran away from the city but was chased down by Zang Tu's army. At last he was killed in a place called Wuzhong (Jixian, Tianjin Municipality).

31. Han Xin Is Appointed Commander-in-Chief of the Army of Han

Liu Bang settled down in Nanzheng, but many of the officers and soldiers of his army did not want to stay in that remote area of Hanzhong and Ba and Shu. They missed their homes in the east. They were quite adamant about returning to their home places, and some of them even took off on their own. This filled Liu Bang with concern, as he fully intended to fight his way back to Guanzhong and to the east, and he would need a capable general to lead his army when the time came.

Han Xin was from Huaiyin (now Huaiyin, Anhui Province), from a poor family. His parents had died early. He was not especially virtuous, so he was not selected as an official. He was not especially good at business, either. He often shared other people's food. Many people resented him. Still, the chief of Nanchang Sub-township had pity on him, and one day he invited Han Xin to come and eat in his house. From then on he went to the house of the chief of Nanchang Sub-township for food every day. He went on showing up for food this way for months. The wife of the chief of Nanchang Sub-township did not like him. So she cooked the family's food very early and let the whole family eat first thing in the morning, in bed. By the time Han Xin came, there was no food left. Han Xin got the message. The chief and his wife resented him, so he turned round and never went to their house for food any more.

Once when Han Xin was fishing by a river, an old lady who was washing clothes saw that he was hungry and gave him some food. From then on, the old lady shared her food with him every day. This went on for more than a month. Han Xin said to the old lady, "I will repay your kindness in the future." The old lady said angrily, "It is a shame on you, that you, as a man, cannot support yourself. I gave you food just because I have pity on you. I don't expect any repayment."

The younger folk wanted to insult him. One day, a young man mocked him in front of many other people. "You are tall and strongly built, and you often walk around with a sword, but actually you are a coward. If you are not afraid of death, stab me with your sword. If you are afraid, then I'll stand with my legs apart and you can crawl between my legs." Han Xin stared at the youth for some time, and then he knelt down and crawled under his legs. All the people in the market laughed at him and took him for a coward.

When Xiang Liang was crossing the Huai River with his army, Han Xin joined Xiang Liang's army as an ordinary soldier. After Xiang Liang was killed in the battle outside the city of Dingtao, Han Xin became a low ranking officer under Xiang Yu. He presented several strategic plans to Xiang Yu, but Xiang Yu did not pay any attention. When Liu Bang went into Hanzhong, Han Xin left Xiang Yu and joined Liu Bang's army. But still nobody knew his ability. He was just a low ranking officer in Liu Bang's army.

Then Han Xin was involved in some offence with thirteen other soldiers and they were all sentenced to death. At the execution grounds, the thirteen others were executed and it was his turn. Han Xin looked up and saw Xiahou Ying, who was in charge of the execution. Han Xin said to Xiahou Ying, "Doesn't Liu Bang mean to fight for the power to rule over all of China? Why would he kill such a warrior as me?" Xiahou Ying was surprised by his words, and took a closer look. And he saw that Han Xin was an extraordinary man. He released Han Xin and talked with him. He understood that Han Xin was a man of great resources. He told Liu Bang about him.

Liu Bang appointed Han Xin to a position in charge of the food supply. He did not take Han Xin as a man of extraordinary ability. Then Han Xin began talking with Xiao He and in the course of several discussions, Xiao He found that he was a man of special talent.

When Liu Bang reached Nanzheng, the capital of the State of Han, many of the officers and men missed their homes in the east part of China so much that they deserted the army. Han Xin thought that by now Xiao He must have talked to Liu Bang several times about him, but still Liu Bang did not put him in a position of any importance. So he decided to run away, too. When Xiao He heard that Han Xin had run away, he jumped on a horse and went run after him. He was in such a hurry that he did not report to the King of Han. When Liu Bang got word that Xiao He had run away, he was very upset. And he was very sorry that he had lost a valuable assistant.

Two days later, Xiao He came back. Liu Bang had mixed feelings; he was glad that Xiao He had come back but he was angry at him for taking off. He asked Xiao He angrily, "Why did you run away?" Xiao He said, "I would not dare to run away. I was chasing down a runaway." Liu Bang asked, "Whom were you chasing down?" Xiao He said, "Han Xin." Liu Bang flared up and said, "You are lying! More than ten generals have run away. You have run after none of them. Why should you run after Han Xin?" Xiao He answered, "Other generals are ordinary. It's easy to find a dozen of them. But Han Xin is unique. If you are satisfied with your position as King of Hanzhong, then you don't need him. If you want to fight for the power to rule all over China, then you won't be successful without him. Whether he stays or not depends on your decision." Liu Bang said, "How can I stay in this corner forever! Of course, I plan to go east to fight for power." Xiao He said, "Since you are determined to go east to fight for power, you can appoint Han Xin to a responsible position and then he will stay. If you don't, then he will leave." Liu Bang said, "I will make him a general." Xiao He said, "Even if you appoint him a general, he will still run away." Liu Bang said, "I will appoint him commander-in-chief of my army." Xiao He said, "That's more like it."

Liu Bang wanted to call Han Xin in and make the appointment right away. Xiao He said, "You have always been rude to people. Now you are going to make an important appointment. You cannot treat it as a trifling matter. You must select a suitable day and you must fast for three days before that day. A platform must be built. Then the solemn ceremony of the appointment may be held." Liu Bang agreed.

Then a platform was built outside the city of Nanzheng. The platform was three meters high with an area of more than 7,000 square meters. There were steps leading to the top of the platform. In front of it there was a big square for the whole army to watch the ceremony.

Liu Bang got up early on the day of the ceremony. Xiao He, leading the generals and ministers, waited outside of the palace. Liu Bang got up into his carriage and the procession went through the south gate, out of the city, to the platform. Liu Bang ascended the platform and sat on a chair in the center of the platform. The generals and ministers with the army stood solemnly in the square. The whole army stood in deep silence and the generals waited for the declaration of the appointment of the commander-in-chief of the whole army. They were wondering who would win such an appointment.

Holding in his hands the gold seal of the commander-in-chief and a battle axe representing supreme military power, Xiao He ascended the platform and handed them over to Liu Bang. Then Xiao He turned to the generals and the army standing in the square, took out the order by Liu Bang, and read out loud: "Now the King of Han hereby appoints Han Xin commander-in-chief of the army of the State of Han. Han Xin, you may come up to the platform to receive the seal of the commander-in-chief and the battle axe."

Everybody was stunned. Han Xin, a coward, a man they knew had once crawled under a man's legs, had been appointed commander-in-chief. Then the band played music and beat the drums. Han Xin stepped out from the rank and file and ascended the platform calmly, step by step. Then he knelt in front of Liu Bang. Liu Bang stood up from the chair and handed the gold seal of the commander-in-chief and battle axe to Han Xin. Han Xin held up his hands over his head and received the seal and the battle axe. Then Liu Bang said to him loudly, "I hereby confer upon you the power to command the whole army. You have the power to make decisions on all military affairs. Do your best to lead the whole army from one victory to another. If anyone despises you and does not obey your order, you may execute him first and report to me afterwards."

The whole army was in awe. Han Xin said loudly, "I hereby express my heartfelt thanks for the kindness of Your Majesty. I will do my best to live up to your expectations." Then Liu Bang sat down in his chair and ordered Han Xin to take a seat.

韓 信 像

Portrait of Han Xin

Liu Bang said, "Premier Xiao He has recommended you many times. What strategic proposals do you have in mind?" Han Xin rose from his seat and made a bow, then asked, "Now Your Majesty is planning to march to the east to fight for power. Is Xiang Yu the enemy of Your Majesty?" Liu Bang answered, "Yes." Then Han Xin asked, "Do you think that you are a match for Xiang Yu in terms of bravery, ferocity, strength and benevolence?" Liu Bang thought for a long time and then said, "No." Han Xin stood up, bowed to him in congratulation, and said, "I don't think so, either. But I have once worked for Xiang Yu and I know more clearly what a person he is. When he roars in anger in battle, all his enemies are so scared that they become paralyzed. But he never trusts his capable generals and never puts them in responsible positions. This is the bravery of an unintelligent person. Xiang Yu is polite and kind to people. When his soldiers fall ill, he weeps for them and shares his food with them. But when his officers and men have rendered outstanding service, he is never generous enough to grant them titles. Sometimes he's had seals carved for the promotion of persons to the rank of an earl; he would play with those seals in his hands for a long time and hold them back in the end. This is the kindness of a woman.

"Xiang Yu has got the power to rule over China and placed all the other kings under his command, but he would not stay in the area of Guanzhong. He has taken Pengcheng as his capital instead. He went against the promise made by King Huai of the State of Chu that the general who first reached the area of Guanzhong would be king of that area. The kings he made of different states were all his friends or those he liked. This has caused in-dignation among the kings. He removed the original kings of several states and made the generals or premiers under them kings of such states. He has moved the Acting Emperor, originally King Huai of the State of Chu, to the south of the Yangtze River.

"He has destroyed cities and massacred people wherever he passed. The people hate him. They have not risen against him because they have been brought to submission by his fame as a conqueror. Now he has lost all support from the people. So although he is strong now, he will become weak very soon. If you know all his weak points and adopt correct policies, contrary to the wrong policies adopted by Xiang Yu, and give full play to the brave and capable people all over the country, then you will be able to overcome any enemy. If you are willing to award cities and big towns in the country to those who have rendered outstanding service, then all the people will obey your orders and be willing to fight for you.

"You may defeat any enemy with the army of officers and men who are longing to go back to the east. The three kings made by Xiang Yu in the areas of Guanzhong, that is, Zhang Han, Sima Xin and Dong Yi, served as Qin generals for several years. Numerous Qin soldiers under them were killed or missing in action. They deceived their officers and men into surrendering to Xiang Yu. Two hundred thousand Qin soldiers who had surrendered were all killed in Xin'an by Xiang Yu, but only Zhang Han, Sima Xin and Dong Yi survived. People in the Qin area hate these men very much but Xiang Yu has forced the people of the Qin area to accept these three men as kings.

"The people of the Qin area love you because when you led your army into Wuguan Pass, your army did not commit the slightest offence to the people. You did away with the cruel laws of the Qin Dynasty. You issued three chapters of law. All the people in the Qin area hoped that you would be made king of Guanzhong. According to the agreement, you should be made king of Guanzhong. People in the Qin area all know that you have not been made king of Guanzhong because Xiang Yu intentionally made you King of Hanzhong instead. The people of the Qin area hate Xiang Yu for this. If you lead your army in the march to the Qin area, you may get support from the people there and take the three states within the Qin area very easily."

Liu Bang was struck by this sound advice and decided to follow it. And the two men stepped down from the platform and went back to the city of Nanzheng.

The next day, Han Xin summoned all the generals to his tent and declared to them the rules he had made and called upon all the officers and men to observe the rules. Then a military training campaign began. Han Xin taught the soldiers all kinds of battle arrays and taught the generals how to use them in real battles. The generals, such as Cao Shen, Fan Kuai and Zhou Bo, had never had such formal training, so they all respected Han Xin very much. Then Liu Bang made strategic plans with his generals and deployed his generals in the military action to take the Qin area. He decided to leave Xiao He in Hanzhong in charge of collecting tax from the Ba and Shu prefectures and the area of Hanzhong and in charge of food supply to the army fighting in the front.

32. LIU BANG'S ACTIONS TO PACIFY THE AREA OF GUANZHONG

One day in August 206 BC, the King of Han and Han Xin with an army of 100,000 men secretly embarked on their northern expedition. They passed Mian Xian and then went up the great mountains of Qin Ling. The mountains were covered with forests. The army went forward with great difficulty. Then they moved westward and reached Gudao (now Fengxian, Shaanxi Province). Han Xin ordered Cao Shen to lead the troops under him to take Gudao. Cao Shen led his troops to attack the town, and they took it.

From the northern end of Gudao, there was a secluded ancient road leading to Chencang (now Baoji, Shaanxi Province) which was located in the west end of the Plains of Weishui River. Han Xin sent out ten soldiers to go first as scouts to assess the situation ahead. Some time after the scouts had left, the Han army marched very quickly along this secluded ancient road. A scout came back and reported to Han Xin, "There is a narrow pass lying ahead. It is guarded by the army of the State of Yong." This was Sanguan Pass, one of the four passes which guarded the area of Guanzhong. Aside from this gorge, the great mountains were impassable. Down below, the Qingjiang River was roiling with rapids. Sanguan Pass was the only access from the southwest into the area of Guanzhong.

Han Xin sent for General Cao Shen. When Cao Shen came, Han Xin said to him, "Select fifty strong and brave soldiers. They shall disguise themselves as woodcutters and enter the pass with other people. They should take the pass at midnight, from within." When sundown was approaching, people came hurrying to get back through the pass. The soldiers of the State of Yong guarding the pass examined everyone who wanted to go through. Some woodcutters came. Every woodcutter carried a heavy load of firewood on his back. The gate guards of the pass examined every one of them. The guards did not find anything suspicious and let them go. The woodcutters hid themselves as darkness fell, and waited. When midnight came, the woodcutters took out their swords that were hidden in the loads of firewood. The gate of the pass had been closed, and most of the guards had gone to sleep. Only a few remained guarding the gate. The woodcutters sneaked back to the gate of the pass, killed the guards, and opened the gate. The Han army rushed through the gate and marched quickly towards Chencang.

The Han army hit the city of Chencang with a surprise attack as soon as they arrived. The general of the State of Yong, defending Chencang, got to the top of the city wall. He could not believe his own eyes. Thousands of soldiers in battle formation with red banners were marching swiftly towards the city. A big red standard with the characters "King of Han" was flying high. He never expected that the Han Army would appear in front of the city. When he saw the attacking army, he thought that they had descended from the heavens. He was not at all prepared for battle. Under the fierce attack by the Han army, the general and his soldiers abandoned the city and ran away. The Han army easily took the city of Chencang.

The general rode quickly to Feiqiu (now Xingping, Shaanxi Province), the capital of the State of Yong, to report to Zhang Han, the King of the State of Yong. The general said to Zhang Han, "The Han army started a surprise attack on the city of Chencang and have taken it." Zhang Han could not believe what he heard and asked in great surprise, "What did you say?" The general said again, "The Han army launched a surprise attack on the city of Chencang and has taken it." Zhang Han said, "Impossible! The plank road has been burned down by Zhang Liang. From which directing did they come?" The general said, "I don't know. They seemed to have come from nowhere."

Zhang Han immediately sent one envoy to Yueyang, the capital of the State of Sai, to ask Sima Xin, the King of the State of Sai, for help, and sent another envoy to Gaonu (now Yan'an, Shaanxi Province), the Capital of the State of Zhai, to ask Dong Yi, the King of the State of Zhai, for help. Then he himself led his army to prevent the advance of the Han army because he knew clearly that the task assigned to him by Xiang Yu was to stop Liu Bang from coming back to Guanzhong.

When his army was near Chencang, they found that Han Xin had arranged the Han army in battle formation. When Zhang Han's army arrived, the army of Yong spread out and formed a battle array with chariots and cavalry. Han Xin ordered Fan Kuai to command his army to attack Zhang Han's army. Fan Kuai led his troops to charge at the army of Yong and broke their battle formation. Zhang Han's army was defeated and Zhang Han led the main part of his army to retreat to Feiqiu; his brother Zhang Ping led the troops under him to Haozhi (now Qianxian, Shaanxi Province).

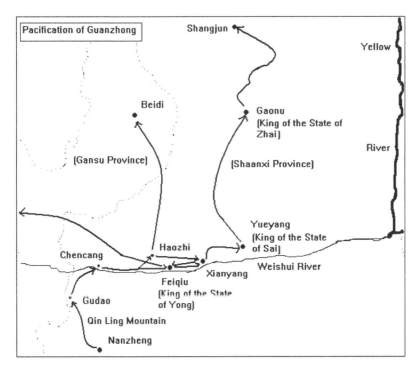

Seeing that the Yong army had split and retreated in two directions, Han Xin thought for a moment. Feiqiu was a strong city, and Zhang Han was an experienced general. It would be difficult to take that city in a short time. Although Zhang Ping was also a good general, the troops under him were fewer than those under Zhang Han. So he decided to deal with Zhang Ping first. He ordered Cao Shen and Zhou Bo to lead their troops to pursue the army of Yong, under Zhang Ping, retreating in the direction of Haozhi. When the Yong army under Zhang Ping retreated to the south of the city of Haozhi, Cao Shen caught up with him. Zhang Ping had to draw up his army in battle formation. The victorious Han army under Cao Shen started a fierce attack, and the Yong army was defeated again. Zhang Ping had to retreat into the city of Haozhi. Cao Shen ordered his troops to lay siege to the city. Not long later, the Han troops under Zhou Bo arrived, and they joined in the siege.

Sima Xin, King of the State of Sai, sent General Zhao Ben to lead an army to reinforce the army of the State of Yong in Feiqiu. An army sent by Dong Yi, the King of the State of Zhai, was hurrying from the north to the Jingshui River area to reinforce the army of the State of Yong. With the reinforcements from the State of Zhai and the State of Sai, Zhang Han led a united army from the three states to march westward to Rangxiang (southeast of Wugong, Shaanxi Province). When Cao Shen received information that the united army of the three states was marching to Rangxiang, he asked Zhou Bo to stay and continue the siege of Haozhi, and he himself led an army to hurry to Rangxiang. A battle was fought in the east of Rangxiang, and the united army was defeated. The Yong army commanded by Zhang Han had to turn back to Feiqiu, and Zhao Ben led the army of the State of Sai to Xianyang to join forces with Neishi Bao, who was the commanding general of the army of Sai, defending Xianyang. Cao Shen led his army back to the siege of Haozhi.

Han Xin thought it was time to take Haozhi so that the Han army could start the campaign to conquer the other areas of Guanzhong. So he went with an army under General Fan Kuai to Haozhi. The armies under Cao Shen, Zhou Bo and Fan Kuai joined forces and started an attack on the city of Haozhi. The Han soldiers put ladders against the city walls and climbed up. General Fan Kuai was the first one to get to the top of the city wall. He killed many soldiers of the Yong army. The defending army fled from the city wall. The Han soldiers opened the city gate, and the main force of the Han army rushed in. Zhang Ping could not resist the assault and had to retreat from the city of Haozhi to the area of Beidi Prefecture to the north of Haozhi. The Han army successfully took the city of Haozhi.

Han Xin ordered Fan Kuai to lead his army to lay siege to the city of Feiqiu and sent Cao Shan and Zhou Bo to attack Xianyang. When Cao Shen and Zhou Bo with their army reached Xianyang, Zhao Ben and Neishi Bao led their army out of the city of Xianyang to have battle with the Han army. A battle was fought outside the city. The army under Zhao Ben and Neishi Bao was no match for the Han army, and they ran away. Cao Shen and Zhou Bo took Xianyang, the former capital of the State of Qin. They sent an envoy to see Liu Bang to report their great victory. Liu Bang issued an order to change the name of Xianyang into Xincheng, meaning "new city."

Cao Shen marched his army to Jingling, which was located east to Xian-yang, and stationed his army there. Jingling was quite close to Yueyang, the capital of the State of Sai. Sima Xin felt that the Han army stationed in Jin-gling was a great threat to the State of Sai, so he led the main force of his army to surround them. Zhang Ping also led his army to march south to join in the attack on the Han army under Cao Shen in Jingling. The Han army defended Jingling bravely for twenty days in very difficult conditions. After a fierce battle, the united army of Sai and Yong was defeated. Zhang Ping retreated to the north, and Sima Xin turned back to Yueyang.

Zhang Ping retreated to Qi (now Bin Xian, Shaanxi Province) in the north. Cao Shen pursued Zhang Ping to Qi. At that time, Dong Yi, King of Zhai, sent a strong army from north to reinforce Zhang Ping. Then Zhang Ping's army became very strong and carried out a counterattack. Cao Shen was hard pressed, and it was doubtful the army under him could resist the counterattack. At this critical moment, a Han army under General Zhou Bo came to reinforce the army under Cao Shen. The Han army under Zhou Bo attacked Zhang Ping's army fiercely and defeated it. Zhang Ping fled further north to Beidi Prefecture (now Maling, Gansu Province). After they had stamped out any resistance in the area of the west part of Long (now west part of Gansu Province), Cao Shen and Zhou Bo led their army back to the south to join in the siege of Feiqiu.

Han Xin sent General Guan Ying to attack Yueyang, the capital of the State of Sai. Because most of his forces had been consumed in the reinforce-ment of Zhang Han and Zhang Ping, Sima Xin did not have enough troops to resist the attack by the Han army under Guan Ying. So when Guan Ying with his army arrived, Sima Xin opened the city gate and surrendered Yuey-ang to the Han army. After Guan Ying had taken Yueyang, Liu Bang moved his headquarters there and he sent a party of soldiers back to Nanzheng, the former capital of the State of Han, to escort Xiao He to Yueyang. After Liu Bang had settled down in Yueyang, Guan Ying led most of his army to join in the siege of Feiqiu.

General Jin She of the Han army conquered the area of Longxi (the west part of Gansu Province).

General Li Shang marched his army to Beidi Prefecture. General Li Shang arranged his army in battle formation and then rode up to the foot of the city wall to challenge for battle. Zhang Ping led his army out of the city of Beidi to take up the challenge. Since the soldiers under Zhang Ping had been defeated several times, the morale of the army of Yong was low. The morale of the Han Army was very high. When the battle began, the Han soldiers charged the enemy formation with loud war cries. The soldiers under Zhang Ping fled in every direction. Seeing that his army was collapsing, Zhang Ping had no heart to go on fighting. He simply rode away. General Li Shang saw him go, and commanded his army to give chase. Zhang Ping saw them coming; he had to turn around to defend himself. General Li Shang rode up to fight with Zhang Ping. After several bouts, Zhang Ping was hit and fell from the horse. The Han soldiers rushed up, caught him and bound him. Very soon the area of Beidi Prefecture was free of fighting.

Now most of the areas of Guanzhong had been taken by the Han army, so Liu Bang and Han Xin decided to attack the State of Zhai in the north. Some troops remained in siege of Feiqiu. The main force of the Han army marched north to Gaonu, the capital of the State of Zhai. Dong Yi, King of the State of Zhai, knew that he could do nothing to save his state from destruction. When the Han army arrived, he opened the city gate and surrendered. Now, apart from the city of Feiqiu which was still in the hands of Zhang Han and was under siege by the Han army, the whole area of Guanzhong had been brought in line.

33. Xiang Yu's Decision to Attack the State of Qi

When Xiang Yu got word that Liu Bang had burst out of Hanzhong and was taking the area of Guangzhong, he was furious. At this time, an envoy sent by Zhang Liang arrived and presented a letter to Xiang Yu. The letter read, "Liu Bang, King of Han, has led his army to the area of Guanzhong. His purpose is to get back what he was entitled to: the designation of King of

Guanzhong. He will stop when he has got what is his due. He has no inten-tion to go further east." After reading the letter, Xiang Yu felt a bit easier.

Not long after, another envoy sent by Zhang Liang arrived in Pengcheng and presented a letter to Xiang Yu. It read, "Information shows that Tian Rong, King of the State of Qi, has made arrangements to threaten the State of Western Chu. He has lent an army to Chen Yu, Marquis of Nanpi, to drive out Zhang Er, King of Changshan, and put Zhao Xie back on the throne of the State of Zhao. The State of Zhao controlled by Chen Yu constitutes a threat to the State of Western Chu. Tian Rong has given a general's seal to Peng Yue, and Peng Yue is also a threat to the Western Chu. And the State of Qi itself is a threat to the State of Western Chu. Tian Rong has formed a united front in the north. The intention of Tian Rong is very clear: he will carry out a comprehensive offensive against the State of Western Chu from the north. Your Majesty must take action before it is too late." So Xiang Yu made up his mind to attack the State of Qi.

The State of Haan was located in a very strategic place, just to the east of Guanzhong. In order to prevent Liu Bang from advancing to the east, Xiang Yu made Zheng Chang King of the State of Haan; and Zheng Chang set out with an army to defend the State of Haan. Now Zhang Liang knew that it was time for him to leave the State of Haan, because Haan Cheng, King of the State of Haan, had been killed by Xiang Yu and Zhang Liang was not needed any more. He decided to go to Guanzhong and serve Liu Bang wholeheartedly. When he arrived in Yueyang, Liu Bang welcomed him warmly, and granted him the title of Marquis of Chengxin. Zhang Liang was not in good health, so he did not command any troops himself; but he often made strategic plans for Liu Bang and often accompanied him.

Xiang Yu urged the Acting Emperor to leave Pengcheng for Chen, south of the Yangtze River. Then in October 206 BC, Xiang Yu sent undercover agents to take secret orders to Ying Bu, the King of Jiujiang, and Wu Rui, King of Hengshan, and Gong Ao, King of Linjiang and they killed the Acting Emperor in the Yangtze River.

Xiang Yu was ready to march his army to the State of Qi. Before he start-ed, Xiang Yu sent an envoy to Liucheng (now Liu'an, Anhui Province), the capital of the State of Jiujiang, to order Ying Bu, King of Jiujiang, to lead an army to assist Xiang Yu in the attack of the State of Qi. But Ying Bu said to the envoy that he was ill and could not lead the army personally to assist Xiang Yu; but he would appoint a general to lead the army in his stead. So the envoy had to go back to the State of Western Chu with an army of 4,000 men of Jiujiang under the command of a general appointed by Ying Bu. When Xiang Yu saw that Ying Bu had not come personally, he was very angry. It was Xiang Yu who had made him King of Jiujiang. By not coming personally, Ying Bu failed to show proper appreciation. Xiang Yu was especially angry because he had placed great hope in Ying Bu. Ying Bu had always commanded the vanguard and was always victorious in battles against the Qin army. Tian Rong was a strong enemy. Xiang Yu had been counting on Ying Bu's help to deal with this enemy. From then on, Xiang Yu hated Ying Bu.

In December 206 BC, Xiang Yu led his army in the march northward to Chengyang (now a place to the north of Heze, Shandong Province). Tain Rong met Xiang Yu's army in Chengyang. A battle was fought in January 205 BC, and Tian Rong was defeated. Tian Rong retreated to Pingyuan (now Pingyuan, Shandong Province). The people there killed him. In January 205 BC, Xiang Yu reinstated Tian Jia as King of the State of Qi. Xiang Yu led his victorious army, fighting all the way north to the sea, destroying cities, burning down houses, killing the Qi soldiers who had surrendered, capturing old people and women. Xiang Yu's army did great harm to the people of the State of Qi, so the people of the State of Qi rose against him.

Tian Heng, Tian Rong's younger brother, gathered the scattered Qi soldiers. He got about 50,000 men. Tian Heng led the army to fight against the army of the Western Chu in Chengyang. In a battle in Chengyang, Tian Jia, the King of the State of Qi made by Xiang Yu, was killed. In March 205 BC, Tian Heng put Tian Guang, Tiang Rong's son, on the throne of the State of Qi. So Xiang Yu was stuck in the State of Qi.

34. Liu Bang's Actions to Conquer the Areas around the Yellow River

After the area of Guanzhong had been basically pacified, Liu Bang decided to begin action to pacify the east. He sent General Xue Ou and General Wang Xi with an army to march out of Wuguan Pass in the south of Guanzhong to the Area of Nanyang to join force with Wang Ling. The purpose of this army was to march back to the Area of Pei, Liu Bang's home place, to escort Liu Bang's father and wife and children to the area of Guanzhong. When Xiang Yu heard that an army of Han was marching eastward, he sent an army to block their way in Xiayang (now Taikang, Henan Province), and ordered Zheng Chang, King of the State of Haan made by Xiang Yu, to send an army to resist the Han army.

After Xiao He arrived at Yueyang, Liu Bang held court to discuss the next action to be taken. He made the decision to take the areas around the Yellow River first. He appointed Xiao He to stay in Yueyang to administer the area of Guanzhong. Han Xin was also to stay in Guanzhong to continue the siege of Feiqiu, which was still in the hands of Zhang Han. Generals Cao Shen, Fan Kuai, Zhou Bo and Guan Ying were also to stay within Guan-zhong to assist Han Xin in the siege of Feiqiu. Liu Bang would personally lead a strong army to march out of Hanguguan Pass to the east.

In September 206 BC, Liu Bang marched out of Hanguguan Pass with a great army of 100,000 men. Liu Bang reached Shan (now Shanxian, Henan Province), and established his headquarters there. He sent out an army to attack the State of Henan. In October 206 BC, when the Han army reached Luoyang (now Luoyang, Henan Province), the capital of the State of Henan, Shen Yang, King of the State of Henan, surrendered to Liu Bang. The State of Henan was turned into Prefecture of Henan.

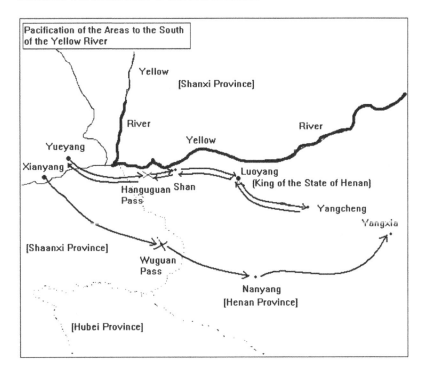

Liu Bang sent an envoy to Zhaiyang (now Yuzhou, Henan Province), the capital of the State of Haan, demanding Zheng Chang to surrender, but Zheng Chang refused. Then Liu Bang summoned Haan Xin, the grandson of the former King of the State of Haan before the State of Haan was conquered by the State of Qin. Liu Bang said to him, "You are the grandson of the former King of the State of Haan. If you can pacify the area of the State of Haan, I will make you King of the State of Haan." Haan Xin took the order and set out with a strong army to take the area of the State of Haan. He successfully took eighteen cities of the State of Haan.

In November 206 BC, the army under Haan Xin and the army under Zheng Chang met in Yangcheng (now a place between Dengfeng and Yuzhou, Henan Province). The two sides had a fierce fight. At last, Zheng Chang surrendered. The whole State of Haan was pacified. Haan Xin turned back to see Liu Bang with his victorious army. Then Liu Bang officially made him King of the State of Haan as he had promised. From then on, Haan Xin, King of the State of Haan, often followed Liu Bang into battle with the troops of the State of Haan against Xiang Yu.

After the State of Henan and the State of Haan, which were located to the south of the Yellow River, were pacified, Liu Bang returned to Yueyang. In November 206 BC, Liu Bang made Yueyang the capital of the State of Han.

One day, a man came to the gate of the palace in Yueyang. He said to the guards of the gate, "Please tell the King of Han that Zhang Er, King of Changshan, requests to see His Majesty." One of the guards went into the palace and reported to the King of Han, "Zhang Er, King of Changshan, has come to see Your Majesty." Liu Bang was surprised to hear that, and said, "Invite him in immediately." When Zhang Er came in, he knelt on one knee and made a salute to Liu Bang. Liu Bang rose from his seat and helped him up, and asked, "King of Changshan, my good friend, why are you here?" Zhang Er said, with tears in his eyes, "Chen Yu with the help of Tian Rong led an army to attack me and occupied the territory of the State of Changshan, and he has put Zhao Xie, the King of the State of Dai, back on the throne of the State of Zhao. Now I have come to ask for help from Your Majesty." Liu Bang comforted him, saying, "Don't worry, I will surely help you get back what belongs to you. You may stay with me for the time being."

Liu Bang next set out to the areas to the north of the Yellow River. This time, Xiao He was to stay within Guanzhong to administer the affairs of the

State of Han and Han Xin was to stay behind to continue the siege of Feiqiu as before, but Generals Cao Shen, Fan Kuai, Zhou Bo and Guan Ying would go with Liu Bang. In March 205 BC, Liu Bang crossed the Yellow River from Linjin (now to the east of Dali, Shaanxi Province) and entered into the area of the State of Western Wei. The Han army marched to Pingyang (now Linfen, Shanxi Province), the capital of the State of Western Wei. Wei Bao, King of the State of Western Wei, opened the city gate to welcome Liu Bang, and put himself and his army under the command of Liu Bang. Then Liu Bang marched his army to Henei (now Wuzhi, Henan Province). The area of Henei belonged to the State of Yin. Sima Wang (King of the State of Yin) led an army from Zhaoge (now Qixian, Henan Province), the capital of the State of Yin, to prevent the advance of the Han army. After a battle, Sima Wang was captured and he surrendered. The State of Yin was pacified, and Liu Bang turned this state into the prefecture of Henei.

This King of Yin had once betrayed Xiang Yu and declared himself in-dependent. Chen Ping, a high-ranking officer in Xiang Yu's army, had been sent to put down the King of Yin's rebellion. Chen Ping attacked the King of Yin and succeeded in bringing him back to submission. When Chen Ping came back from the battle, Xiang Yu granted him a promotion in rank and gave him two hundred kilograms of gold for his outstanding service. But when the King of Yin was captured by Liu Bang and surrendered, Xiang Yu was very angry and unreasonably held Chen Ping responsible for Liu Bang's success in capturing King of Yin. Chen Ping was afraid. He asked a person to return the seal and the gold to Xiang Yu and then secretly disappeared. He decided to go over to Liu Bang.

He crossed the Yellow River and joined Liu Bang's army in Xiuwu (now Huojia, Henan Province). Through Wei Wu Zhi, he sought an audience with Liu Bang. Liu Bang invited him to dinner. After the dinner, Liu Bang sent him back to a guesthouse. Chen Ping said, "I have come for important matters. What I am going to tell Your Majesty must be said today." Then Liu Bang talked with him and liked him very much. Then Liu Bang appoint-ed him to a responsible position as a supervisor of the generals. When the generals learned of the appointment, they were all angry. They said, "Chen Ping is only an officer who has just betrayed Xiang Yu's army. The King does not know him well, but has appointed him to supervise us generals who are much more senior than he." In spite of all their complaints, Liu Bang still had confidence in him.

Liu Bang crossed the Yellow River and went south to Luoyang (now Luoyang, Henan Province). An old man stopped the King of Han's horse and said to the King, "I have heard that those who uphold justice will win. Those who are against justice will fall. The army that carries out an expedition against an enemy must be sent with a justifiable reason. Otherwise, the cause of the expedition will fail. Your Majesty should openly declare what crime your enemy has committed, so that you may condemn your enemy and subdue him. Now, Xiang Yu has committed a serious crime. He has moved King Huai of the State of Chu, that is, his former king, to the south of the Yangtze River and had him killed in the river. So he is the common enemy of the people all over China. People all over China will come over to your side because of your benevolence and justice, not only because of your bravery and strength. I suggest that Your Majesty order all the officers and men in your army to wear white clothes to mourn for King Huai of the State of Chu. Then Your Majesty may call upon the kings of different states all over China to launch an expedition against Xiang Yu. Then people all over China will admire your kindness. This is the act of a wise king."

The King of Han took his advice and held a mourning ceremony for the death of the Acting Emperor (King Huai of the State of Chu). The mourning ceremony lasted for three days. Then Liu Bang sent out envoys to all the kings with the message to this effect: "The Acting Emperor is the emperor over all the people. We are all his subjects and should place ourselves in his service. Now Xiang Yu has removed the Acting Emperor to the south of the Yangtze River and had him killed in the river. He has committed a serious crime. I have sent all the troops in the area of Guanzhong and the armies of Henei, Henan, and Hedong areas to embark on an expedition together with the forces of the kings of all the states against the one who has ordered the assassination of the Acting Emperor."

When Liu Bang's envoy reached the State of Zhao with the message, Chen Yu said, "If the King of Han kills Zhang Er, then I will do what he has instructed." Liu Bang found a person who resembled Zhang Er in appearance and had him killed. Then he sent an envoy with the head of this person to Chen Yu. Then Chen Yu sent his army to the King of Han.

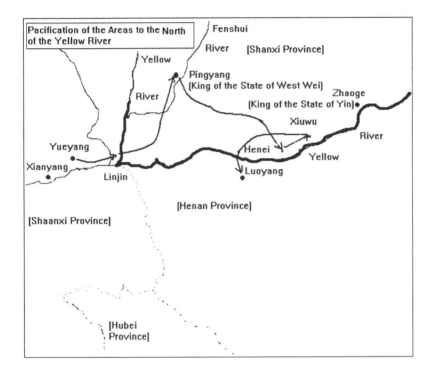

35. The Battle of Pengcheng

After Tian Rong died, his brother Tian Heng collected the scattered soldiers; he collected more than 30,000 soldiers and stationed his army in Chengyang. In April 205 BC, Tian Heng made Tian Rong's son Tian Guang King of the State of Qi to resist Xiang Yu's attack. Xiang Yu attacked Cheng-yang several times but could not take it. Although he learned that Liu Bang was advancing eastward, he would not withdraw from Chengyang to stop the advance of the King of Han. He wanted to defeat the army of Qi first before he coped with the King of Han. So Liu Bang commanded the united army of the kings of other states, 560,000 in all, in an expedition against Xiang Yu.

In April 205 BC, the Han army and the armies of other kings marched towards Pengcheng in three routes: the north route, the middle rout and the south route. The north route mainly comprised of the Han army under Gen-erals Cao Shen, Fan Kuai, Zhou Bo and Guan Ying. They started from Henei. They marched to Xiuwu (now Huojia, Henan Province). They continued marching to the Port of Baima (now Huaxian, Henan Province) situated on the west bank of the Yellow River. From the Port of Baima, the Han army crossed the Yellow River. They marched south to Dingtao (now Dingtao, Shandong Province). Generals Long Ju and Xiang Tuo of the army of the Western Chu led the army under them to fight with the Han army. The army of the State of Western Chu was defeated, and Long Ju and Xiang Tuo ran to join Xiang Yu. The Han army marched to Dang (in the southwest of Henan Province) and Xiao (Xiaoxian, Jiangsu Province) and was ready to enter Pengcheng.

The army of the south route comprised of the Han army commanded by Generals Wang Ling, Xue Ou and Wang Xi, which had already marched to the area of Yangxia (now Taikang, Henan Province) and was stopped by the army of the Western Chu. The Han army started an attack and took Yangxia. This route of the army marched towards Pengcheng.

Liu Bang led the middle route. Zhang Liang, Chen Ping, Xiahou Ying, Jin She, Lu Wan, Haan Xin (King of the State of Haan), Wei Bao (King of the State of Western Wei), Zhang Er (original King of the State of Changshan), Shen Yang (original King of the State of Henan), Sima Xin (original King of the State of Sai), Dong Yi (original King of the State of Zhai), Sima Wang (original King of the State of Yin) were in this route. This route of the army took Quyu (now Zhongmao, Henan Province) and marched to Waihuang (now a place near Minquan, Henan Province). Peng Yue joined Liu Bang with 30,000 men under his command. Liu Bang said to Peng Yue, "Since you have occupied more than ten cities in the Wei area. I sincerely wish to make the descendant of the former King of the State of Wei as the King of the State of Wei. Now Wei Bao, the King of the State of Western Wei is a true descendant of the former King of the State of Wei. I appoint you as the premier of the State of Wei. You may lead an army to conquer the whole area of Wei." So Peng Yue commanded his army in taking the area of Wei. Liu Bang's army marched to Pengcheng and took the city. Liu Bang confiscated all the treasures and beautiful women in Xiang Yu's Palaces. Then Liu Bang held banquets day and night to celebrate the victory.

Xiang Yu got word that Liu Bang had entered Pengcheng. He ordered other generals to continue the fighting with the Qi army while he himself with an army of 30,000 hand-picked troops all on horses moved quickly and secretly south through Lu (now Qufu, Shandong Province) to Huling (in the southwest of Shandong Province), then to Xiao (now Xiaoxian, Anhui

Province) which was situated to the west of Pengcheng. Liu Bang did not notice the movement of the army of the Western Chu at all, because he thought that Xiang Yu was still busy fighting with the army of the State of Qi. He still held celebrations every day without taking the least preventive measures.

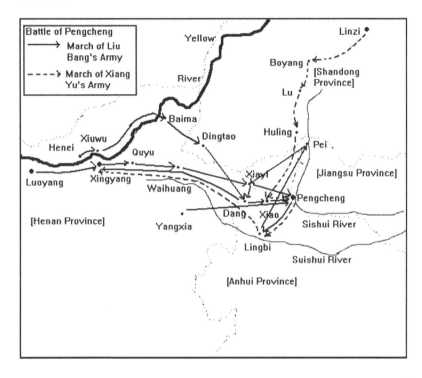

One day in April 205 BC, in the early morning, Xiang Yu commanded the Western Chu army to launch a surprise attack on the Han army, sweeping from west to east to Pengcheng. The Han army was caught entirely off guard, and it collapsed. At noon, the Western Chu army inflicted a crushing blow upon the Han army. The Han soldiers ran for their lives and they all rushed into the Sishui River and the Gu River. More than 100,000 Han soldiers were killed. The Han soldiers ran southward to the hills. The Western Chu army was in hot pursuit to the Suishui River in the east of Lingbi (now Suixi, Anhui Province). The Han soldiers were driven into the waters. About 100,000 Han soldiers were in the Suishui River, so many that the river was blocked and the water in the river stopped flowing.

Xiang Yu spotted Liu Bang in the confusion and ordered his soldiers to surround him. The Western Chu army surrounded the King of Han in three rings. But suddenly, a fierce wind blew up from the northwest. The wind was so strong that big trees broke and houses were lifted from the ground. Sand and stones were blown up into the air. The day went dark. The wind blew directly against the Western Chu army and the Western Chu army was in great confusion and then scattered. Liu Bang and about ten followers on horseback seized the chance to make their escape.

36. Liu Bang Meets Qi Ji

Liu Bang sped away from the battlefield and rode to the hills. Some soldiers of the Western Chu army saw him and pursued him. When he reached a village, he saw a well, and he jumped off his horse and into the well while his horse continued to gallop forward. The Western Chu soldiers stopped to check the well and saw that the opening was covered with spider webs, and it did not seem that anybody had jumped into it. So the Western Chu soldiers got back on their horses and continued their pursuit in the direction in which Liu Bang's horse was galloping. Sometime later, Liu Bang's horse rode back to the well and neighed. A beautiful girl named Qi Ji heard the neighing of the horse and came out of her house. She saw the horse by the well and looked down into the well; and she saw Liu Bang in the bottom of the well, which was dry. She ran back to her house and called her father. And she and her father came to the opening of the well with a rope. They dropped one end of the rope to the bottom of the well and pulled Liu Bang out of it. When Liu Bang was pulled out of the well, he made a bow to Qi Ji and her father and expressed his deepest thanks for their saving him. When the girl saw that Liu Bang was a tall and handsome man, she fell in love with him. Qi Ji's father invited Liu Bang into his house and served him good food. Liu Bang stayed in the house for the night. Qi Ji's father offered his daughter to Liu Bang for the night. The next morning, before he left, Liu Bang said to Qi Ji, "Since you have slept with me, you are one of my concubines. If you get pregnant, and give birth to a boy, he will be a prince of the State of Han. If you give birth to a girl, she will be a princess of the State of Han." Not long later after Liu Bang had left, Qi Ji found that she was indeed pregnant, and nine months later she gave birth to a baby boy.

In the meantime, Liu Bang rode out of the village and met many Han soldiers who were looking for him. On their way, Liu Bang wanted to go past Pei and take his family with him, but at the same time Xiang Yu sent an army after them. Liu Bang's family got wind that Xiang Yu had sent an army after them and they ran away, so that when Liu Bang got there, he could not find them. On their way, Liu Bang found his son Liu Ying and daughter Liu Yuan. He took them in his carriage and went on. The Western Chu cavalry-men were hot on their trail. With the extra weight slowing them down, Liu Bang was afraid that they might not avoid capture. When the Western Chu cavalrymen were close, he pushed his two children down from the carriage. General Xiahou Ying, who was the driver of the king's carriage, stopped the carriage and took the two children back. Three times Liu Bang pushed his children from the carriage; and three times Xiahou Ying got them back. He said, "They are your own children. Although the enemy is close, you should not abandon them." Liu Bang was so angry that he wanted to kill Xiahou Ying many times, but at last, they succeeded in making their escape, and Xiahou Ying saved the two children.

At that time, Liu Bang's wife's brother Lü Ze was a general under Liu Bang and stationed his army in Xiayi (now Dangshan, Henan Province). Liu Bang went into Lü Ze's camps and put Lü Ze's army under his own com-mand. But Liu Bang's wife, his father, and Shen Yi Ji were unlucky. They tried to run away along the side roads to look for the King of Han. They did not meet the King of Han. Instead, they fell into the hands of Xiang Yu. And Xiang Yu kept them in his army as hostages.

37. Liu Bang's Strategic Decision in Xiayi

When Liu Bang got the army from General Lü Ze, he began to retreat. On the way, when he was leaving Xiayi, an idea struck him. He got off his horse, put one hand on the saddle and fell deep into thought. Then he called for Zhang Liang. He said to Zhang Liang, "I am thinking of granting the land east to Hanguguan Pass to those who make the greatest contributions in defeating Xiang Yu. Who do you think can make such contributions and be granted the land?"

Zhang Liang said, "Ying Bu, King of Jiujiang, is a brave general who made great contributions in battles to overthrow the rule of the Qin Dy-nasty. Xiang Yu always assigned the most difficult tasks to him. Recently,

Xiang Yu called upon him to lead the army of Jiujiang personally to assist him in the battles against Tian Rong, but Ying Bu did not go personally. He only appointed a general to lead the army to assist Xiang Yu. This made Xiang Yu very angry. Peng Yue united with Tian Rong against Xiang Yu. He is now carrying out military operations in the area of Liang, a place of strategic importance. Your Majesty may mobilize these two men immediately. As for the generals under Your Majesty, only Han Xin may assume such great responsibility alone. If Your Majesty wants to grant the land east to Hanguguan Pass to anybody, Your Majesty may grant the land to these three people. Then Xiang Yu may be defeated." Liu Bang accepted Zhang Liang's suggestion readily. He sent an envoy to Peng Yue to convey his decision to grant him land if he could make great contributions in defeating Xiang Yu.

After Liu Bang was defeated by Xiang Yu, many kings who were originally on Liu Bang's side betrayed him and turned to Xiang Yu's side. Sima Xin, the King of Sai, and Dong Yi, King of Zhai, went over to join Xiang Yu. Sima Wang, the former King of Yin, was missing in action.

The King of Han moved his army from Xiayi to Yu (now a place near Yucheng, Henan Province). Liu Bang said to the officials around him, "You men are so mediocre. I can't get much help from you when it really matters." Sui He, in the retinue of the King of Han, said, "I'm not sure I understand what Your Majesty means..." Liu Bang said, "I wonder if any one of you can be sent as my envoy to persuade the King of Jiujiang to betray Xiang Yu and raise an army to attack the State of Chu, and keep fighting with Xiang Yu for several months. Then I may be sure of winning the power to rule over the whole country." Sui He said, "I am willing to be the envoy." Then Liu Bang sent Sui He as his envoy to the King of Jiujiang with twenty followers.

In May, the King of Han arrived in Xingyang (now Xingyang, Henan Province). All the troops which had been defeated and scattered in the battle of Pengcheng congregated in Xingyang. And Xiao He sent all the men he could recruit in the area of Guanzhong to reinforce Liu Bang's army. Han Xin left some troops to continue the siege of Feiqiu, and led an army to Xingyang to join Liu Bang. So Liu Bang's army was revitalized.

Xiang Yu recovered Pengcheng. Then he led his army from Pengcheng in the march west to Xingyang to fight against the King of Han. Xiang Yu sent many cavalrymen into battle; so Liu Bang needed to select someone particularly competent as the general to command his cavalry. The generals recommended Li Bi and Luo Jia, who were from the former Qin area. Liu Bang wanted to make the appointment right away, but Li Bi and Luo Jia said, "We are people of the former State of Qin. We are afraid that we cannot gain the trust of the officers and men under us. Let us suggest that Your Majesty select as the commander of the cavalry a general who has followed Your Majesty for a long time; and we will assist him in commanding the cavalry in battles." The King of Han appointed Guan Ying as the commander of the cavalry, with Li Bi and Luo Jia in the role of assistant commanders.

Then they led the cavalry into battle against the cavalry of Western Chu. A battle was fought to the east of Xingyang. The Han cavalry won a great victory over the Chu cavalry. From then on, the march of the Western Chu to the west was stopped. The troops were blocked before Xingyang and could not go further west. The King of Han stationed his army in Xingyang. Xingyang was a strategic place, situated just south of the Yellow River. To the west of Xingyang was Chenggao (now Sishui Town of Xingyang City, Henan Province), where there were food warehouses at a place named Aocang. The King of Han ordered to have a road constructed, protected by walls all along its length, leading to Aocang. Via this protected road, the King of Han ensured a sufficient food supply from Aocang.

Generals Zhou Bo and Guan Ying said to the King of Han, "Chen Ping looks handsome and is well dressed, but actually he is not a virtuous man. We hear that when he was young, he caused his sister-in-law to be abandoned by his brother. When he worked for the former King of the State of Wei, the King of the State of Wei drove him out. Then he ran away and went over to Xiang Yu. Again he could not make himself acceptable to Xiang Yu. Now he has come over to the State of Han. Your Majesty has put him in a responsible position to supervise generals. We hear that Chen Ping accepts money from the generals. Those who give more money are well treated. Those who give little money are ill-treated. Chen Ping has changed sides frequently. He is not a devoted officer. We hope that Your Majesty will look into this matter."

Their accusation aroused the King of Han's suspicion. He called upon Wei Wu Zhi, who had introduced Chen Ping to the King of Han, and quizzed him over his recommendation of Chen Ping. Wei Wu Zhi said, "I have recommended Chen Ping to Your Majesty for his ability. Now Your Majesty is asking about his virtue. Whether he is a virtuous man or a dutiful son has nothing to do with Your Majesty's great cause of winning the power to rule over the whole country. Your Majesty, the King of Han, and Xiang Yu, the King of Western Chu are fighting desperately against each other. I have recommended a resourceful and astute man. My only consideration is whether his strategy is going to serve the state and the cause of your Majesty. As for whether he has caused his sister-in-law to be abandoned by his brother or whether he has taken money from the generals, these are trivial matters. Why should Your Majesty be suspicious of him for such trivial reasons?"

Then the King of Han called upon Chen Ping and accosted him, saying, "You served the former King of Wei, but he drove you out. You once worked for Xiang Yu, but you left him and came over to me. Are you a disloyal person?" Chen Ping said, "When I served the former King of Wei, he would not accept my advice. So I left him and went over to Xiang Yu. But Xiang Yu does not trust people other than his family members, men who bear the family name of Xiang, and his relatives. People of great ability and talent cannot earn responsible positions under him. I heard that Your Majesty is a generous man and offers good positions to talented people. So I have sided with Your Majesty. I left Xiang Yu in haste and I did not bring anything with me. If I do not accept money from the other generals, I don't have the money to do my job. If Your Majesty thinks that any of the suggestions I have provided to Your Majesty are useful, Your Majesty just adopts them. If Your Majesty thinks that none of them has been useful, all the money I received from the generals is still here. It can be sealed and delivered to the government treasury. I beg Your Majesty to accept my resignation and let me go back home to live out the rest of my life." At these words, the King of Han immediately apologized to Chen Ping; he gave him many gifts and appointed him supervisor over the whole army. The generals did not talk about it anymore.

In June 205 BC, the King of Han returned to Yueyang, the capital of the State of Han in the area of Guanzhong. Han Xin and Fan Kuai accompanied him back to Guanzhong. Liu Bang appointed his son Liu Ying Crown Prince of the State of Han. The troops of Han had surrounded Feiqiu for a long time. Liu Bang decided to conquer Feiqiu. Han Xin made an inspection around the city; and after he made his inspection, a plan formed in Han Xin's mind. The Weishui River flowed through south to the city of Feiqiu. Han Xin decided to have water diverted from the Weishui River to destroy the walls of the city of Feiqiu. He ordered Fan Kuai to do the job. The soldiers under Fan Kuai worked very hard to dig a channel from the side of the Weishui River to the foot of the city wall. When the channel had been dug, Han Xin issued the order to let water flow. The water flooded through the channel to the foot of the city wall, and the city wall was softened. Several days later, the city wall fell. The Han soldiers entered the city of Feiqiu. The people of the city surrendered, and Zhang Han saw that he could not do anything to save the State of Yong. He drew out his sword and killed himself. From then on, the three states in the Qin area became three prefectures.

In August, the King of Han went back to Xingyang. Before he left, he ordered Xiao He to stay in the area of Guanzhong to help the Crown Prince, to make laws to rule over the people, and to build temples and palaces. He gave Xiao He the power to make decisions and take action by himself on urgent matters before he reported to the King. Xiao He had the number of households in the area of Guanzhong calculated so that he could properly impose taxes, requisition food supplies and recruit soldiers to support Liu Bang's army. Xiao He did such a good job that the supply of food and new recruits had never stopped.

38. Wei Bao's Betrayal of Liu Bang

Wei Bao, King of the State of Wei, had a concubine named Bo Ji. Bo Ji's father had died early. Bo Ji's mother, Lady Wei, was the daughter of the former King of the State of Wei before the State of Wei was destroyed by the State of Qin. After the State of Wei was reinstated and Wei Bao became King of the State of Wei, Lady Wei brought Bo Ji back to the State of Wei and married Bo Ji to Wei Bao. Lady Wei invited Xu Fu, a famous fortune-teller, to the palace of Wei in Pingyang (now Linfen of Shanxi Province), the capital of the State of Wei, to foretell Bo Ji's fortune. After reading Bo Ji's face carefully, Xu Fu said to Lady Wei, "Your daughter will give birth to an emperor!" Lady Wei exclaimed, "Really!" Then she said, "Will you go to Xingyang to tell the King about this?"

Xu Fu traveled all the way from Pingyang to Xingyang where Wei Bao, King of the State of Wei, was staying. Wei Bao was allied with Liu Bang. Wei Bao had led his army to help Liu Bang attack Pengcheng. But later they were defeated by Xiang Yu, and they all ran back to Xingyang. When Xu Fu arrived, Wei Bao invited her to a private room. Xu Fu said, "I have read your concubine Bo Ji's face. I can predict that she will give birth to an emperor!"

Wei Bao said excitedly, "My concubine will give birth to an emperor! That is to say, I shall be the father of an emperor!" He paid Xu Fu generously and sent her back. Wei Bao thought, "Since my concubine is going to give birth to an emperor and I shall be the father of an emperor, why should I be subordinated to the King of Han and obey his orders? I shall be my own master." So he decided to leave Liu Bang.

Wei Bao went to see Liu Bang. He said, "Yesterday, a messenger was sent from Pingyang. He told me that my mother is ill and wants to see me. May I ask for a period of leave? I shall be back as soon as my mother recovers." Liu Bang said, "You are a devoted son. If your mother is ill, you should hurry back to take care of her. I grant you the leave you ask for. Just come back as soon as possible."

In May 205 BC, as soon as he crossed the Yellow River and stepped on the territory of the State of Wei, Wei Bao immediately ordered the army of Wei to block all the ports by the Yellow River to prevent Liu Bang's army from crossing the Yellow River and attacking the State of Wei. When he arrived at Pingyang, he openly declared that the State of Wei was no more an ally of the State of Han. Later he even declared that he would be on the side of Xiang Yu.

39. The Battle to Defeat the King of the State of Wei

When Liu Bang got the news that Wei Bao had openly declared his betrayal and gone over to Xiang Yu's side, he was worried. The situation was unfavorable to Liu Bang. Xiang Yu was confronting with him in the area of Xingyang. He had to cope with Xiang Yu's great army in the east. Liu Bang said to Li Yi Ji, "Will you go to the State of Wei to persuade King of the State of Wei to resume his alliance with us? If you succeed in persuading him to give up his hostile position against us, I shall make you a marquis enjoying the tax on 10,000 peasant households." Li Yi Ji went to the State of Wei as the envoy of the King of Han, to try to persuade the King of the State of Wei to turn back to the side of the King of Han. Li Yi Ji conveyed Liu Bang's intention to call upon him to discuss the matter. But King of the State of Wei refused and said, "Life in this world is short. It is as short as a blink of an eye. I just want to be the master of my own self and not to be a subordinate to somebody else. The King of Han is very rude and very impolite to kings of other states. He often abuses the other kings and his courtiers as if they were his servants. I cannot stand that and I will not see him anymore."

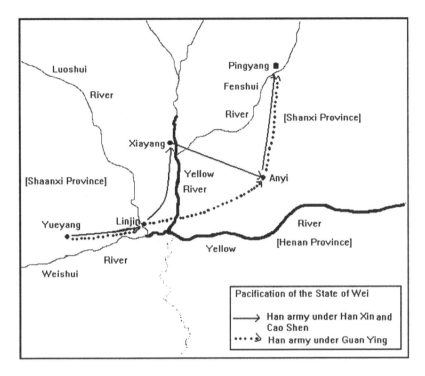

When Li Yi Ji went back to Xingyang and reported the attitude of the King of the State of Wei, Liu Bang decided to attack the State of Wei and to bring Wei Bao to his knees. In August 205 BC, Liu Bang appointed Han Xin as the deputy premier of the State of Han and sent him, together with Guan Ying and Cao Shen, to attack the State of Wei. Liu Bang asked Li Yi Ji, "Who is the commander-in-chief of the army of Wei?" Li Yi Ji answered, "Bo Zhi." Liu Bang said, "He is still a greenhorn. He is no match for Han Xin. Who is the general in charge of the cavalry?" Li Yi Ji answered, "Feng Jing." Liu Bang said, "He is the son of Feng Wu Ze, a former general of the Qin Dynasty. He is a virtuous man, but he is no match for Guan Ying. Who is the general in charge of the infantry?" Li Yi Ji answered, "Xiang Ta." Liu Bang said, "He is not a match for Cao Shen. Then I don't need to worry about anything now."

Han Xin commanded his army to advance to Linjin (now to the east of Dali, Shaanxi Province). Wei Bao deployed his army in Puban (now Pu-zhou, west to Yongji, Shanxi Province) to prevent the army commanded by

Han Xin from crossing the Yellow River from Linjin. Han Xin ordered his soldiers to collect ships along the southern bank of the Yellow Rive and gather them in Linjin. In a few days, about a hundred big ships were lined up along the riverside of Linjin. Han Xin ordered the soldiers to bedeck the ships with red flags marked with the character of "Han," and ordered the soldiers to beat drums and to shout loudly on board the ships, showing the army of the State of Wei that the Han army was going to cross the Yellow River from Linjin to Puban. Wei Bao sent General Bo Zhi and Feng Jing and Xiang Ta with 100,000 men to reinforce the Wei army in Puban.

One night, Han Xin summoned General Guan Ying to his tent. He said, "I will leave here with General Cao Shen and his 20,000 men up north. You and your 10,000 cavalrymen shall remain here. You must do your best to attract the attention of the army of the State of Wei and let them believe that the whole army of Han is still in Linjin. When the Wei army on the east bank begins to retreat, you will immediately cross the river and give chase." General Guan Ying said resolutely, "Yes, I shall do my best to fulfill my task."

That night, Han Xin directed the 20,000 soldiers under the command of General Cao Shen secretly to march further north to Xiayang (now Xiayang Village, Heyang County, Shaanxi Province) where the bank of the Yellow River was low, and the water flowed slowly, and there were no Wei soldiers guarding the opposite bank. After the Han army had pitched camp, Han Xin summoned General Cao Shen and some other officers to his tent. He said, "I'm going to assign you an important task: Send half of your soldiers out to buy from the people as many big storage jars as possible, the ones with narrow necks, and send half of your soldiers to the forest to cut long branches to make poles. And those who accomplish their task best will be granted a reward." In five days, thousands of jars had been collected and more than 10,000 poles were ready.

When Cao Shen and the other officers went to see Han Xin to report that they had accomplished their tasks, Han Xin produced several sketches and distributed to them and said, "Now make rafts according to these sketches." And the whole army set to making rafts out of poles and jars. The soldiers first inserted wooden plugs to seal the mouths of the jars, then took a pair of poles and lashed the neck of a jar between them at one end of the poles, and another jar between the other end of the poles. Then they made another pair of poles and jars. Then they made a square by lashing poles between the two sets of jars and poles, with more poles across the square to form a platform on which soldiers could stand. In a few days, they had a thousand rafts of jars and poles and a lot of paddles too.

One morning in August 205 BC, the soldiers of the Han army assembled and marched toward the river bank carrying the rafts. They put the rafts on the Yellow River, and eight to ten soldiers got on each raft, and in a moment, a thousand rafts began to ferry across the Yellow River. The soldiers paddled hard, and the rafts moved quickly. When the rafts reached the opposite bank, the soldiers got off, and two soldiers paddled back to take more soldiers. Han Xin and Cao Shen also got on the rafts and got to the opposite bank. All the horses and equipment were also ferried across. That night, the army of Han marched quickly towards Anyi (now Xiaxian, Shanxi Province). They did not meet with any resistance because there were no Wei soldiers on their way at all. At dawn, the army of Han reached Anyi. General Wang Shang, the commanding general defending Anyi, led an army to go out to fight with the Han army. Cao Shen galloped forward to meet him. In the fight, Cao Shen intentionally showed a flaw. Wang Shang saw his chance and thrust his spear at Cao Shen. But Cao Shen dodged quickly as Wang Shang was thrown forward, very close to Cao Shen. Cao Shen caught him by his belt and threw him to the ground. The soldiers of the Han army caught him and tied him up. When the soldiers of Wei defending Anyi saw that their commanding general had been captured, they all surrendered. The army of Han successfully took Anyi.

When the news of the fall of Anyi reached Pingyang, Wei Bao immediately sent a messenger to order Generals Bo Zhi, Feng Jing and Xiang Ta, who were in Puban, to come back to defend the capital. When they got the order, they immediately retreated. When a soldier of the Han army at the observation post on a ship in the port of Linjin saw that the Wei army had begun to retreat, he immediately reported the situation to General Guan Ying. General Guan Ying ordered all his cavalrymen to get on board the ships and cross the Yellow River. General Bo Zhi led his great army of about 100,000 men quickly back to Pingyang. General Guan Ying and his cavalrymen joined forces with Han Xin and Cao Shen and began to attack Pingyang. Wei Bao personally led his army out of the city of Pingyang to fight against the Han army. The Han army under Cao Shen surrounded him. Wei Bao fought face to face with Cao Shen. Cao Shen hit him with his spear. Wei Bao fell from his horse. The Han soldiers bound him up and put him into a coarse wagon drawn by an ox. Wei Bao was forced to approach the front gate of Pingyang; when the guards of Pingyang saw that their king had been captured by the Han army, they opened the gate and surrendered. The Han army went to the imperial harem where Wei Bao's concubines lived. Wei Bao's concubines were taken as prisoners of war. Bo Ji, with other concubines, escorted by the Han soldiers, walked slowly and with heavy hearts to Xingyang. When Xu Fu predicted that she would give birth to an emperor, Bo Ji had been very happy. But now she had become a prisoner. There was no hope of her giving birth to an emperor.

Wei Bao was brought before Liu Bang. Liu Bang scolded him angrily, "You traitorous wretch. I have treated you kindly and I let you go back to take care of your mother. Why did you betray me?" Then he ordered the soldiers, "Take him out and chop off his head!" Wei Bao broke into a cold sweat and crawled at Liu Bang's feet, begging him to spare him. Then Liu Bang burst into loud laughter and said, "I know you are a coward and you can't accomplish anything. I shall let you live for the time being, and give you a chance to redeem yourself." Then Wei Bao was untied and was sent to the army to defend the city of Xingyang. The territory of the State of Wei was divided into three prefectures: Hedong Prefecture, Shangdang prefecture and Taiyuan Prefecture. Then Liu Bang ordered that all the concubines of Wei Bao, including Bo Ji, be sent to work as slaves in a weaving room to weave cloth. In recognition of Cao Shen's contributions in taking Pingyang, Liu Bang made Cao Shen Marquis of Pingyang.

40. THE BATTLE OF JINGXING

When the Han army was defeated in Pengcheng by the Chu army, Chen Yu, the premier of the State of Zhao, found that Zhang Er was still alive. So the State of Zhao controlled by Chen Yu turned against Liu Bang.

Since Han Xin had squelched any resistance in the State of Wei, he sent an envoy to Liu Bang to ask for permission to attack the State of Zhao, the State of Yan, and the State of Dai in the north, and the State of Qi in the east with 30,000 troops. Liu Bang gave him permission.

In September 205 BC, Han Xin, Zhang Er, the former King of the State of Changshan, and General Cao Shen marched their army to the area of the State of Dai. The King of the State of Dai was Chen Yu. He had not gone to the State of Dai to take the throne of that state. He continued to stay in the State of Zhao to assist Zhao Xie, the King of the State of Zhao. He just entrusted the state affairs of the State of Dai to Xia Yue, the premier of the State of Dai. When the Han army arrived at the east of Wuxian (now Jiexiu, Shanxi Province), Xia Yue led an army to block their advance. General Cao Shen led his army into battle against the Dai army under the command of Xia Yue. Cao Shen and Xia Yue fought. After several bouts, Cao Shen killed Xia Yue, and the Dai army surrendered. Han Xin decided to continue his march to Jingxing with Zhang Er. He ordered Cao Shen to lay siege to Wuxian which was defended by the Zhao army under General Qi of the State of Zhao. General Qi abandoned the city and tried to escape, but was caught up by the Han army under the command of General Cao Shen and was killed. The State of Dai was pacified in a very short time. After the State of Dai was pacified, General Cao Shen led his army back to Aocang to join Liu Bang.

In October 205 BC, Han Xin and Zhang Er maneuvered an army of 30,000 men eastward to the State of Zhao. When Zhao Xie and Chen Yu got word that the Han army was advancing to the State of Zhao, they concentrated their army of 200,000 men in the entrance of Jingxing Pass.

Li Zuo Ju, a general of the army of the State of Zhao, said to Chen Yu, "Han Xin and Zhang Er have just won a great victory. Their army is a victorious army. This army has left its base to fight in a distant place. It is difficult to fight head on with this army. But it is said that if an army is a thousand miles away from its base, the soldiers will surely suffer from hunger because it is very difficult to transport so much food such a great distance. Now the roads in Jingxing area are so narrow that carts carrying food supplies can move only in single file. It is a general rule that when the army has to march several hundred miles, the food supply will surely drag behind the troops. I hope you will give me 30,000 men. With this army, I will go by side roads to attack the Han troops escorting the food supply and destroy their food supplies entirely. You can reinforce the camps by digging deep ditches around the camps and building higher battlements. When the Han army arrives, don't fight. Just let your army to stay inside the camp fences. Then the Han army cannot move any further and cannot turn back either. They cannot get food from the fields. In no more than ten days, I will present the heads of these two persons to you. Otherwise, we will be captured by them."

Chen Yu said, "An army fighting for a just cause will win victories without using treacherous schemes. Han Xin has an army of only 30,000 men and the soldiers of this army are tired because they have marched such a long way here. We have an army of 200,000 men. If we avoid fighting against this small army, the kings of other states will think that I am a coward and look down upon me, and they will invade our state at their own will."

Han Xin sent some spies to Jingxing to get information. When he received the information that Chen Yu had turned down Li Zuo Ju's suggestion, he was extremely happy. Then he gave the order to march forward to Jingxing. When the army was fifteen kilometers away from the Jingxing Pass, he ordered the army to stop marching and to pitch camps for the night. At midnight, he ordered the soldiers to get up. He selected 2,000 men from the cavalry, each of whom carried a red flag. They were ordered to go through side roads in the Bi Mountain to get to a place overlooking the camps of the Zhao army. Han Xin said to them, "I will pretend I have been defeated by the Zhao army and in retreat. All the Zhao soldiers will come out of their camps to run after me. Then you ride as quickly as you can into the camps of the Zhao army. Pull up all the Zhao flags and put up the red flags of Han." Then he asked a general to send his order to the official in charge of food to prepare a banquet for all the soldiers to celebrate the victory over the Zhao army that same day.

The generals did not believe that they would defeat the Zhao army, but they all pretended that they were happy about having a banquet after the victory. Han Xin said to the generals, "Now the Zhao army has built their camps on advantageous ground. The Zhao army will not come out of their camps to fight until they see from my commander-in-chief flag that I have entered the narrow, dangerous pass." Then Han Xin sent 10,000 troops into the pass and the troops were deployed in a battle formation with the Jinman River at their backs. When the Zhao officers and soldiers saw that the Han troops were deployed in battle formation with a river behind them, they all laughed out loud. For it was a general rule, written in the military books, that an army should be deployed facing a river; if the army is deployed with a river behind them, they cannot retreat. Only foolish generals would deploy their armies in such a way.

In the morning, Han Xin and his officers and men marched into the pass with the big flag of commander-in-chief flying high. The army marched to the beat of the drums. The gates of the camps of the Zhao army opened, and the Zhao soldiers came out of their camps to fight with the Han army. The battle went on for some time, and then Han Xin and Zhang Er pretended that they were defeated and abandoned the flags and drums. When the Zhao soldiers remaining in their camps saw that the Han army was defeated, they all came out of their camps to run after Han Xin and Zhang Er. Han Xin and Zhang Er and their army ran to the battle formation by the river. The formation opened to accept Han Xin and Zhang Er and their army. A fierce fight began. Since there was a river behind them, the Han soldiers had nowhere to escape. So the Han soldiers fought bravely for their own lives. They held their ground. When the 2,000 cavalrymen hiding in the hills near the camps saw that all of the Zhao soldiers had left their camps, they rode as quickly as they could into the empty camps and pulled up all the flags of Zhao and put up the red flags of Han. The Zhao soldiers could not catch Han Xin and Zhang Er, so they wanted to get back to their camps. To their great surprise, all their flags had been replaced by the red flags of Han. This made them think that the King of the State of Zhao and the commander-in-chief of the Zhao army had been captured. So the Zhao army was in great disorder and the soldiers scattered and began to run for their own lives. The generals of the Zhao army tried to stop the soldiers from running away by killing some of the deserting soldiers, but even so they could not control the situation. The Han army attacked the Zhao army from two sides. They won a glorious victory. They killed Chen Yu in battle and took prisoner Zhao Xie, the King of the State of Zhao.

After the battle, the generals of the Han army presented to Han Xin all that they had captured in the battle. After the ceremony, the generals quizzed Han Xin. "According to the rules of the art of war, battle formations should be deployed with high ground to the back and the right side of the army and with a river or marshes at the front and left side of the army. But you gave orders to deploy the troops with a river at their backs; and you told us that a banquet would be given after the defeat of the Zhao army. We did not believe it. But in the end, we won. What kind of strategy is this?" Han Xin said, "Actually, this is also a rule of the art of war. According to this rule, the troops must be confronted with the fear of death and they will fight for their lives. The soldiers must be put in a desperate position before they will fight to survive. The men I have are not well-trained soldiers. This is like forcing ordinary people from the marketplace to fight in a battle. They must have a real sense of the danger of death, and then every one of them will put up a desperate fight for his own life. If I put them in a place where they could survive without a desperate fight, they would all run away. How can I get such people to fight for me?" All the generals were impressed.

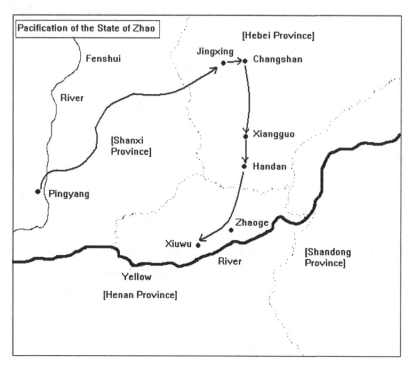

Han Xin put up a notice to the effect that anyone who captured Li Zuo Ju would be given a handsome reward. Several days later, Li Zuo Ju was captured and bound, and was brought to Han Xin. As soon as Li Zuo Ju was brought before him, Han Xin untied the ropes and invited him to sit in a seat facing east. Then, treating him with the respect due to a teacher, Han Xin asked politely, "I want to launch an expedition against the State of Yan in the north and the State of Qi in the east. What shall I do so that I can accomplish my goal?" Li Zuo Ju said politely, "I am your prisoner and a general of an army defeated by you. What right do I have to discuss a matter of such importance?" Han Xin said, "When Bai Li Xi served as premier of the State of Yu, the State of Yu was conquered by the State of Jin and Bai Li Xi was captured by the Jin army. Then, when the Duke of Jin's daughter was married to the Duke of Qin, the Duke of Jin gave Bai Li Xi to the Duke of Qin as a present. The Duke of Qin treasured Bai Li Xi for his talent and appointed him premier of the State of Qin. And due to his efforts, the State of Qin became prosperous. This is not because Bai Li Xi was a fool when he was in the State of Yu and wise when he was in the State of Qin. It is because the Duke of Yu paid no heed to his advice—but the Duke of Qin adopted every suggestion he provided. Now, if Chen Yu had adopted your suggestion, you would have captured all of us. I have won the victory and I can talk to you here only because Chen Yu did not take your advice. I value your advice. I hope you will not decline my request."

Then Li Zuo Ju said, "You crossed the Yellow River and captured Wei Bao, the King of the State of Wei. You marched to the east and took Jingxing Pass. You started the battle in the early morning and defeated an army of 200,000 men before the morning was over. You killed Chen Yu in the battle. You captured the King of the State of Zhao. Your great fame has spread far and wide. The peasants all over the different states stopped their work in the fields and wondered when you would conquer their states. This is your strength, your advantage. But now your soldiers are all very tired. If you use this army of tired soldiers to attack the heavily defended cities of the State of Yan with its formidable city walls, your army will be stuck there. The Yan army will not step outside the cities to fight with you. When you attack such cities, you cannot take them. Then your strength will be weakened. If this situation goes on for long, food will run short. Since you will not be able to force the State of Yan into submission, the neighboring State of Qi will take its time to prepare and strengthen their forces to resist you. As long as the stalemate lasts, the outcome of the war between Liu Bang and Xiang Yu will be pending. This is your disadvantage. A wise general will avoid his disadvantages and make use of his own advantages."

Han Xin prodded further. "Then what shall I do?" Li Zuo Ju said, "The best plan for you is to stop marching forward to the State of Yan and let your soldiers have a good rest. You might appease the people of the State of Zhao. Then the people of the State of Zhao will love you and they will bring gifts such as cows and wine to your army every day. You can let your officers and men have good food every day. When the army is ready for the expedition against the State of Yan in the north, you can send a persuasive envoy to the King of the State of Yan with a letter. Let the envoy show all your advantages and strengths to the King of the State of Yan. The King of the State of Yan will obey your instructions. Then you can move your army east to the State of Qi. When that happens, not even the wisest general will be able to save the State of Qi from destruction. Then you may be sure of a victory all over China. It is a rule of the art of war that you may overawe your enemy by displaying your strength." Han Xin took his suggestion and sent an envoy to the King of the State of Yan; and the King of the State of Yan agreed to submit to the King of Han. Then Han Xin sent an envoy to the King of Han to report their success and ask permission to make Zhang Er King of the State of Zhao. The King of Han gave his permission.

41. Ying Bu Turns against Xiang Yu

In November 205 BC, Sui He, the envoy sent by the King of Han to per-suade Ying Bu to betray Xiang Yu, arrived in Liucheng, the capital of the State of Jiujiang. In the interview by Ying Bu, Sui He demonstrated with persuasive arguments that Liu Bang, even if he seemed to be weaker, would surely win, and that Xiang Yu, who looked powerful, would surely lose. Ying Bu was convinced and promised to come over to Liu Bang's side, but said he wanted to keep it secret for the time being.

At that same time, an envoy sent by Xiang Yu was in Jiujiang. In the interview, the envoy urged Ying Bu to send troops to help Xiang Yu. Sui He walked directly into the meeting room. He said to the envoy, "The King of Jiujiang has changed sides and is with the King of Han. Why should he send his army to help the King of Chu?" Ying Bu was stunned. The Chu envoy stood up and made ready to leave. Sui He said to Ying Bu, "Now your betrayal of Xiang Yu is manifest. You must kill the envoy. Don't let him go back. You should join forces with the King of Han and fight against Xiang Yu." The King of Jiujiang could only agree, and he killed the envoy and sent his army to attack the State of Chu.

Xiang Yu sent Xiang Sheng and Long Ju to attack Jiujiang. Several months later, Long Ju defeated the army of Jiujiang. The King of Jiujiang wanted to lead all his troops to join the King of Han, but he was afraid that the Chu army would pursue him. So he and Sui He and several followers went along the by-roads to the King of Han. In December, Ying Bu arrived in the State of Han. When he was introduced to Liu Bang, Liu Bang was sitting on his bedside washing his feet. Ying Bu was very angry. He was so sorry that he'd come to the State of Han that he wanted to kill himself. But when he went to his suite, he found that everything in the house, the food served to him, and the number of servants, were the same as those of the King of Han. So he was very pleased. He sent an envoy back to Jiujiang.

The envoy found that Xiang Yu had ordered Xiang Bo to take away all the troops of Jiujiang. The Chu army had killed Ying Bu's wife and children. The envoy gathered some former officials under Ying Bu and brought back about a thousand men to Han. The King of Han gave some troops to Ying Bu and let him station his army in Chenggao.

42. Chen Ping's Tricks to Drive a Wedge between Xiang Yu and His Devoted Followers

Chen Ping   Fan Zeng

Things were not looking very good for the King of Han. He was worried. He sent an envoy to see Xiang Yu. He suggested to Xiang Yu to divide the realm in two. The western part of Xingyang would belong to the State of Han, and the eastern part of Xingyang would go to the State of Chu. This seemed to be a good offer, and Xiang Yu was about to accept it. But Fan Zeng, Xiang Yu's military adviser, stopped him, saying, "The King of Han cannot stand for long because his food supply is short. He can easily be de-feated. If you accept his suggestion and give up the chance to defeat him now, you will regret it." In that light, Xiang Yu realized that Liu Bang's sug-gestion was only a measure to stave off his attack. So he sternly rejected Liu Bang's offer. And Xiang Yu intensified the attack on Xingyang.

The King of Han spoke to Chen Ping. "The whole realm has been in great disorder for a long time. When will peace and order be resumed?" Chen Ping said, "Xiang Yu is a polite person. He always respects others. This is one of his merits. Many honest and polite men go over to his side. But he is not at all generous in granting rewards to those who have made great contributions. So those who pursue titles of nobility will not be on his side. Your Majesty is rude and impolite, so those who are honest and polite are not likely to come to the side of Your Majesty. But Your Majesty is gener-ous in granting noble titles to those who have made great contributions to your cause. So those who pursue titles and who have no sense of shame have come to the side of Your Majesty. If Your Majesty would stop being rude and treat people more courteously, while continuing to be generous in granting ranks, it would not be long before Your Majesty gained the power to rule over the whole realm."

He went on: "There are only a few people who are devoted and true to Xiang Yu. They are Fan Zeng, Zhong Li Mei, Long Ju and Zhou Yin. If Your Majesty will invest several thousand kilos of gold into a stratagem to sow distrust and discord, we may drive a wedge between Xiang Yu and his true followers and arouse suspicion among them. Xiang Yu is always suspicious anyway. He is prone to believing rumors. Then there will be killings among them. And if the Han army launches an assault, the Chu army will be surely defeated." The King of Han took his advice and put 20,000 kilos of gold at Chen Ping's disposal. The King of Han did not ask how Chen Ping spent the money.

Chen Ping spread the money far and wide. He spent a lot of money spreading rumors among the Chu army about General Zhong Li Mei, Long Ju and Zhou Yin. They had been generals for Xiang Yu for a long time and had rendered outstanding services, but they had not been made kings of any place. Surely they would unite with the King of Han to destroy Xiang Yu and then divide his territory and make themselves kings of his lands.

The stratagem worked wonderfully. Just as expected, Xiang Yu felt he could not trust Zhong Li Mei, Long Ju and Zhou Yin anymore. One day, an envoy sent by Xiang Yu arrived. Chen Ping entertained the envoy on behalf of the King of Han. Wonderful dishes of food were brought to serve in front of the envoy. Then Chen Ping walked in and saw the envoy. He said in great surprise, "I thought this was an envoy sent by Fan Zeng, but this is actually an envoy sent by Xiang Yu." Then he ordered the servants to take away all the good food and served the envoy with distinctly inferior food. The envoy went back and told Xiang Yu what had happened in the reception. This aroused Xiang Yu's suspicion of Fan Zeng. The more Fan Zeng urged Xiang Yu to step up his attack on Xingyang, the more Xiang Yu suspected Fan Zeng's true intention. Xiang Yu stopped listening to his advice. When Fan Zeng understood that he was under suspicion, he said angrily to Xiang Yu, "The outcome of the war is now clear. Your Majesty is on your own and you will have to do your best to save yourself from destruction. I am too old to do anything for you. I hope Your Majesty will let me retire so that I may die at home." Xiang Yu gave his permission. Fan Zeng left Xingyang for Pengcheng. But he died of skin ulcers on his back before he even reached Pengcheng.

43. Ji Xin Dies for Liu Bang and Xingyang Falls

In May 204 BC, the situation became worse and worse. Food rations for the Han army became very short. The Western Chu army attacked the city of Xingyang fiercely. The city could fall at any moment. General Ji Xin said to the King of Han, "The situation is critical. Now, I bear a strong resemblance to Your Majesty. I am willing to disguise myself as Your Majesty to deceive Xiang Yu. Then Your Majesty can escape Xingyang in secret." The King of Han hesitated. Chen Ping said, "I am afraid this is the only way out."

At night, Chen Ping sent about 2,000 women in armor out through the east gate of Xingyang. The troops of the Western Chu army all gathered near that gate to attack those who were trying to get out of the besieged city. Then Ji Xin, dressed up in the King of Han's clothes, was driven out through the east gate in the King of Han's carriage. From the carriage, he declared to the army of Western Chu, "I am King of Han. My army has run out of food. I have decided to surrender." When the soldiers of the Western Chu army got news that the King of Han had surrendered, they cheered, "Victory! Victory!" and rushed to the east gate to watch the great scene of the surrender of the King of Han.

Meanwhile Liu Bang and about thirty followers rode on horses out of the city of Xingyang from the west gate.

When Xiang Yu arrived and saw that the man in the carriage was not Liu Bang but Ji Xin, he asked, "Where is the King of Han?" Ji Xin said with a smile, "He has gone out of the city." Xiang Yu was so angry that he ordered his soldiers to collect bundles of firewood and set Ji Xin atop the bonfire and burned him to death.

The Western Chu army continued to lay siege to Xingyang. Before Liu Bang left Xingyang, he ordered Haan Xin (the King of the State of Haan), Zhou Ke, the Minister of Justice, General Zong Gong, and Wei Bao, the former King of the State of Wei, to stay behind to defend the city. In May 204 BC, Wei Bao stood at the top of the city wall and watched the Western Chu army attacking the city. Secretly, he felt happy. He hated Liu Bang, and he had once declared himself to be on Xiang Yu's side. If the city fell, he would certainly go over to Xiang Yu. He had waited for a long time for Xiang Yu, and it seemed this day had at last come. When he thought of this, he even smiled.

General Zhou Ke was standing not far from him, and he saw the smile on Wei Bao's face. He said to General Zong Gong, "Wei Bao is treacherous. He betrayed the King of Han once and declared himself to be on the side of Xiang Yu. I think he has been waiting for this day for a long time. He is not reliable. It is dangerous to defend Xingyang with such a person. We'd better kill him first before he does something for Xiang Yu from inside the city." General Zong Gong agreed. Zhou Ke drew his sword and went up to Wei Bao. Wei Bao was still deep in reverie when Zhou Ke shouted loudly, "Wei Bao!" Wei Bao unconsciously turned to face him. Zhou Ke drove his sword into Wei Bao's chest and killed him.

After the King of Han left Xingyang, he went to Chenggao. When Xiang Yu heard that Liu Bang had escaped to Chenggao, he sent his army in pursuit. The Han army could not resist the attack by the Western Chu army, and Liu Bang had to leave Chenggao; he went into the area of Guanzhong through Hanguguan Pass. He raised an army there and wanted to go back to Xingyang. But Yuan Sheng, one of Liu Bang's advisers, said to the King of Han, "The Han army and the Western Chu army have been at a stalemate in Xingyang for several years. The Han army is often in a difficult situation. This time, I hope, Your Majesty will go through Wuguan Pass in the south. Then Xiang Yu will surely command his army south to fight with Your Majesty. Your Majesty should build strong camps with deep ditches around them. Your Majesty should stay in the camps and not give him any fight. In this way the army of Your Majesty in Xingyang and Chenggao can have a chance to rest. At the same time, Your Majesty can allow Han Xin and Zhang Er to settle things down in the area of the State of Zhao to the north of the Yellow River. Your Majesty should unite with the State of Yan and the State of Qi. Later Your Majesty may go back to Xingyang. Then Xiang Yu will have to divide his forces to deal with many enemies. This way, the Han army can have a rest. After the army has regained its strength, it may start an assault against the Western Chu army. The Han army will surely defeat the Western Chu army."

The King of Han took his advice and maneuvered his army through Wu-guan Pass in the south to the area between Wan (now the area around Nan-yang, Henan Province) and Ye (now Yexian, Henan Province). Ying Bu was also there with the King of Han. When Xiang Yu heard that the King of Han was in the area between Wan and Ye, he led his army to the south to meet the army of the King of Han. The King of Han ordered his army to stay in the camps and strongholds and not fight with the Western Chu army.

When the King of Han was defeated in Pengcheng and retreated to the west, Peng Yue also lost all the cities he had occupied in the area of Wei. Then he led his army to the areas along the Yellow River to carry out guerrilla attacks. He launched raids on the food transportation units of the Western Chu army. This greatly disrupted the food supply of the Western Chu army. Xiang Yu was annoyed. In May 204 BC, Peng Yue crossed the Su-ishui River and fought the Western Chu army commanded by Xiang Sheng and Xue Gong in Xiapi (now northwest of Suining, Jiangsu Province). Peng Yue defeated the army led by Xue Gong and killed Xue Gong. At the same time, General Han Xin and Zhang Er led a great army to march south; they marched down to the north bank of the Yellow River, forming a threat to the army of Western Chu.

Xiang Yu decided to deal with Peng Yue and Han Xin first, so he sent an army across the Yellow River to fight with Han Xin and Zhang Er's army. Xiang Yu ordered General Zhong Gong to take some troops to defend Chenggao and he himself commanded his army to march east to deal with Peng Yue.

The King of Han seized the chance to move his army north to Chenggao; they defeated the Western Chu army at Chenggao under General Zhong

Gong, and they took the city of Chenggao. Liu Bang stationed his army there. In June, Xiang Yu defeated Peng Yue and drove Peng Yue out of the area of Xiapi. In June 204 BC, when Xiang Yu got the news that Liu Bang had taken Chenggao and stationed his army there, he moved swiftly west and made a severe strike at Xingyang and broke into the city.

Zhou Ke, General Zong Gong and Haan Xin (King of the State of Haan) were captured and were brought before Xiang Yu. Xiang Yu said to Zhou Ke, "If you surrender, I will appoint you commander-in-chief of my army and grant you the tax on 30,000 peasant households." Zhou Ke said resolutely, "If you don't surrender right now, you will be captured by the King of Han very soon. You are not at all a match for the King of Han." Xiang Yu was so incensed that he had Zhou Ke cooked in a big pot. Then Xiang Yu turned to General Zong Gong. Xiang Yu said, "Surrender now. Otherwise, you will also be killed." General Zong Gong said resolutely, "No. I will not surrender." Xiang Yu swung his sword and killed Zong Gong. Zhou Ke and Zong Gong were both from Pei. When Liu Bang rebelled in Pei, they joined him. They had followed Liu Bang in every battle. Zhou Ke had a cousin named Zhou Chang. Zhou Chang had also joined Liu Bang when he stood up in Pei. He was at that time defending Aocang as the Minister of Supervision.

When Xiang Yu had killed Zhou Ke and Zong Gong, he turned to Haan Xin, the King of the State of Haan. Xiang Yu said to him, "Surrender now! Otherwise you will meet the same fate as these two." Haan Xin was shocked by the terrible killings. He knelt down on his knees and answered in a trembling voice, "I will surrender." Then Xiang Yu ordered his soldiers to unbind Haan Xin. Later, when the men dropped their guard, Haan Xin seized his chance and run away. He went to Chenggao, to Liu Bang. Liu Bang forgave him and made him King of the State of Haan again.

Then Xiang Yu directed his army north to lay siege to Chenggao. The King of Han and Xiahou Ying drove away from the north gate of Chenggao in a carriage. They crossed the Yellow River to the north bank. They stayed in Xiuwu (now Huojia, Henan Province) for the night. Early the next morning, they reached the camp of the Han army under the command of Han Xin and Zhang Er. The guards of the camp stopped them and would not let them into the camp. Liu Bang said, "We are envoys sent by the King of Han. We have important matters to tell Han Xin and Zhang Er on behalf of the King of Han." The guards had to let them into the camp. At that time, Han Xin and Zhang Er were still sleeping fast. The King of Han went into Han

Xin's tent and Zhang Er's tent and seized their seals for the command of their army. With the seals in his possession, the King of Han had the army under his own command.

When Han Xin and Zhang Er got up and found that their general seals had been taken by the King of Han, they were stunned. They hurried to the tent where Liu Bang was. The King of Han said to Zhang Er, "You have been in the State of Zhao for a long time. You may recruit the native people in this area to organize them into an army. With this army, you may defend the area of the State of Zhao and prevent Xiang Yu from entering this area. I shall make you King of the State of Zhao when you have completed your task." Zhang Er said, "I will do my best to fulfill my task." Then the King of Han said to Han Xin, "I hereby appoint you as the premier of the State of Han. I shall assign you the task of taking the State of Qi. This is an important task because after you have taken the State of Qi, you can threaten the State of Western Chu directly from the north. I shall place an army under your command. And I shall send General Cao Shen with an army and General Guan Ying with his cavalrymen to follow you to attack the State of Qi." Han Xin said, "I will do my best to fulfill my task." Then Liu Bang appointed Cao Shen deputy premier of the State of Han. He sent an envoy to convey his order to Cao Shen and Guan Ying, ordering them to lead their army to join Han Xin in the expedition of the State of Qi.

The generals of Han who were defending Chenggao withdrew from the city, one group at a time, to join the King of Han. Xiang Yu recaptured the city of Chenggao. He wanted to move west, but the King of Han had deployed troops along the natural barriers in the area of Gong (now Gongyi, Henan Province) to prevent the advance of the Western Chu army. The Western Chu army was stopped in Gong and could not move further west.

After the King of Han got the army under the command of Han Xin and Zhang Er, he stationed the army in Xiuwu. in August. He was worried about Guanzhong. He had been defeated by Xiang Yu several times. He had been away from Guanzhong for quite a long time. He had entrusted state affairs for the State of Han to Xiao He. Now he had left Xingyang and Chenggao. The people in Guanzhong did not know his whereabouts. So he sent an envoy back to Guanzhong to send his best regards to Xiao He. When the envoy reached Yueyang and saw Xiao He, he conveyed Liu Bang's greetings. Xiao He was very happy and put up the envoy in a guesthouse. After the envoy left, an official named Bao Sheng in the office of the premier said to

Xiao He, "Now the King of Han is fighting a hard war with Xiang Yu. His Majesty is always exposed to danger. His Majesty has experienced all kinds of hardships and difficulties. But still he sends envoys to convey his regard for you. This shows that he doubts your loyalty. I think the best thing you can do to win his trust is to send all your brothers, sons, grandsons, cousins and nephews to the place where the king is now to take part in the war against Xiang Yu. Then the King will have great confidence in you." Xiao He accepted his suggestion. He gathered all his brothers, sons, grandsons, cousins and nephews together. There were over thirty of them. He said to them, "The King of Han is fighting hard at the front. His Majesty has experienced so many hardships. We must share the hardships with His Majesty. I hope you will all go to the front to fight for the King."

Then Xiao He recruited several thousand young men from Guanzhong. Then this army marched to Xiuwu where Liu Bang was. When this army arrived, Liu Bang received the sons and relatives of Xiao He with special warmth. He was satisfied with Xiao He. He didn't doubt Xiao He's loyalty anymore.

Liu Bang wanted to get started against Xiang Yu. But Zheng Zhong, one of his attendants, succeeded in persuading the King of Han to stay inside the camps on the north bank of the Yellow River and not to start any battles with Xiang Yu. Liu Bang sent Generals Liu Jia and Lu Wan with 20,000 troops and several hundred cavalrymen across the Yellow River from the port of Baima (now Huaxian, Henan Province) into the area of Western Chu. They assisted Peng Yue by burning the food stores of the Western Chu army so that the Western Chu army ran short of provisions. When the Western Chu army came to attack them, they stayed in their camps and did not go out to fight. Peng Yue started his military operations in the area of Wei and took seventeen cities including Suiyang (now south of Shangqiu, Henan Province) and Waihuang (now northwest of Minquan, Henan Province).

In September, Xiang Yu said to Cao Jiu, the general in charge of military affairs for the State of Western Chu, "You must take the greatest precautions in defending Chenggao. If the King of Han comes to challenge you to battle, just ignore him and don't fight with him. Your task is only to prevent him from moving east. I will win back the cities which have been captured by Peng Yue in fifteen days. I will come back to join you in fifteen days' time." Cao Jiu said, "I will do as Your Majesty has said." Xiang Yu also assigned Sima Xin, the former King of Zhai, to assist General Cao Jiu in defending Chenggao.

After Xiang Yu made these arrangements to defend Chenggao, he commanded his army to march east and attacked the city of Chenliu (now a place southeast to Kaifeng, Henan Province) and took it. But when Xiang Yu attacked the city of Waihuang, he met with strong resistance. Peng Yu's army and the people of Waihuang defended the city bravely. Xiang Yu only took the city after several days of hard fighting with severe casualties. Then Xiang Yu marched his army to east again. When Xiang Yu reached Suiyang, the people of Suiyang surrendered.

44. Li Yi Ji's Advice to Take Chenggao

The King of Han had been besieged in Xingyang several times, so he was planning to give up Xingyang and Chenggao and station his army in the area of Gong (now Gongyi, Henan Province) and Luo (now Luoyang, Henan Province) to prevent Xiang Yu from advancing to the west. Li Yi Ji said, "If a king knows what is the most important thing among all the important things, he will succeed in winning the power to rule over the whole realm. If he does not know this, he will certainly lose. For a king, the people are the most important thing. For the people, food is the most important thing. During the reign of the Qin Dynasty, all kinds of grain were transported from all over the realm to Aocang. I hear that there is huge food storage center in Aocang. Xiang Yu took Chenggao, but he did not realize the importance of Chenggao and he did not assign special troops to defend Chenggao; instead, he only assigned ex-convicts to defend Chenggao while he himself has led a great army to the east to fight with Peng Yue. This is the chance that the Heavens have granted to Your Majesty. If Your Majesty gives up Chenggao and Xingyang and establishes your defensive line in the area between Gong and Luo, Your Majesty will miss the chance the Heavens have granted. I think this would be a mistake on the part of Your Majesty. Now Your Majesty is fighting a desperate war with Xiang Yu. It is impossible for both Your Majesty and Xiang Yu to exist in this world. Only one of you two will win; and the loser will be killed. The confrontation between the State of Western Chu and the State of Han has lasted for a long time. The people are suffering from this protracted war, and the whole realm is in great chaos. The peasants cannot work in the fields, and the women have stopped weaving cloth, because the whole realm is still in disorder. I suggest that Your Majesty quickly move his army to take Changgao and seize the grain stores in Aocang. Your Majesty can take advantage of the natural barriers in Chenggao to prevent Xiang Yu from advancing to the west." Liu Bang followed his advice and took action immediately.

45. Li Yi Ji's Plan to Persuade the King of the State of Qi to Surrender

Li Yi Ji suggested to the King of Han, "Now the States of Yan and Zhao are quiet. Only the State of Qi still resists. The members of the Tian family are powerful people. The State of Qi is a big state with the sea to the east and Mount Tai in the south. The Yellow River runs through it. The neighbor to the south is the State of Western Chu. The people of Qi are treacherous. Even if Your Majesty sends a strong army of tens of thousands there, Your Majesty will not pacify the state in a year. I suggest that Your Majesty appoint me as Your Majesty's envoy to the State of Qi. I will try my best to persuade the King of Qi to become the king of a vassal state to the State of Han." The King of Han agreed and sent him to the State of Qi.

When Li Yi Ji arrived and met with the King of the State of Qi, he asked the King, "Do you know to whom this whole realm is going to belong?" The king said, "I don't know. Do you know?" Li Yi Ji said, "The whole realm is going to belong to the King of Han." The King of the State of Qi asked, "What makes you say so?" Li Yi Ji said, "Liu Bang was the general who first occupied Xianyang, the capital of the Qin Dynasty. According to the promise made by King Huai of the State of Chu, he should be king of Guanzhong. But Xiang Yu went against that agreement. He made Liu Bang King of Hanzhong instead. Xiang Yu moved the Acting Emperor to the area to the south of the Yangtze River—and killed him. When the King of Han got the news, he raised a great army in Shu and Hanzhong to put down the unrest in the three states in the Qin area. Then he moved his army out of the passes. He named Xiang Yu as the killer of the Acting Emperor. He reinstated the descendants of the kings of the former six states. He has united the kings' armies. Whenever a general takes a city, he will make the general marquis of that city. Whenever he has received presents, gifts, and goods, he will share them with his generals. He is willing to share all the benefits with the people all over China. Therefore, all the great talented, capable and competent people are willing to work for the King of Han.

"As for Xiang Yu, he is infamous for his breach of the agreement; he is accused of the crime of killing the Acting Emperor; he never gives recognition for the outstanding services his generals have rendered but he never forgets their mistakes; when a general has captured a city, he never makes the general marquis of that city; he does not grant any rewards to his generals who have won great victories; only the members of the Xiang family can be appointed to responsible positions. Therefore all the people have betrayed him. Competent people will not serve him. It is clear that China will belong to Liu Bang and not to Xiang Yu.

"The King of Han raised all the soldiers of Hanzhong and Shu and conquered the three states in the Qin area; he crossed the Yellow River and defeated the King of Wei. He sent Han Xin with an army to Jingxing and they killed Chen Yu in battle. Now he has taken the natural barriers of Chenggao; he has blocked the port of Baima to prevent anyone from crossing the Yellow River; he has blocked all the routes leading to the area of the State of Zhao and the State of Yan. Those who refuse to obey him will perish. So, if you surrender to the King of Han, the State of Qi may survive. Otherwise, the State of Qi will perish very soon."

The King of the State of Qi took his advice. Previously, when the King of the State of Qi had got the news that Han Xin was marching east with a strong army, he had sent Hua Wu Shang and Tian Xie with an army to Lixia (now Jinan, Shandong Province) to block Han Xin's advancing army. After getting Li Yi Ji's advice, he sent an envoy to make peace with the King of Han. Then the King of the State of Qi told his two generals in Lixia that they did not need to be vigilant against the army of Han. The King of the State of Qi himself entertained Li Yi Ji with good food and wine every day.

46. HAN XIN DEFEATS THE STATE OF QI

When Han Xin reached Pingyuan (now Pingyuan, Shandong Province), he heard that Li Yi Ji had succeeded in persuading the King of the State of Qi to surrender to the King of Han, so he wanted to stop advancing. Kuai Che, one of Han Xin's advisers, said to him, "You were ordered by the King of Han personally to attack the State of Qi. But the King of Han sent a secret envoy to persuade the King of the State of Qi to surrender. Has the King of Han sent you any order to stop attacking the State of Qi? Why should we stop marching to the State of Qi without any order from the King of Han?

Li Yi Ji is only a scholar. But he has taken more than seventy cities of the State of Qi by smooth-talking the King of the State of Qi into coming over to the side of the King of Han. You have tens of thousands of soldiers under your command. You have fought tenaciously for more than a year. You have taken about fifty cities so far. Why should the contributions you have made by fighting hard as a general for years on end be less than those of a scholar?" Han Xin agreed with that view and ordered his army to cross the Yellow River. In October 204 BC, Han Xin suddenly attacked the Qi army in Lixia and defeated them. Then the Han army pursued the defeated army to Linzi, the capital of the State of Qi (now Linzi, Shandong Province). The King of the State of Qi thought that Li Yi Ji had deceived him. So he killed Li Yi Ji and had him cooked.

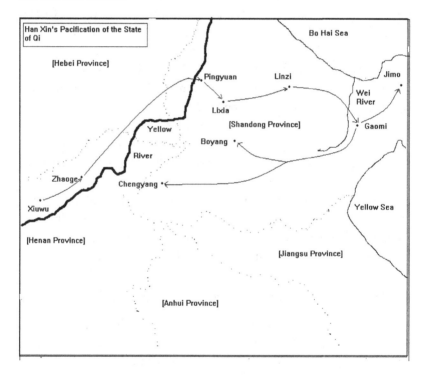

The King of the State of Qi appointed Tian Guaang as the acting premier to defend Linzi and he maneuvered his army to cross the Wei River to Gaomi (now Gaomi, Shandong Province). He sent an envoy to Xiang Yu to ask for help. Tian Heng, the premier of the State of Qi, retreated to Boyang with an army. When the Han army attacked Linzi, Acting Premier Tian Guaang fled to Chengyang. General Tian Ji stationed his army in Jiaodong (now Jimo, Shandong Province).

47. The Battles of Chenggao

Liu Bang took Li Yi Ji's advice and decided to take Chenggao. The Han army marched along the north bank of the Yellow River to the Port of Pin-gyin, where they crossed the river to the south bank. Then they marched east to attack Chenggao. At that time the general defending Chenggao was Cao Jiu. Before Xiang Yu left Chenggao to head east to go after Peng Yue, he had told Cao Jiu to stay in the city and not to fight with the King of Han. So when the Han army came to challenge him to battle, he just shut the city gates tight and would not take up the challenge. Then the King of Han ordered his soldiers to shout insults against Cao Jiu for five days. Cao Jiu got so angry that he forgot what Xiang Yu had said, and led his army out of the city to cross the Sishui River and fight the King of Han. When only half of the soldiers of the Western Chu army under Cao Jiu had crossed the river, the Han army struck the Western Chu soldiers and defeated them. Cao Jiu and Sima Xin killed themselves in the river. The King of Han took Chenggao again and took great quantities of booty. He stationed his army on a hill west of Guangwu Mountain (now Guangwu, Henan Province) and established food supply lines from Aochang.

Guangwu Mountain was situated to the north of Xingyang and east of Chenggao. It rose abruptly on the south bank of the Yellow River and ex-tended to the south. There was a great ravine, the Guangwu Ravine, which was 200 meters deep and 100 meters wide that cut Guangwu Mountain into two parts—the Western Guangwu Hill and the Eastern Guangwu Hill. At the bottom of the ravine there was a canal dug by the people of the State of Wei during the Period of Warring States for the purpose of irrigation. Liu Bang stationed his army on the Western Guangwu Hill and ordered his soldiers to build a wall 1,200 meters long and 10 meters high around the hill to defend the camps.

48. Bo Ji Becomes Liu Bang's Concubine and Liu Heng Is Born

When Liu Bang went back to Chenggao, he went to the weaving room where the concubines of Wei Bao, the former King of the State of Wei, were working. He saw a particularly pretty young lady sorrowfully working at the looms. He asked one of the keepers, "Who is that young lady?" The keeper said, "She is Bo Ji, one of Wei Bao's concubines." Liu Bang had pity on her and said, "I have decided to select her as one of my concubines. Send her to my harem." But for quite a long time, he did not invite her to his bed. One day, Liu Bang was sitting with two of his favorite concubines. One of them was Lady Guan and the other was Zhao Zi Er. These two ladies were good friends of Bo Ji. They had once made a promise with each other, "Anyone who first becomes the favorite of the king will help the others to have the same favor." At that time, the two ladies mentioned their promise to the King of Han. The King of Han felt compassion for Bo Ji, and that night, he called her to his bed. When she was undressed and lying in the bed of the King of Han, she said shyly, "Last night, I dreamed that a dragon coiled upon my belly." King of Han said, "I will make your dream come true." They spent the night together. Not long later, Bo Ji found that she was pregnant, and in nine months, she gave birth to a baby boy. He was named Liu Heng. But from then on, Liu Bang rarely called Bo Ji to his bed.

49. The Confrontation between Liu Bang and Xiang Yu in Guangwu Mountain Area

Xiang Yu went east to fight with Peng Yue and won back more than ten cities from Peng Yue. When he heard the news that Cao Jiu had been defeated and Chenggao had been taken by Liu Bang, he immediately went back with his army. At that point, the Han army had just laid siege to the city of Xingyang which was defended by the Western Chu army under General Zhong Li Mei. When the Han army found out that Xiang Yu was coming, they all retreated to tenable defensive positions on the Western Guangwu Hill. Xiang Yu stationed his army on Eastern Guangwu Hill opposite them. He also ordered his soldiers to build a wall 1,000 meters long, 15 meters high and 26 meters wide. The two hostile armies were at a stalemate for several months.

50. Xiang Yu Threatens to Cook Liu Bang's Father into Soup

As the Western Chu army's food supplies began to run short, when Xiang Yu went back west to Xingyang, Peng Yu began to attack the food supply lines of the Western Chu army. Xiang Yu was worried. One day, Xiang Yu ordered his soldiers to build a platform at the foot of Eastern Guangwu Hill beside the canal. Then a big block for cutting meat was put on the platform, and a big pot was set there over a big fire. Then Liu Bang's father was dragged to the platform by an executioner with a big axe in his hand.

Liu Bang's father stood on the platform in the wind blowing across the Yellow River. Xiang Yu shouted to the other side of the canal, "Liu Bang, if you don't surrender immediately, I will chop your father to pieces and cook him into soup!" From the other side of the channel Liu Bang could see his father's mournful and helpless eyes. He felt pain in his heart. His struggle with Xiang Yu had dragged his father into disaster. His heart was breaking and tears were about to run down his face. But with a great effort, he held back his tears, and he shouted back, "When we both served King Huai of the State of Chu and were fighting side by side against the rule of the Qin Dynasty, we swore to be brothers. Since we were sworn brothers, my father is also your father. If you are so cruel as to cook your father into soup, when it is ready, please give me a bowl of the soup." Xiang Yu was so angry at these words that he ordered the executioner to chop Liu Bang's father to pieces. The executioner dragged Liu Bang's father to the big block and pressed his head to the block. Then he raised his axe high and was about to chop off Liu Bang's father's head. But Xiang Bo intervened. He stopped the executioner and said to Xiang Yu, "Now, we cannot tell who will win the final victory. Liu Bang is an ambitious man and will reach his goal regardless of his family. He will not care even if you kill his father. It will only bring you more trouble." Xiang Yu backed down, and ordered Liu Bang's father to be taken back into custody.

The confrontation between Liu Bang and Xiang Yu continued. One day, Xiang Yu shouted to Liu Bang, "The whole country has been in great chaos for several years only because of you and me. Let's fight a battle now to decide once and for all who will be the final winner so as to spare the people all over China from their suffering." The King of Han smiled and said, "I would like to beat you with wits, not with strength." Xiang Yu ordered three warriors to challenge the King of Han. The King of Han sent Lou Fan, a cavalry-man who could shoot arrows accurately while on horseback, to ride out of the camps. Lou Fan shot three arrows and dispatched the three soldiers of the Western Chu army in short order. Xiang Yu was furious. He put on his armor and rode out with a trident in his hand in challenge. When Lou Fan was ready to pull back his bowstring, Xiang Yu glared at him and shouted so loud that Lou Fan was shocked; he lost his nerve. He did not dare to look at him and he could not let go the arrow. Lou Fan rode back into the camps and did not dare to go out. The King of Han was surprised and sent a soldier to find out who that man in armor was. Not long later, the soldier came back and reported that the man was Xiang Yu himself. Xiang Yu rode up and asked Liu Bang to come out and talk. Liu Bang rode out of his camps and they had a conversation across the canal. Xiang Yu said, "In order to end the sufferings of the people, I would like to fight a duel with you single-handedly to decide who the winner is." The King of Han listed all of Xiang Yu's wrongdoings. "When you and I were assigned the task to march into Guanzhong, King Huai of the State of Chu promised that the general who first entered into Guanzhong would be made King of Guanzhong. I was the first general who marched into Guanzhong. You broke the promise. You made me King of Hanzhong instead of King of Guanzhong. This is your first offence. You killed Song Yi on a false order from King Huai of the State of Chu. This is your second offence. After you relieved the State of Zhao, you did not go back to report to King Huai of the State of Chu. Instead, you commanded all the other kings and generals into the area of Guanzhong without orders from King Huai of the State of Chu. This is your third offence. You burned the palaces of the Qin Dynasty. You tried to dig up the tomb of the First Emperor of the Qin Dynasty. You took all the treasures from the palaces as your own. This is your fourth offence. You killed Ying Zi Ying, the King of the State of Qin, who had surrendered. This is your fifth offence. You killed 200,000 Qin soldiers who had surrendered in Xin'an. This is your sixth offence. You made the general kings of good places and moved the original kings to bad places. This is your seventh offence. You drove the Acting Emperor out of Pengcheng and made Pengcheng your own capital. You took the land from the King of the State of Wei and made yourself king of both the areas of Chu and Wei. You took lands from other kings as your own. This is your eighth offence. You secretly sent someone to kill the Acting Emperor in the Yangtze River. This is your ninth offence. You have carried out unfair policies. You never keep your promises. You have become the common enemy of the people all over China. You have committed the crime of treason. This is your tenth offence. I have raised an army and united with all the other kings to embark on a just cause to put you, the common enemy of the people, to death. I will not kill you by myself. I will send soldiers who are convicted criminals to kill you. Why should I fight a duel with you?"

Xiang Yu was furious and gave the signal to hidden archers to shoot. An arrow hit the King of Han in the chest, but he bent down to touch his toe and shouted, "That soldier has shot my toe." He rode back to his camps in great pain. The King of Han lay in bed with a serious wound. Zhang Liang suggested that the King of Han should get up in spite of his serious wound and go among the soldiers to show his recognition of the service they had rendered. This would allay any panic among the soldiers and forestall rumors that the King of Han had been wounded, and deter the Western Chu army from trying to take advantage and launch an attack. The King of Han accepted his suggestion and got up from the bed and visited his soldiers. But his wound was so serious that he had to be moved into Chenggao for treatment.

51. Han Xin Pacifies the State of Qi

After Han Xin took Linzi, he commanded his army in the pursuit of the King of the State of Qi in the east. Xiang Yu sent Long Ju with an army of 200,000 men to relieve the State of Qi. Long Ju joined the King of the State of Qi in Gaomi. A man suggested to Long Ju, "The Han army has come from afar to fight. The soldiers are eager for battle. It will be difficult to defeat this army. Since the Qi soldiers are fighting in their home area, they may be easily defeated and flee. The best thing to do is to order the soldiers to stay in their camps and not to give battle. You may ask the King of the State of Qi to send envoys to the cities which have been occupied by the Han army. If the people of these cities know that the King of the State of Qi has survived and that the army of Western Chu has come for help, they will surely rise up against the Han army. The Han army is a thousand kilometers away from its base in this hostile land of Qi, and the people of the fallen cities will rise against them. They cannot get any food from the State of Qi. Then you can defeat the Han army without fighting." But Long Ju said, "I know very well what kind of man Han Xin is. He is a coward and very easy to deal with.

He took food from an old lady who was washing clothes by the river. He humbly accepted a man's insult and crawled between his spreading legs. He is not a man of valor. Why should I be afraid of him? I have been ordered to relieve the State of Qi. If I defeat the Han army without a fight, then what services have I rendered? If I defeat the Han army in battle, then half of the State of Qi will belong to me."

In November 204 BC, the armies of Qi and Western Chu were stationed on the east bank of the Wei River, and the army of Han commanded by Han Xin was stationed on the west bank of the same river. The two rivals confronted each other with the Wei River in between. Han Xin had 10,000 bags made and sent troops upstream in the night. They filled the bags with sand and blocked the course of the river. Downstream, there was little water flowing. When morning came, Han Xin and his army crossed the river to attack the Western Chu army under Long Ju. Long Ju started a counterattack and Han Xin's army pretended to be defeated and fled back to the west bank. Long Ju laughed and said, "I have said that Han Xin is a coward. He really is."

Then he commanded his army to cross the river and pursue the Han army. Han Xin gave the signal to the troops upstream to lift up the bags. Water rushed down and the river was full again. Only Long Ju, General Zhou Lan and a small number of Western Chu soldiers reached the west bank. Most of the troops under Long Ju could not cross the river. The Han army under Han Xin, Cao Shen and Guan Ying turned back and fought with the Western Chu troops who had crossed the river. General Guang Ying led his cavalrymen to pounce on the Western Chu soldiers, killing many of them. In the battle, the cavalrymen under Guan Ying killed Long Ju and captured Zhou Lan. Since the Western Chu army on the west bank had lost their commander, they scattered and ran away. Tian Guang, the King of the State of Qi, escaped. Han Xin went after Tian Guang and captured him at Chengyang (now a place to the north of Heze, Shandong Province). General Guan Ying pursued Tian Guaang, the premier of the State of Qi, and captured him, too. Then he moved his army to Boyang (now a place near Tai'an, Shandong Province).

When Tian Heng got news that the King of the State of Qi had been killed, he made himself King of the State of Qi and commanded his army into battle against the army of Han under the command of Guan Ying. A battle was fought in Ying (now a place near Laiwu, Shandong Province) and Tian Heng was defeated. He escaped and joined Peng Yue who was operating in the area of Wei. Then Guan Ying marched his army to Qian-sheng (now northeast to Gaoqing, Shandong Province) to fight with Tian Xi, commander-in-chief of the army of the State of Qi. Tian Xi was killed in battle. Cao Shen attacked Tian Ji in Shandong Peninsula and killed him. And the State of Qi was pacified.

52. HAN XIN IS MADE KING OF THE STATE OF QI

In November 204 BC, Liu Bang made Zhang Er King of the State of Zhao. Since Han Xin had pacified the whole of the State of Qi, he sent an envoy to see Liu Bang. The envoy conveyed Han Xin's words to the King of Han: "The people of the State of Qi are treacherous, disobedient and fickle. The State of Western Chu is situated just to the south of the State of Qi. The People of Qi might go over to the State of Western Chu any time. I hope that Your Majesty will make me Acting King of the State of Qi so that I can suppress the rebellions by the people of Qi." After that the envoy presented to Liu Bang a letter written by Han Xin to the same effect, asking the King of Han to make him King of the State of Qi. After reading the letter, the King of Han was so angry that he began to curse out loud. "You dirty scoundrel! I have been stuck here for a long time, looking forward to your coming to help me. But now you have made yourself king!" Zhang Liang and Chen Ping were standing behind him; they squeezed his heels and whispered in his ear, "Right now the situation is not favorable for the State of Han. How can we prevent him from making himself King of the State of Qi? It would be better to make him King of the State of Qi and treat him well and let him defend the State of Qi. If you don't make him king, he will betray you."

Liu Bang realized the danger immediately and he began shouting again, but with a difference. "Well, since you have pacified the State of Qi, why should you be acting king? I hereby make you true King of the State of Qi."

In February 203 BC, Liu Bang sent Zhang Liang to the State of Qi with the seal of the King of the State of Qi to make Han Xin King of the State of Qi. And then Liu Bang ordered Han Xin to attack the State of Western Chu.

When Xiang Yu heard that Long Ju had been killed, he was shocked. He sent Wu She to the State of Qi. When Wu She saw Han Xin, the King of the State of Qi, he said, "The people of China suffered from the cruel rule of the Qin Dynasty for a long time. Thanks to the efforts of the generals, the rule of the Qin Dynasty has been overthrown. Xiang Yu made the generals kings of different places according to the contributions they have rendered so that the soldiers and people can have a rest. But the King of Han raised an army and started the war again. He moved his army east and invaded the territory of other kings. He defeated the three kings in the Qin area and took their lands from them. Then he maneuvered his army through the passes and marched east to attack the State of Western Chu. This shows that he is ambitious. He is greedy. He wants to take all of China for his own. This is the reason why the whole country is in great chaos. The King of Han may not win the whole country. Xiang Yu has defeated him several times. He survives to this day only because Xiang Yu had mercy on him. But as soon as he escaped, he forgot the kindness Xiang Yu had shown to him and attacked Xiang Yu again. This man has no faith at all. Now you think that you have profound friendship with the King of Han. You have spared no effort to fight for him. But in the end, you will be his prisoner. Perhaps you are alive still today only because Xiang Yu still survives. Now Xiang Yu and Liu Bang are confronting with each other in a stalemate. You are important for both of them because if you side with Xiang Yu, Xiang Yu will win, and if you side with Liu Bang, Liu Bang will win. If Xiang Yu is destroyed today, you'll be destroyed tomorrow. You once served under Xiang Yu, so in a sense, you are a friend of Xiang Yu. Why don't you turn against Liu Bang and make peace with Xiang Yu? In that case, you three will divide China in three parts and each of you will be a king of one part. If you miss this chance and you are determined to fight for the King of Han against Xiang Yu, you will regret later. This is not what a wise man should do." Han Xin said, "It's true that I once served under Xiang Yu. But the position he offered me was only that of a low-ranking officer. I was only one of his guards. He never listened to me. He never adopted any of my advice. So I left him to join Liu Bang. Liu Bang has appointed me commander-in-chief of his army. He has entrusted me with an army of tens of thousands. He has given me what I want. He listened to me and adopted every plan I ever proposed. I owe all of my achievements to him. He has great faith in me. If I betrayed him, it would not be a righteous act. I won't do that even I die for it. But still, please convey my thanks to Xiang Yu."

After Wu She left, Kuai Che knew that Han Xin held the power to decide the outcome of the struggle between Liu Bang and Xiang Yu. So he went to see Han Xin as a fortuneteller. Kuai Che said to Han Xin, "I learned fortunetelling when I was young. I can tell your fortune from your face. You will be made marquis of some place at the most and you will always live in precarious conditions and face danger. But from your back, I can tell that you have endless fortune." Han Xian asked, "What do you mean?" Kuai Che said, "When people all over China rose up to fight against the cruel rule of the Qin Dynasty, they all hoped that the Qin Dynasty would be overthrown as soon as possible. But now, Xiang Yu and Liu Bang are fighting against each other for the power to rule all over China. Many people have been killed. The bones of men are spread all over the battlefields. Liu Bang once took Pengcheng, but very soon Xiang Yu drove him out of it and commanded his victorious army in a sweep from east to west. Xiang Yu is known all over China for his military power. But now his army has been stuck in the area of Xingyang and Chenggao for three years. He is near the mountains in the west but cannot move a step forward.

"As for the King of Han, he is commanding an army of 100,000 men in resistance to Xiang Yu's army in the area of Gong and Chenggao. He made use of the advantages of natural barriers of the Yellow River and the mountains. In that area, several battles were fought in a day. Liu Bang cannot gain an inch of land. He has lost some land but he has no ability to recover it. Liu Bang has come to the end of his courage and wits. The people are extremely tired and hate this war. They do not know whom they should turn to. As I see it, neither Liu Bang nor Xiang Yu is able to end this trouble. Now the destiny of these two kings depends on you. If you are for the King of Han, then the King of Han will win. If you are for Xiang Yu, then Xiang Yu will win. My suggestion is that you not help either of them. Then the whole China is divided in three parts like the three legs of a tripod. This situation of stalemate will continue for some time. No one will dare to take the first step to break this stalemate. You are a wise and virtuous man. You have a strong army. You own the State of Qi, a state with vast territory You may unite with the States of Yan and Zhao. You can lead an army to march through the areas without resistance to the back of your enemies. After you have gained the controlling position to the west, you may express the demand of the people and call on the two kings to stop the war. The people all over China will respond to your call to stop the war and support you. With this great power, you may overcome anyone who is against you. Then you may divide the country in even parts and make the generals kings of each part. Then the kings will owe all they have to you and obey all your orders. All the kings will come to the State of Qi and pay respects to you. I have heard that if the Heavens have offered you something and you refuse to take it, it will cause great trouble to you. If you do not take action at the right time, it will also cause you great trouble. I hope you will consider my advice seriously."

Han Xin said, "The King of Han has treated me very well. How can I betray him for my own interest?" Kuai Che said, "When Zhang Er and Chen Yu were still ordinary people, they were friends sworn to death. But later they turned against each other after the battle of Julu and had a heated quarrel over Chen Ze and Zhang Yan. In the end, Zhang Er killed Chen Yu in the battle in Jingxing. Why did these two best friends end up killing each other? Troubles are often caused by greed. You can never tell the true intention of other people. Now you are dealing with the King of Han with good faith and devotion. But your friendship with the King of Han is far less close than that between Zhang Er and Chen Yu. You think that so long as you are devoted to the King of Han, you will be secure. That is a wrong idea. Long ago, Wen Zhong, the premier of the State of Yue, made great contributions to the survival of the State of Yue, which had been defeated by the State of Wu. He helped Gou Jian, the defeated King of the State of Yue, become a powerful king in the period of Spring and Autumn. He rendered great contributions to the State of Yue and gained great fame for himself. But it was at that time that he was killed by Gou Jian, the King of the State of Yue. It is common practice that when all the wild game has been hunted down and killed, the hunter will kill the hunting dog and cook it. As far as friendship is concerned, no friendship between any two people is closer than the friendship was between Zhang Er and Chen Yu. As far as devotion and faith to a king are concerned, no minister was truer in his devotion and faith to his king than Wen Zhong to Gou Jian. These two examples are strong signs. You'd better consider them seriously. And I have also heard that anyone who is so courageous and so resourceful that his master feels that he is a threat to him is in great danger. Anyone whose contribution is greater than everybody else's will not be granted any reward. Now you are so courageous and so resourceful that you are already a threat to your master. You have rendered such outstanding military service that you will not be granted any reward. If you turn to Xiang Yu, he will not trust you. If you turn to Liu Bang, Liu Bang will feel that you are a threat to him. Do you think that you will be secure either way?" Han Xin thanked him for his wise insights. He said to Kuai Che, "You may go back and have a rest. I will think over what you have said."

Several days later, Kuai Che went to see Han Xin again. He said to Han Xin, "A person who is willing to listen to a good stratagem may have a chance to succeed. A stratagem is the opportunity to succeed. Anyone who has listened to a stratagem without taking action, who misses the moment to implement the stratagem, will never be safe. A wise man will take resolute action when he is offered the opportunity. Hesitation will ruin everything. Any wise man knows that it is not enough to be very careful in small matters but to ignore matters of life and death. Trouble will follow if you have made a decision but don't dare to implement it. Success is extremely difficult to obtain but easy to lose. Opportunity knocks but once." Han Xin still hesitated and could not make up his mind to betray the King of Han. He also thought that he had rendered outstanding services and the King of Han would not deprive him of his rights as the King of the State of Qi. So he refused to take Kuai Che's advice. Kuai Che left Han Xin and pretended to lose his mind; as a madman he might avoid future trouble.

In July 203 BC, Liu Bang made Ying Bu King of the State of Huainan and sent him back to Jiujiang. Ying Bu's task was to block Xiang Yu's way to return to the south.

53. THE DECISIVE BATTLE IN GAIXIA

In August 203 BC, Xiang Yu realized that he could not get help from anywhere; he had run out of food for his army. At that time Han Xin's army was advancing from the State of Qi to attack the State of Western Chu. Xiang Yu was in a bind. While he was pondering his options, a guard in his camp came to his tent and said, "The King of Han has sent his envoy Hou Gong. He is asking to see Your Majesty." Xiang Yu said, "Let him in." Then he sat solemnly on a chair. Hou Gong walked in calmly and made a bow to Xiang Yu. Xiang Yu asked angrily, "What does your master want? He does not come out to fight. He does not withdraw either." Hou Gong asked, "Does Your Majesty want to fight or to withdraw?" Xiang Yu said, "I want to fight!" Hou Gong said, "It is dangerous to fight. It is hard to tell who will win. The war between Your Majesty and the King of Han has lasted for more than four years. The people are suffering and the soldiers on both sides are very tired. I have come to put an end to the war to relieve the people from more suffering."

"Then you have come to make peace with me?" Xiang Yu asked. Hou Gong said, "The King of Han does not want to compete with you. If you are so kind as to have pity on the suffering people and make peace with the King of Han, the King of Han is ready to make peace with you." Xiang Yu asked, "What are your conditions for peace?" Hou Gong answered, "The King of Han has set out two important conditions. The first is to draw a demarcation line to divide the whole realm into two parts. You will take the eastern part and the King of Han will take the western part. Each will stay in his own territory and will not invade the territory of the other. The second is that you will release the King of Han's father and wife. The King of Han will be very grateful to you if you return his father and wife and the people all over the realm will know that you are a kindhearted person and sing your praise." Xiang Yu thought that the conditions were reasonable. Then he summoned Xiang Bo into his tent and appointed him the representative to negotiate the detailed terms for peace.

Hou Gong on behalf of the King of Han and Xiang Bo on behalf of the King of Western Chu held negotiations for several days. They reached an agreement on the terms for peace. They decided where to mark the limits of the territories of the State of Han and the State of Western Chu. They decided that the demarcation should be along Honggou. Honggou was the name of an ancient canal taking water of the Yellow River from the north of Xingyang through the north of Kaifeng to the Yingshui River in the southeast of Huaiyang of Henan Province. It ran between Western Guangwu Hill, where the camp of Liu Bang's army was situated, and the Eastern Guangwu Hill, where the camp of Xiang Yu's army was situated. The areas to the east of Honggou belonged to Xiang Yu, the King of Western Chu. The areas to the west of Honggou belonged to Liu Bang, the King of Han.

Then Hou Gong and the envoy sent by Xiang Yu went to Liu Bang's camp. Liu Bang read the agreement and approved the terms. After that, Hou Gong and Xiang Yu's envoy went back with the agreement approved by Liu Bang to Xiang Yu. Then Xiang Yu released Liu Bang's father and wife, and Shen Yi Ji who had been captured together with them. When Liu Bang's father and wife arrived at the camp of Liu Bang's army, Liu Bang went out of the gate of the camp to welcome them. The soldiers of the whole army were so excited to see Liu Bang's father and wife that they all cheered loudly. Hou

Gong had made great contributions in negotiating with Xiang Yu for the release of Liu Bang's father and wife. In return, Liu Bang made him Marquis of Ping Guo.

In September, since the peace agreement had been made, Xiang Yu left Xingyang on his way back to the east with his army. He was eager to return to Pencheng, his capital. His soldiers longed to go back home. So his army marched very quickly east.

The King of Han wanted to go back to the west. He ordered his army to get ready to return to Guanzhong. But Zhang Liang and Chen Ping said to Liu Bang, "Your Majesty has owned over half of the realm now. The kings of other states are all on your side. The troops of the Western Chu army are very tired now and they are out of food. This is the chance Heaven has offered us to destroy Xiang Yu. If we do not seize this chance to destroy Xiang Yu now, that would be letting the tiger go back to the jungle. Later he will bring you great trouble." The King of Han took their advice. He sent a party of soldiers to escort his father and wife to Yueyang. Then he led his army of 100,000 men to cross Honggou, the demarcation, to pursue the army of Western Chu.

In October 203 BC, the King of Han pursued Xiang Yu to Yangxia (now Taikang, Henan Province). Then Liu Bang stopped advancing. He ordered his army to pitch camp there. He sent out envoys to Han Xin, King of the State of Qi, and Peng Yue, premier of the State of Wei, ordering them to lead their armies to join with him in Guling to destroy Xiang Yu's army. Several days later, Liu Bang calculated that Han Xin and Peng Yue would be joining him in Guling (now a place between Taikang and Huaiyang of Henan Province), and he ordered his army to march there. But to his great disappointment, Han Xin and Peng Yue did not come.

The Western Chu army attacked the Han army and defeated it. The King of Han had to order his troops to withdraw into their camp and stay inside. The King of Han asked Zhang Liang, "Han Xin and Peng Yue did not obey my order. What shall I do?" Zhang Liang said, "When Han Xin asked Your Majesty to make him King of the State of Qi, Your Majesty made him King of the State of Qi with great reluctance, and Han Xin was not sure whether Your Majesty really meant he was King or had only granted him the title. Peng Yue has made great contributions in pacifying the areas of the State of Wei and he was entitled to be named King of the State of Wei. But Your Majesty made Wei Bao King of the State of Wei, and Peng Yue was only appointed premier. Now that Wei Bao is dead, Peng Yue wants to be King of the State of Wei, but Your Majesty has not made him king. I suggest that Your Majesty should promise Han Xin and Peng Yue that if Xiang Yu is destroyed, Peng Yue will be made king of the territory from Suiyang to Gucheng in the north; the territory from Chen to the sea in the east will be given to Han Xin, King of the State of Qi. The King of the State of Qi wants his hometown to be included in the territory of the State of Qi. This will satisfy his desire. Otherwise they will not come and Xiang Yu will not be destroyed." Liu Bang took his advice and sent out envoys to Han Xin and Peng Yue.

When the envoy reached the State of Qi and conveyed Liu Bang's offer, Han Xin immediately held a military meeting to make arrangements to lead his army to destroy Xiang Yu. He ordered Cao Shen to stay in the State of Qi to quell any remaining unrest among the people of the State of Qi. He himself led an army of 300,000 men to join the King of Han. General Kong Xi and General Chen Bao went with him. Guan Ying, General of the cavalry, led 5,000 cavalrymen to go with the King of the State of Qi. Peng Yue led all the army under him to march to Gaixia (a place near Suiyang, Henan Province) from the area of Wei. General Liu Jia led an army to march to Gaixia from Shouchun (now Shouxian, Anhui Province).

General Zhou Yin of Xiang Yu's army betrayed Xiang Yu and led the army under him to march from Jiujiang to join General Liu Jia and marched to Gaixia. Ying Bu, King of the State of Huainan, also led his army from Huainan to Gaixia to participate in the battle to destroy Xiang Yu.

In December Liu Bang's great army of over 500,000 men had gathered in Gaixia and was ready to attack Xiang Yu's army. There were about 100,000 men in Xiang Yu's army. Now over 600,000 men gathered in Gaixia to fight a decisive battle.

Xiang Yu's army pitched camp on high ground. Liu Bang's great army marched to Xiang Yu's camp to challenge them to battle. Liu Bang's great army was arranged in several battle formations. Han Xin personally commanded the middle formation. General Kong Xi commanded the left wing and General Chen Bao commanded the right wing. Liu Bang was behind them with Zhang Liang and Chen Ping on both sides. Behind them were General Zhou Bo and General Chai. General Guan Ying led his cavalrymen as reserve.

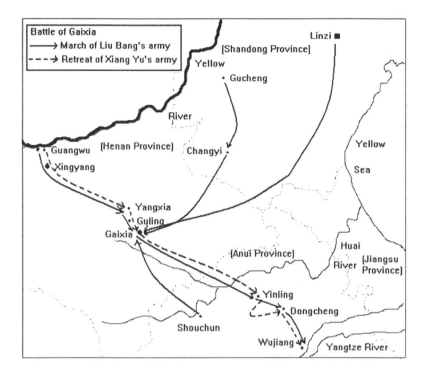

Xiang Yu led his army out of his camp and arranged his army in battle formation. Then the great battle began.

Han Xin issued the order to attack. With loud war cries, the soldiers of his middle formation marched forward. Xiang Yu waved his soldiers forward to meet the Han army. The two armies engaged. Xiang Yu and his men fought fiercely and Han Xin's army was pushed back. At a certain moment, General Kong Xi commanding the left wing and General Chen Bao commanding the right wing led their troops to attack the flanks of Xiang Yu's army. Xiang Yu had to send soldiers to resist the attack on the flanks; this weakened the front formation. Han Xin took this chance to press forward again. The battle cries rose to the sky. Many soldiers were killed. Blood soaked the ground. The battle went on for a long time. Nearly half of the men of Xiang Yu's army fell. Xiang Yu was defeated. He retreated with his remaining army into his camp.

Yu Ji, a beautiful young lady, was the concubine whom Xiang Yu loved most. She always accompanied Xiang Yu in wartime. She welcomed her husband back to the tent and helped him wipe the spilt blood off his face and battle garb. Xiang Yu was disheartened and Yu Ji tried her best to comfort him. Then she served food, and they ate. Night fell. Xiang Yu was exhausted and he fell into a deep sleep.

The Han army surrounded Xiang Yu's camp in three rings. At midnight, all was silent. Then Zhang Liang stood on the top of a hill and began playing his flute. The tone of the flute was mournful. All the Han soldiers surrounding the camp of the Western Chu army began to sing to the tune of a traditional Western Chu song. The tune was melancholy and the words they sang were heartbreaking. The song went:

> It is already late autumn,
> Frost covers the fields.
> The sky is clear and the brooks have gone dry.
> The lonely wild goose flies in the cold sky,
> Winging its way, hear its bitter cry.
> On a barren hill the lonesome soldier stands,
> Weighed down with armor, a spear in his hand.
> For ten years he's been away from his home and his land.
> He will never see his mother and father again.
> His wife yearns for his return,
> His grey-haired mother stands at the doorway
> Longing for him.
> His young son weeps sadly for his father.
> The land is left untilled and weeds all grow high;
> Where will the soldier's soul go, should he die?
> What have you fought for, dear soldier?
> The King of Han is a kind-hearted king,
> He never kills soldiers who surrender;
> Xiang Yu's days are numbered,
> Why die with him?
> I sing this song to show your destiny to you.
> When you hear it, don't hesitate. You know what to do.

This song was sung again and again all night long. When the soldiers of the Western Chu army heard this tune from their homeland, they shed tears. Then the soldiers stood up, sneaked out of the camp and left. Even Xiang Bo, Xiang Yu's uncle, ran out of the camp and turned over to the side of the King of Han. Only eight hundred soldiers remained.

Xiang Yu woke up from his deep sleep and heard the song of the Chu being sung all around. He was greatly surprised and said, "Has the King of Han occupied the whole State of Western Chu? Are there so many Chu people in the Han army?" He sat with Yu Ji in his tent and poured drinks for them both. He sang sadly, repeatedly, with tears in his eyes:

My might can lift mountains,
My aspiration is wide as the world,
But luck has deserted me; it's done.
Even my horse would not gallop, it won't run.
My horse would not gallop.
What shall I do?
My dear Yu Ji, what will you do?

Yu Ji danced and sang the following lines:

The Han Army has taken all the lands of Chu,
The air resounds with the song of the Chu;
Luck has deserted my dear husband the king;
I will not live alone in this world, not for anything.

All those standing around were in tears and could not look up. Suddenly, Yu Ji drew a sword and killed herself. Xiang Yu clung to Yu Ji's dead body and cried bitterly. He asked the soldiers to dig a grave at the corner of the camp, and he lowered her corpse into it. The soldiers found some slate stones and placed them around her to make a stone coffin. Then they covered the stone coffin with earth. Xiang Yu stood lost in sadness in front of the grave for some time. And it came to him that he must make his breakthrough before dawn; galvanized, he realized he had to act immediately.

Xiang Yu and his eight hundred followers all jumped on the back of their horses and galloped quickly southward. After a short clash, they broke through the encirclement. It was dawn when the Han army found out that Xiang Yu had escaped. Liu Bang ordered General Guan Ying, the commander of the cavalry, to go after him with 5,000 cavalrymen. When Xiang Yu crossed the Huai River, only a hundred men followed. When he reached Yinling (now northwest to Dingyuan, Anhui Province), he lost his way. He has to stop and ask a farmer. The farmer deceived him, telling him to go westward. He went westward and galloped several miles, only to find that he was trapped in a big stretch of marshes. The Han cavalrymen caught up with him. He headed eastward again to Dongcheng (now southeast to

Dingyuan, Anhui Province). Only twenty-eight men on horseback were still with him.

Xiang Yu says farewell to his concubine Yu Ji

There were several thousand Han cavalrymen pursuing him. It was hopeless. He said to his followers, "Since I led an army in rebellion against the Qin Dynasty, eight years have already passed. I have experienced over seventy battles. I never lost one. So I have the ability to control the realm. I have won fame as the Conqueror. But in the end, now, I am trapped here. That is not my fault. That is not because I am not good at fighting. It is destiny that has led to my destruction. It is not because I am not a capable warrior. I am doomed to die today and I intend to fight a quick battle for you. In order to show that my failure is Heaven's will and not because of my inability to fight, I will gallop straight into the battle formation of the Han army and make a breakthrough for you, kill a general, and cut down a flag." He divided his men into four groups, four groups that would make a breakthrough in four directions. The Han troops had encircled them, ring upon ring.

Xiang Yu pointed at the general leading the Han army and said to his followers, "I will kill that general for you." Beforehand, they agreed to meet at three places east of the mountain. Then Xiang Yu charged the Han cavalry-men fiercely with a loud war cry. The Han soldiers fled as he galloped close. He killed a general of the Han army. Another general pursued him. Xiang Yu turned back and in a booming voice bellowed, "How dare you run after me!" The man and horse were both so scared by his thundering shout that they turned and ran back for a mile.

The Defeated Xiang Yu

Then Xiang Yu and his men met up, the east of the mountain, gathering in bands in three different places. The Han army caught up with them, but they did not know in which of the three places Xiang Yu was. So the Han army was divided into three groups to surround the three places. Then Xiang Yu started galloping again and killed one high-ranking officer and over a hundred Han soldiers. Then they met again. He had only lost two men. There was no doubt in the minds of his men that he was indeed a superlative warrior and that his failure was caused by his bad luck.

Then they reached Wujiang (now Wujiang, Anhui Province), situated on the west bank of the Yangtze River. A local official was waiting for him in a boat. He said to Xiang Yu, "Although the area to the east of the Yangtze River is not very large, it is still a place with an area of more than a thousand square miles with tens of thousands of people. It wouldn't be bad to be a king of that area. I hope Your Majesty will get on board. I will ferry Your Majesty to the east bank of the river. This is the only boat in the area. When the Han soldiers reach here, they cannot get across the river to pursue Your Majesty." Xiang Yu smiled and said, "I am destined to die today. What is the use of my going to the east bank? When I crossed the Yangtze River heading westward eight years ago, I brought with me 8,000 sons and brothers of the people in the area to the east of the river. But none of them has come back with me. Even if the people of the area to the east of the river have pity on me and make me their king, I am too ashamed to see the fathers and brothers of those 8,000 men. Even if they do not mention it, I cannot meet them with a clear conscience." Then he said to the man, "I know you are a kindhearted person. My horse is five years old. This horse has carried me in many victorious battles. It can cover three hundred miles a day. I am not hardhearted enough to kill it. I will give it to you." So the man pulled the horse on board his boat and rowed away.

All of his remaining followers dismounted and fought on foot with short weapons. Xiang Yu killed several hundred Han soldiers but he also sustained many wounds. Then he saw Lü Ma Tong, an officer of the Han cavalry. Xiang Yu asked, "Were you once my friend?" Lü Ma Tong had served in Xiang Yu's army but later turned to the side of Liu Bang. Lü Ma Tong was ashamed to face Xiang Yu squarely, so he turned aside and said to his fellow officer Wang Yi, "This is King Xiang Yu!" Xiang Yu said, "I hear that the King of Han has offered 10,000 catties of gold for my head and the person who gets it will be made a marquis enjoying the tax on 10,000 peasant households. I will offer my head to you." With these words, he put his sword to his neck and killed himself. He died at the age of thirty-two. Wang Yi rode up and got his head. Then the Han soldiers rushed up trying to seize the dead body of Xiang Yu. Yang Xi, Lü Ma Tong, Lü Sheng and Yang Wu each took one part of it. These five persons were all made marquises later by Liu Bang.

The whole State of Western Chu had been brought under control by the King of Han except the city of Lu (now Qufu, Shandong Province). The city of Lu refused to surrender because Lu was the first piece of land granted to Xiang Yu by King Huai of the State of Chu. The people of Lu tried to keep this land for Xiang Yu and they were willing to die for their lord. The King of Han reached the city and showed the head of Xiang Yu to the people of that city. Then the people of Lu surrendered. Xiang Yu was buried in Gucheng (now Pingyin, Shandong Province) with the honor of a duke. The King of Han personally attended the funeral and when he left, there were tears in his eyes. The King of Han did not kill any of Xiang Yu's family members. He made Xiang Bo Marquis of Sheyang, and granted him the family name of Liu, and made Xiang Shang Marquis of Tao and Xiang Tuo Marquis of Pinggao, and they were also granted the family name of Liu.

54. Peace and Order Resumes in the Realm

All the other kings submitted to the King of Han except for Gong Wei, King of Linjiang. Gong Wei was the son of Gong Ao. It was Xiang Yu who had made Gong Ao King of Linjiang. After Gong Ao died, Gong Wei succeeded to the throne of the State of Linjiang. Gong Wei could not forget Xiang Yu's kindness in making his father King of Linjiang, so he refused to submit to Liu Bang. Liu Bang sent General Liu Jia and General Lu Wan with an army to subdue the area of Linjiang. Not long later, Gong Wei was captured and the area of Linjiang was pacified. Gong Wei was brought to Luoyang and was executed there.

Then Liu Bang led his army to Dingtao (now Dingtao, Shandong Province). At that time, the army of the State of Qi under Han Xin, King of the State of Qi, was stationed in Dingtao. Liu Bang had secretly discussed Han Xin's military might with Zhang Liang and Chen Ping. Zhang Liang and Chen Ping both thought that Han Xin's military might was too great and should be taken away before he caused any trouble. One day, Liu Bang rode into Han Xin's camp and right up to the tent where Han Xin was staying. Han Xin stood up to welcome Liu Bang. Liu Bang sat down on a chair and said to Han Xin, "You have made great military contributions in the war against Xiang Yu. Now Xiang Yu has been killed and I will never forget the great contributions you have made. The whole realm is now at peace and there will be no more wars. So it is not necessary for you to hold the power to command a great army. You may return your military tally to me." He was referring to the tiger-shaped metal symbol given to military command-ers to indicate their right to command armies. "You may keep some troops, enough to maintain peace and order in the State of Qi." Han Xin could not find any way out of it, so he had to hand his military tally to Liu Bang. After Liu Bang took the tally from Han Xin, he immediately left.

In January 202 BC, the King of Han sent an envoy to the State of Qi with an order to Han Xin. The order read, "Now order has been brought to the State of Western Chu. The original King of Chu, Xiong Xin, is dead, and he has no descendant. You were born in the area of Chu and grew up there. You know the customs of the State of Chu very well. You are the best candidate to be the King of the State of Chu. I hereby make you King of the State of Chu. The capital of the State of Chu will be Xiapi. I will turn the State of Qi into a prefecture." Although Han Xin knew very well that Liu Bang did not want him to be King of the State of Qi, he was glad to take the offer, because Chu was a big state and it was his home place. He would return to his home place gloriously.

At the same time, Liu Bang sent an envoy to Peng Yue with an order. The order read, "You have made great contributions in overthrowing the rule of the Qin Dynasty and in the wars against Xiang Yu. You have brought order to the area of Wei. I hereby make you King of the State of Liang. The capital of the State of Liang will be Dingtao." When Peng Yue got the order, he was very glad to see that all his efforts had not been in vain. He set out for Dingtao immediately to see Liu Bang. He knelt down in front Liu Bang and received the seal of King of the State of Liang.

When Han Xin saw Liu Bang, he returned the seal of King of the State of Qi to Liu Bang, and accepted the new seal of the King of the State of Chu. Cao Shen, the premier of the State of Qi, also went to see Liu Bang and re-turned the seal of the premier of the State of Qi.

Han Xin went to Xiapi to take the throne of the State of Chu. He sent someone to look for the old lady who had given him food when he was fishing by the river. When the old lady came, he granted her a thousand catties of gold. Then he summoned the chief of Nanchang Sub-township to the palace. He granted him a small sum of money and said, "You are a mean man. You could not carry out a virtuous act to the end." He summoned the man who had asked Han Xin to crawl under his spreading legs. When the man came to the palace, he was trembling all over because he thought that Han Xin was going to punish him for his insults. So when he saw Han Xin sitting on the throne, he knelt down and touched his forehead to the ground and said, "I am sorry I insulted Your Majesty. I hope Your Majesty will spare me." Han Xin laughed and said, "I will not punish you. I will appoint you a captain in my army." The man could not believe his own ears and said, "I only beg Your Majesty to spare my life. I dare not ask for more than that." Han Xin let him stand up, and then said to the generals and courtiers around, "He is a brave man. When he insulted me, I would have killed him. But that was not a justifiable excuse to kill a person. So I suppressed my anger and crawled under his legs. Otherwise, I would not have become King of the State of Chu today."

55. LIU BANG BECOMES EMPEROR OF THE HAN DYNASTY

In February 202 BC, Han Xin (King of the State of Chu) together with Peng Yu (King of the State of Liang), Ying Bu (King of the State of Huainan), Haan Xin (King of the State of Haan), Wu Rui (who was King of the State of Hengshan until Xiang Yu deprived him of that title and demoted him to Lord of Po, that is, the Ruler of the Barbarian Areas to the south of the Yangtze River), Zhang Er (King of the State of Zhao), and Zang Tu (King of the State of Yan), jointly presented a memorandum to Liu Bang, King of the State of Han, proposing that he ascend the throne as emperor. The memorandum read, "We, Han Xin, King of the State of Chu, Peng Yu, King of the State of Liang, Ying Bu, King of the State of Huainan, Haan Xin, King of the State of Haan, Wu Rui, the former King of the State of Hengshan, Zhang Er, King of the State of Zhao, Zang Tu, King of the State of Yan, take the liberty to present the following memorandum to Your Majesty: In the wars to overthrow the cruel rule of the Qin Dynasty, Your Majesty was the first to enter the capital of the Qin Dynasty and captured the King of Qin. Your Majesty pacified the area of Guanzhong. In these wars, Your Majesty made the greatest contributions. Your Majesty has fought very hard to preserve the states once destroyed by the Qin Dynasty and has brought peace and order to the whole realm. Your Majesty has granted us the title of kings.

Your Majesty is the king of kings. The merits and virtues of Your Majesty are unprecedented and unrepeatable. Your Majesty has been very kind to the kings of the other states and bestowed benefits upon them. Your Majesty deserves the title of Emperor. We hereby suggest that Your Majesty ascend the throne of emperor."

Premier Xiao He and the civil officials and the generals also presented a memorandum to Liu Bang proposing that he ascend the throne of emperor.

After Liu Bang read the memoranda, he discussed the matter with his courtiers. Liu Bang said, "I hear that, in ancient times, the title of Emperor was for the most virtuous kings. I am not at all as virtuous as those virtuous ancient emperors. I don't deserve the title of Emperor." The courtiers said, "Your Majesty rose up from the grassroots. Your Majesty has led the people to overthrow the cruel rule of the Qin Dynasty and defeated Xiang Yu. Your Majesty has granted titles of kings and marquises to those who have made great contributions. Now the whole realm has been pacified. Peace and order have been resumed in the whole realm. If Your Majesty does not ascend the throne of emperor, the people of the whole realm will be disappointed." Three times Liu Bang declined the title, but at last he was persuaded to ascend the throne as Emperor.

Liu Bang appointed Lu Wan and Shusun Tong to make preparations for the ceremony of his ascension to the throne. They selected a place to the south of Jishui River, south of Dingtao. They ordered soldiers to build a stage there. One day in late February 202 BC, a grand ceremony was held. Liu Bang stepped up onto the stage and sat on the throne in the middle of the stage. Han Xin, Peng Yu, Ying Bu, Haan Xin, Wu Rui, Zhang Er, and Zang Tu went up onto the stage and knelt down in front of Liu Bang and touched their foreheads to the ground three times, and they expressed their congratulations to Liu Bang upon the occasion of his ascension to the throne of the Emperor of the Han Dynasty. Then they went down from the stage. Then the civil officials and generals went up and repeated the same procedures. During the ceremony, it was declared that Lü Zhi, the Queen of the State of Han, had become the Empress of the Han Dynasty. Liu Ying, the Crown Prince of the State of Han, became the successor to the throne of the Han Dynasty. The Emperor decided to make Luoyang (now Louyang, Henan Province) the capital of the Han Dynasty.

Liu Bang issued an imperial edict to make Wu Rui King of the State of Changsha. Wu Rui became the king of a big state which covered the areas of

Changsha (now Hunan Province), Yuzhang (now Jiangxi Province), Xiang (now the west part of Guangxi Zhuang Autonomous Region), Guilin (the east part of Guangxi Zhuang Autonomous Region and the west part of Guangdong Province) and Hainan (now Guangdong Province).

Liu Bang issued another imperial edict, making Wu Zhu King of the State of Minyue. Wu Zhu became the King of the State of Minyue, which covered the area of Min (now Fujian Province) and Yue (now northeast part of Guangdong Province).

Considering that the soldiers had been fighting continuously for eight years, and the people had suffered from the war for so long, Liu Bang demobilized the armies and let the soldiers go home.

56. Happy Family Reunion

After the ceremony of Liu Bang's ascension to the throne of the Emperor of the Han Dynasty, the kings left Dingtao for their own states. Liu Bang, the new Emperor, set out for Luoyang, his new capital. Before he left Dingtao, he sent out courtiers to Yueyang, the provisional capital of the State of Han, to escort his father Liu Zhi Jia, his wife Lü Zhi (the Empress), and his son Liu Ying (the Crown Prince) and his daughter Princess Lu Yuan, to Luoyang. He sent out courtiers to Pei, his home place, to escort his second elder brother Liu Zhong, his nephew Liu Xin, and his younger brother Liu Jiao to Luoyang. He sent out courtiers to escort Lady Cao and Liu Fei to Luoyang. Lady Cao was Liu Bang's first lover before Liu Bang married Lü Zhi. Lady Cao and Liu Bang had a son, and that was Liu Fei. So Liu Fei was actually Liu Bang's first-born son. Other envoys were sent by Liu Bang to the mountain village in Lingbi to fetch Qi Ji and her son and her father to Luoyang. Bo Ji and her son Liu Heng were also brought to Luoyang, capital of the Han Dynasty.

When all of them gathered together in the palace at Luoyang, Liu Bang was very happy. When Qi Ji and her son were brought before Liu Bang, Liu Bang was especially happy. At that time, the child was just three years old. He was a lovely boy. Liu Bang said happily, "This child looks like me very much. I hereby name him Liu Ru Yi." Qi Ji was especially loved by Liu Bang because she was so beautiful, and from then on she always accompanied Liu Bang even when Liu Bang went out for war.

57. THE THREE OUTSTANDING PERSONS OF THE HAN DYNASTY

One day, Liu Bang held a banquet to entertain his ministers and generals in the South Palace of Louyang. During the banquet, he said, "Marquises and generals, please answer my question frankly and honestly. Please don't conceal your ideas. My question is: What is the reason why I have won the power to rule over China while Xiang Yu lost it?"

Wang Ling stood up and said, "Your Majesty is rude and impolite to people. Xiang Yu is very polite to those who are under him. But when Your Majesty sent a general to take a city, and when the city was taken, you granted that city to the general who has taken it. You share the benefit of the victory with all the people. But Xiang Yu did otherwise. He disliked those who had rendered outstanding services. He distrusted those who were capable and virtuous. He did not reward those who won victories. He did not give any benefits to general who conquered cities. That is the reason why he lost." The Emperor said, "This is one of two reasons, and it is the minor one. The other and more important one is this: When it comes to planning strategies within the command tent to ensure victory on a battlefront 1,000 miles away, I am no match for Zhang Liang. When it comes to stabilizing the state, pacifying the people, and assuring the food supply for the army, I am no match for Xiao He. When it comes to commanding a million men in occupying cities and winning victories, I am no match for Han Xin. These three persons are outstanding. I have allowed them to give full play to their abilities. That is the reason why I have won the whole realm. Xiang Yu had an outstanding person, namely Fan Zeng, but Xiang Yu did not listen to his advice. That is the reason why he was defeated by me." All the ministers and generals were convinced.

58. TIAN HENG, THE FORMER KING OF THE STATE OF QI, AND HIS FIVE HUNDRED FOLLOWERS

Since Liu Bang had made Peng Yue King of the State of Liang, Tian Heng, the former King of the State of Qi, who had joined Peng Yue when Han Xin had defeated him, was afraid that he might be punished. So he and his five hundred followers escaped to an island in the East China Sea. Liu Bang considered that Tian Heng, as the former King of the State of Qi, was supported by the local people. And many virtuous men of the Qi area had joined him. Now they were on an island in the sea. If they were not dealt with now, they might cause trouble later. So he sent an envoy to the island to pardon Tian Heng for his crimes and summoned him to Luoyang. Tian Heng declined the kindness of Liu Bang and said in all frankness to the envoy, "I cooked His Majesty's envoy Li Yi Ji. I hear that Li Yi Ji's younger brother Li Shang is a general of Han. I am afraid of him. So I dare not obey His Majesty's order. I hope His Majesty will let us live on as commoner and stay on this island." The envoy went back and reported it to the Emperor.

The Emperor summoned General Li Shang and said to him, "Tian Heng, the former King of the State of Qi, is coming soon. If you dare to do anything harmful to him, to any of his followers, and even to his horses, I will kill you and all your family members." Then he sent an envoy to the island to tell Tian Heng that he had warned Li Shang not to do anything against Tian Heng. The envoy further conveyed Liu Bang's order: "If Tian Heng comes, he may be made a king or marquis. If he does not come, I will send an army to punish him." Tian Heng accepted the order and traveled to Luoyang with the envoy and two of his followers. When they were fifteen kilometers away from Luoyang, they stopped at a stage inn along the way. Tian Heng asked the envoy to leave him and his two followers alone for some time, saying, "As a subject of the Emperor, I am going to see His Majesty. Before I see him, I must take a bath. Will you excuse us and let us take a bath?" When they were left alone, Tian Heng said to his two followers, "In the past the King of Han and I were both kings. But now the King of Han has become the Emperor but I have become his subject because he has conquered the State of Qi. I shall have to serve him and call him His Majesty. It is a great insult to me. And I cooked Li Shang's brother Li Yi Ji, and now I shall have to serve the Emperor side by side with Li Shang. Even if Li Shang does not act against me because the Emperor has warned him not to, I will always feel guilty in my heart. The Emperor has summoned me. He just wants to know what I look like. You can take my head to the Emperor. It is only fifteen kilometers from here. My head won't change much by the time you get there. And the Emperor will know what I really looked like." Then he drew out his sword and killed himself. One of his followers took his head and drove to the palace to see the Emperor. When the Emperor saw Tian Heng's head, he said with great admiration, "What great people the three brothers of the Tian family are! They rose from common people and they became the King of the State of Qi one after another. They were really virtuous people." The Emperor wept for Tian Heng and appointed the two followers to a high-

ranking position in the army. He sent 2,000 soldiers to dig a tomb and buried Tian Heng with a funeral ceremony fit for a king. After the funeral, the
two officers dug a hole on the side of the tomb and killed themselves there.
The Emperor was shocked when he heard about their death. The Emperor
knew that Tian Heng's followers were all virtuous people, so he sent an
envoy to the island to summon them to the capital. When the 500 men got
the news that Tian Heng had died, they all drew out their swords and killed
themselves.

59. Liu Bang Moves His Capital from Luoyang to Guanzhong

A man named Lou Jing was sent from the area of Qi (now Shandong
Province) to garrison the frontier in Longxi (now west part of Gansu Province). When the group of people being sent to Longxi passed Louyang, Lou
Jing set down the cart he was pulling and went to see General Yu, who was
also from the area of Qi. He asked General Yu to make an appointment for
him to see the Emperor. General Yu succeeded in making the appointment.
Before Lou Jing set out to see the Emperor, General Yu asked him to take off
his coarse clothes and put on better clothes. But Lou Jing insisted on meeting the Emperor in his coarse clothes.

In the interview, Lou Jing asked the Emperor, "Your Majesty has made
Luoyang the capital of the Han Dynasty. Is it because Your Majesty wants
to show the people all over China that the Han Dynasty is as great and prosperous as the Zhou Dynasty?" The Emperor answered, "Yes." Lou Jing said,
"The forefathers of the Zhou Dynasty performed a lot of good deeds for the
people and accumulated virtue for more than ten generations before King
Wu of Zhou defeated the Shang Dynasty and established the Zhou Dynasty.
He became King of all China. When King Cheng of the Zhou Dynasty ascended the throne, Zhou Gong was the premier. He began the construction
of palaces in Luoyang because Luoyang was situated in the center of China
and he thought that all the dukes of the states would pay their tribute from
all directions to this center. Well, when the King of the Zhou Dynasty was
virtuous, capable and strong, he could easily rule over China from Luoyang.
But if the king was not virtuous, or not capable, he would be easily attacked
and killed. When the Zhou Dynasty was strong and prosperous and China
was at peace, the dukes were obedient and they did pay tribute to the King
of the Zhou Dynasty. But when the Zhou Dynasty became weak, none of

the dukes paid any tribute. The King of the Zhou Dynasty could do nothing about it. Not only was the King of the Zhou Dynasty himself weak; he was also in a geographically disadvantageous position."

And he went on: "Now Your Majesty rose from Pei as an ordinary man. Your Majesty became King of Han, ruling over Hanzhong and Shu. Your Majesty defeated the three kings in the Qin area and pacified the three states. Your Majesty fought against Xiang Yu in the area of Xingyang and Chenggao. More than seventy grand battles and more than forty smaller battles were fought. Countless people were killed and the bones of the dead soldiers are still exposed in the wild. The bitter cries of the families of the dead soldiers are still heard everywhere. The wounded have not yet recovered. The situation is not yet stable, and the country is far from being prosperous. The Qin area is protected by the Xiao Shan Mountain and the Yellow River. It is not easily accessible. So it is easily defended. And if there is an emergency, an army of a million men can be raised instantly. There are rich resources in the Qin area and leagues upon leagues of fertile land. It is the land of abundance. If Your Majesty establishes your capital in the Qin area, even if there is disorder in the areas to the east of the Xiao Shan Mountain, there will still be order and peace in the area of Qin. When you are fighting with another man, you must try to strangle him by the throat and hit him on the back. If Your Majesty occupies the area of Qin, Your Majesty is actually controlling the throat of the whole country and you are in an advantageous position to hit the back of your enemy."

Liu Bang asked his ministers for their opinions. Most of the ministers were from the east part of China, so they said, "The Zhou Dynasty lasted for several hundred years but the Qin Dynasty lasted for only two generations. Luoyang is protected by Chenggao in the east, the Xiao Shan Mountain (in the west of Henen Province) and Mianchi (now Mianchi, Henan Province) in the west, the Yellow River in the north and the Yi River and the Luoshui River in the south. So Luoyang is also an easily defended city." Liu Bang asked Zhang Liang for his opinion. Zhang Liang said, "Although Luoyang has the advantages mentioned by the ministers, the area protected is too small, no more than a hundred square kilometers. The lands are not fertile. It is easily attacked from all sides. It is not a good place for a capital in war times. But the Qin area is protected by the Xiao Shan Mountain and Han-guguan Pass in the southeast and Long Shan Mountain in the west. There is over a thousand square kilometers of fertile land in the area. From there, you can control the kings in the east and the kings dare not rebel against Your Majesty. The Yellow River and the Weishui River facilitate the transportation of food to the capital and to places all over China. If any king rebels, troops and food may be sent down the Yellow River to suppress the rebellion. The Qin area is securely defended and really is the land of abundance and a good place for a capital. Lou Jing's opinion is right."

Liu Bang decided immediately to establish the capital of the Han Dynasty in the area of Guanzhong. He appointed Lou Jing to a high-ranking position just next to the position of the premier. Liu Bang said to Lou Jing, "Your family name is Lou. The word Lou is the same as the word Liu. So I hereby grant you the family name of Liu." From then on, Lou Jing became Liu Jing.

Not much later, the Emperor of the Han Dynasty selected a date to start his journey to Guanzhong. The procession of the royal family and the ministers and courtiers and generals moved from Luoyang through Hanguguan Pass into the area of Guanzhong. They first reached Yueyang, the former provisional capital of the State of Han. After discussing it with Xiao He, the premier, Liu Bang decided to make Chang'an (now Xi'an, Shaanxi Province) the capital of the Han Dynasty. Chang'an was a place south to Xianyang, the capital of the Qin Dynasty. All the palaces in Xianyang had been burned down to the ground by Xiang Yu, so it was not suitable to be the capital of the Han Dynasty. New palaces would have to be built in Chang'an. The Emperor put Xiao He in charge of the building of new palaces in Chang'an.

60. Zhang Liang Retires from the Scene of State Affairs

Zhang Liang had made great contributions to the establishment of the Han Dynasty. But his health had always been poor. So after he had followed Liu Bang into the area of Guanzhong, he did not attend to state affairs any more. He stayed at home and led a very quiet life. He devoted himself to practicing a form of the Taoist disciplines to become an immortal. When he was asked why he had retired, he said, "My forefathers were premiers of the State of Haan. When the First Emperor of the Qin Dynasty conquered the State of Haan, I spent all my money to avenge the State of Haan on the First Emperor of the Qin Dynasty. I sent a warrior to assassinate the First Emperor of the Qin Dynasty by throwing a big hammer at his carriage in Bolangsha. Now I have become the military counselor of the Emperor of the Han Dynasty. This is the highest rank one can expect. I am very satisfied with it. I just want to abandon the trouble in this world and practice to become an immortal."

Portrait of Zhang Liang

61. THE REBELLION OF ZANG TU, THE KING OF THE STATE OF YAN

In July 202 BC, Zang Tu, King of the State of Yan, rebelled against the Han Dynasty. He sent an army to attack the area of Dai (now an area around Weixian in the north part of Hebei Province) and took it.

When the news reached the Emperor, he was irate. He said, "Zang Tu did not make any contribution in the wars against Xiang Yu. I let him keep the title of the King of the State of Yan only because he surrendered to me. He is an ungrateful man. I will carry on an expedition to put down his rebellion personally." A great army was mobilized. The Emperor appointed Fan Kuai as premier, Li Shang as general and Guan Ying as the general of the cavalry to command this army to suppress Zang Tu's rebellion. General Lu Wan and General Chen Xi also took part in this expedition. Li Shang led an army in the vanguard. He defeated the Yan army in the border area between the State of Zhao and the State of Yan. Then he marched his army to Yi (now Yixian, Hebei Province). A battle was fought there, and the army of Yan was defeated there. Li Shang took the city of Yi. In September, the main force commanded by Fan Kuai and Guan Ying quickly marched to Ji (now Beijing), the capital of the State of Yan. Zang Tu had to come out of the city of Ji to fight with the army sent by the Emperor. But very soon he was defeated and turned back to the city. The Emperor ordered his army to lay siege to the city. Three days later, the army of the Han Dynasty under the command of Fan Kuai and Guan Ying launched a fierce attack and the Han army entered the city of Ji. Zang Tu was captured. His son escaped through the north gate of the city and ran away to the Huns in the north. Zang Tu was executed and his head was exhibited to the rest of the State of Yan, and there was no more trouble in whole area of the State of Yan.

62. Lu Wan Is Made King of the State of Yan

Lu Wan was born on the same day of the same month and the same year in the same village as Liu Bang. Lu Wan and Liu Bang had grown up together and were childhood playmates. When Liu Bang rose from Pei, Lu Wan joined him and became Liu Bang's most trusted follower. He was given the most important position, to take care of Liu Bang's personal life. Any one who wanted to see Liu Bang had to get Lu Wan's permission. Liu Bang showed special favor to him. When Liu Bang granted properties to his sub-ordinates, Lu Wan always got the greatest share. Lu Wan was granted the title of the Marquis of Chang'an (now Xi'an, Shaanxi Province). Since Zang Tu, the King of the State of Yan, had been captured and executed, a new king of the State of Yan could be appointed. Liu Bang intended to make Lu Wan King of the State of Yan. But he knew that Lu Wan had not provided any especially great services, so he let the ministers to discuss the new position. The ministers knew perfectly well that the Emperor intended to make Lu Wan King of the State of Yan. So they all recommended Lu Wan. In this way, Lu Wan became King of the State of Yan.

63. Han Xin's Conspiracy for Rebellion

Zhong Li Mei, one of the fiercest generals of Xiang Yu, was a good friend of Han Xin. After Xiang Yu died, Zhong Li Mei escaped to Han Xin for protection. Liu Bang hated Zhong Li Mei very much. When Liu Bang knew that Zhong Li Mei was in the State of Chu under the protection of Han Xin, he sent an order to the State of Chu to arrest Zhong Li Mei.

In October 202 BC, the Emperor received a secret written statement informing him that Han Xin was plotting a rebellion. The Emperor discussed the matter with his generals. They all suggested that an army should be sent to kill Han Xin. The Emperor did not give any comment. Then he asked Chen Ping for his opinion. Chen Ping asked the Emperor, "Does Han Xin know that somebody has spread the word that he is going to rebel?" The Emperor answered, "No." Then Chen Ping asked, "Are Your Majesty's soldiers better fighters than those under Han Xin's command?" The Emperor answered, "No." Chen Ping asked again, "Are the generals under Your Majesty better versed in the art of war than Han Xin?" The Emperor answered, "No." Chen Ping said, "The soldiers of Your Majesty are not better fighters than his. The generals under Your Majesty are not better versed in the art of war than he. If you attack him with an army, you actually accelerate his rebellion. The result can only be disaster." The Emperor asked, "Then what shall I do?"

Chen Ping said, "In ancient times, the emperors made hunting trips in designated places and met the kings and dukes there. I suggest that Your Majesty make a hunting trip to the Marsh of Yunmeng. An appointment may be made with all the other kings to meet in the area of Chen. The State of Chu is very close to that area. Han Xin will think that since Your Majesty is making a hunting trip and meeting the kings, there would be no danger in meeting Your Majesty in the borderlands of Chu. Then Your Majesty can arrest him with just two strong warriors." The Emperor took his advice and sent out envoys to the kings informing them to meet the Emperor in the area of Chen (now an area in the east of Henan Province and the west of Anhui Province) and then follow him in a hunting trip to the Marsh of Yunmeng (now in the area south to Qianjiang City, Hubei Province).

When Han Xin got the notice, he was afraid and did not know what to do. One of his followers said to him, "If you kill Zhong Li Mei and go to meet the Emperor with Zhong Li Mei's head, the Emperor will be happy and there will be no trouble." Han Xin accepted his idea. Han Xin called Zhong Li Mei to discuss this matter. Zhong Li Mei said, "The Emperor does not attack the State of Chu precisely because I am in the State of Chu. If you want to please the Emperor with my head, you will be destroyed soon after I die." Han Xin insisted that Zhong Li Mei should kill himself. Then Zhong Li Mei cursed loudly, "You are not a virtuous man. Disaster will fall on you very soon." Then he drew his sword and killed himself with it.

In December, the Emperor met the kings in the area of Chen. Han Xin brought Zhong Li Mei's head and went to see the Emperor. As soon as he arrived, the Emperor gave the order to two strong warriors to arrest Han Xin. Han Xin shouted for all to hear, "Now that the whole realm has been conquered, it is time that I should be cooked." The Emperor looked at him and said, "Shut up! It is clear that you are plotting a rebellion." Then the Emperor ordered the guards to put Han Xin in a carriage just behind his own carriage. Han Xin said, "I have got what I deserve. People say, when all the rabbits have been hunted, the hunting dog will be killed and cooked; when all the swans flying in the sky have been shot down, the bow will be put away; when all the enemy states are conquered, the military counselors will be put to death. Now the whole realm has been brought under control, it is time that I should be killed." The Emperor said to Han Xin, "You are accused of conspiring rebellion." The Emperor brought Han Xin back to Luoyang, then pardoned him and made him Marquis of Huaiyin (now Huaiyin, Jiangsu Province).

Han Xin knew that the Emperor disliked him because of his ability, so he seldom went to court to see the Emperor, often excusing himself on the grounds of being ill. He was always sad. He felt shameful to be in the same rank as such generals as Guan Ying and Fan Kuai. Once the Emperor had a chat with Han Xin about how many soldiers certain generals could command. The Emperor asked Han Xin, "How many soldiers do you think I can command?" Han Xin answered, "100,000 at the most." The Emperor asked, "Then how many can you command?" Han Xin answered "The more the better." The Emperor laughed and said, "The more the better! Then why have you been captured by me?" Han Xin said, "Your Majesty has no ability in commanding soldiers but Your Majesty has great ability in commanding generals. That is why I have been captured by Your Majesty. The ability of Your Majesty is granted by the Heavens. This is the reason why my ability cannot be comparable to that of Your Majesty."

Tian Ken, a courtier, went to see the Emperor. He first expressed his congratulations to the Emperor. He said, "Your Majesty has captured Han Xin and deposed him as the King of the State of Chu. This is the first thing for which I express my congratulations. Your Majesty has decided to move the capital to Guanzhong. This is the second thing for which I express my congratulations. Guanzhong, the area of Qin, has the geographical advantages. It is protected by the Yellow River and the Xiao Shan Mountains. In this area, Your Majesty can control all the other kings. I have a suggestion. The area of the former State of Qi also has geographical advantages. In the east of the area of Qi, there are the areas of Langya and Jimo which are close to the sea. These areas are extremely rich. In the south of Qi, there are the Taishan Mountains which provide a natural protection for the area of Qi. The area of Qi is protected by the Yellow River in the west and Bo Hai Sea to the north. Rich resources can be obtained from that sea. The area of Qi is vast and well populated. An army of a million men can be mobilized in a very short time. The area of Qi is comparable to the area of Guanzhong. I may say the area of Qi is the area of Guanzhong in the east. Only the closest relative of Your Majesty can be made king of the area of Qi." The Emperor said, "Very good suggestion! I will consider this matter seriously." The Emperor granted Tian Ken five hundred catties of gold. Then the Emperor made Liu Fei, his eldest son, King of the State of Qi, which had seventy counties. The Emperor appointed Cao Shen the premier of the State of Qi to assist Liu Fei.

Since Han Xin was deposed as the King of the State of Chu, the Emperor divided the State of Chu into two states: the State of Jing, which had fifty-three counties, and the State of Chu, which had thirty-six counties. He made Liu Jia, his cousin, King of the State of Jing, and made his younger brother Liu Jiao King of the State of Chu.

64 THE CREATION OF MARQUISES

Since the whole of China had been brought under control, Liu Bang began to give the title of marquis to those who had made great contributions. In December 202 BC, the Emperor first created Xiao He the Marquis of Zan (now in the west of Yongcheng, Henan Province), entitled to the tax on 8,000 peasant households. All the generals who had shown outstanding military merit said, "We all risked our lives fighting in the battlefields wearing heavy armor, with weapons in our hands. Some have lived through more than a hundred battles. Some have lived through at least several dozen battles. Xiao He has not rendered any military service. He has only performed some administrative work and made some suggestions. Why should he be given a higher rank than ours?" The Emperor said, "Do you know anything about hunting? It is the hunting dogs that do the job of hunting. But it is the human beings who instruct and send the dogs to hunt. Now, you all have the merits of the dogs. Xiao He has the merits of a human being instructing and sending the dogs. You generals joined me alone. Some of you joined me together with two or three relatives at the most. But Xiao He sent more than thirty of his own family members to assist me in the war against Xiang Yu. I will never forget this contribution Xiao He has made." The generals didn't dare to say anything anymore.

Zhang Liang had not fought in any battle either. He was a military counselor. The Emperor said, "Planning strategies within a command tent to ensure victory on a battlefront a thousand miles away is Zhang Liang's great contribution." The Emperor let him select a place with 30,000 peasant households. Zhang Liang said, with deep feelings, "I started from Xiapi and met your Majesty in Liu. The Heavens designated me to assist Your Majesty. Your Majesty adopted my plans and some of my plans luckily worked successfully. I will be satisfied if Your Majesty creates me Marquis of Liu, the place where I first met Your Majesty. The tax on 30,000 peasant households is too much for me. Ten thousand will be enough." So the Emperor created Zhang Liang Marquis of Liu (now to the southeast of Peixian, Jiangsu Province).

The Emperor created Chen Ping Marquis of Huyou (now in Chenliu, Henan Province), entitled to the tax on 5,000 peasant households. Chen Ping said, "This merit does not belong to me." The Emperor said, "I defeated my enemy by using your stratagem. Isn't that your merit?" Chen Ping said, "Without Wei Wu Zhi, how could I have had the chance to work for Your Majesty?" The Emperor said, "You are a man who never forgets the kindness other people have shown you." Then the Emperor granted handsome awards to Wei Wu Zhi as well.

Cao Shen was created Marquis of Pingyang (now Linfen, Shanxi Province), enjoying the tax on 10,600 peasant households. Of all the generals, Cao Shen had rendered the greatest military services. He was wounded more than seventy times. He conquered many cities and captured vast lands from the enemies.

The Emperor created twenty-nine marquises in the period from December 202 BC to January 201 BC. The following table sets out the name, the title of the marquis, his merits, the number of the peasant households taxed for his support, and the time when he was created marquis.

Name	Title	Merits	Number of peasant households	Time in Which the Marquis was created
Cao Shen	Marquis of Pingyang (now Linfen, Shanxi Province)	He joined Liu Bang in Pei, entered Hanzhong as a general, took part in the pacification of Guanzhong, took part in the expedition of the State of Wei and the State of Qi	10,600	December 202 BC
Jin She	Marquis of Xinwu	He joined Liu Bang in the area of Wan as a retinue, entered Hanzhong as a high ranking officer of the cavalry, took part in the pacification of Guanzhong, took part in the war against Xiang Yu	5,300	December 202 BC
Wang Xi	Marquis of Qingyang (now Qinghe, Hebei Province)	He joined Liu Bang in Feng as a retinue, followed Liu Bang to Bashang, entered Hanzhong as a general of the cavalry, took part in the war against Xiang Yu as a general	3,100	December 202 BC
Xiahou Ying	Marquis of Ruyin (now Bengbu, Anhui Province)	He helped Liu Bang to take the city of Pei, served as the driver of Liu Bang's carriage, always accompanied Liu Bang during the war times	6,900	December 202 BC
Fu Kuan	Marquis of Yangling (now Gaoling, Shaanxi Province)	He joined Liu Bang in Hengyang as a retinue, followed Liu Bang to Bashang, entered Guanzhong as a general, took part in the pacification of Guanzhong, took part in the pacification of the State of Qi under the command of Han Xin	2,200	December 202 BC

	Marquis of Guangyan	He joined Liu Bang in Pei as a retinue, followed Liu Bang to Bashang as a high ranking officer, entered Hanzhgong as a general, took part in the pacification of the State of Zhao and the State of Yan as a general	2,200	
Zhao Ou				December 202 BC
Xue Ou	Marquis of Guangping (now Jize, Hebei Province)	He joined Liu Bang in Feng as a retinue, followed Liu Bang to Banshang, entered Hanzhong as the commander of Liu Bang's Guards, took part in the war against Xiang Yu as a general	4,500	December 202 BC
Chen Bi	Marquis of Boyang (now in the area of Shangcai, Henan Province)	He joined Liu Bang in Dang as a retinue, entered Hanzhong as a general, died in the battle of defending the walled road for transportation of food from Aocang to Xingyang when Xiang Yu attacked that walled road. He was granted the title of marquis posthumously		December 202 BC
Chen Ping	Marquis of Huyou (now in Chenliu, Henan Province)	He joined Liu Bang in 204 BC in Xiuwu, was appointed supervisor of the army, presented six effective stratagem to help Liu Bang to pacify the whole realm	5,000	December 202 BC
Chen Ying	Marquis of Tangyi (now north to Liuhe, Jiangsu Province)	During the war against the Qin Dynasty, he pacified the area of Dongyang. He joined Xiang Liang, and was appointed Premier of the State of Chu. After Xiang Yu died, he turned over to the State of Han and pacified the areas of Yuzhang (now Jiangxi Province) and Zhejiang (now Zhejiang Province).	1,800	December 202 BC

Lü Ze	Marquis of Zhoulü (now in the area of Dingtao, Shandong Province)	He was Lü Zhi's elder brother. He joined Liu Bang as a reti-nue. He followed Liu Bang to Hanzhong. He took part in the pacification of Guanzhong. He first led an army to march to Dang. When Liu Bang was defeated by Xiang Yu in Pengcheng, Liu Bang went to Dang to get help from Lü Ze. He assisted Liu Bang in the pacification of the whole realm.		January 201 B.C
Lü Shi Zhi	Marquis of Jiancheng (now in the area of north Jiangsu Province)	He was Lü Zhi's elder brother. He joined Liu Bang as a reti-nue. He followed Liu Bang to Hanzhong. He took part in the pacification of Guanzhong. He was sent by Liu Bang back to the area of Feng-Pei to escort Liu Bang's father and wife to Guanzhong. But Liu Bang's father and wife fell into the hands of Xiang Yu. He carried out military operations in that area.		January 201 BC
Zhang Liang	Marquis of Liu (now to the southeast of Peixian, Jiangsu Province)	He rose in Xiapi, joined liu Bang in Liu, assisted Liu Bang in the march to Guanzhong, protected Liu Bang in the banquet of Hongmen, helped Liu Bang to obtain the area of Hanzhong, presented strata-gem to assist Liu Bang in the pacification of the whole realm.	10,000	January 201 BC
Liu Chan (original name: Xiang Bo)	Marquis of Sheyang (now Sheyang, Jiangsu Province)	He took part in the war against the rule of the Qin Dynasty, protected Liu Bang in the banquet of Hongmen.		January 201 BC

Xiao He	Marquis of Zan (now in the west of Yongcheng, Henan Province)	He joined Liu Bang in Pei, followed Liu Bang to Hanzhong, served as premier to administrate the areas of Hanzhong and Guanzhong for Liu Bang, provided food and soldiers to Liu Bang from Guanzhong, assisted Liu Bang in the pacification of the whole realm, made laws and decrees.	8,000	January 201 BC
Li Shang	Marquis of Quzhou (now Quzhou, Hebei Province)	He joined Liu Bang as a general in the area of Chenliu, followed Liu Bang to Hanzhong, took part in the pacification of Guanzhong, and took part in the war against Xiang Yu.	4,800	January 201 BC
Zhou Bo	Marquis of Jiang (now Jiangxian in the southwest of Shanxi Province)	He joined Liu Bang in Pei, followed Liu Bang to Bashang, took part in the pacification of Guanzhong as a general, and took part in the war against Xiang Yu.	8,100	January 201 BC
Fan Kuai	Marquis of Wuyang (now Wuyang, Henan Province)	He joined Liu Bang in Pei as a retinue, followed Liu Bang to Bashang, then entered Hanzhong, took part in the pacification of Guanzhong as a General, took part in the war against Xiang Yu.	5,000	January 201 BC
Guan Ying	Marquis of Yingyin (now in Xuchang, Henan Province)	He joined Liu Bang in Dang as a retinue, followed Liu Bang to Hanzhong, took part in the pacification of Guanzhong, took part in the pacification of the State of Qi as general of cavalry under the command of Han Xin, and took part in the decisive battle in Gaixia to exterminate Xiang Yu.	5,000	January 201 BC

Zhou Chang	Marquis of Fenyin (now in Wanrong, Shanxi Province)	He joined Liu Bang in Pei, took part in the war against the rule of the Qin Dynasty as a civil official, followed Liu Bang to Hanzhong, defended Aocang resolutely as an official in charge of civil affairs, and served as the Minister of Supervision in the pacification of other kings.	2,800	January 201 BC
Wu Hu	Marquis of Liangzhou (now Zhouping, Shandong Province)	He joined Liu Bang when Liu Bang rose in Pei, followed Liu Bang in the war to overthrow the rule of the Qin Dynasty, took part in the war against Xiang Yu as a general	2,800	January 201 BC
Dong Xie	Marquis of Cheng (now Tai'an, Shandong Province)	He joined Liu Bang when Liu Bang rose in Pei, followed Liu Bang in the war to overthrow the rule of the Qin Dynasty, took part in the war against Xiang Yu as a general	2,800	January 201 BC
Kong Xi	Marquis of Liao (now Tanghe, Henan Province)	He joined Liu Bang in Dang as a body guard, entered Hanzhong as an officer in charge of food supply for the army, took part in the war against Xiang Yu as a general under the command of Han Xin, took part in the decisive battle in Gaixia to exterminate Xiang Yu.		January 201 BC
Chen He	Marquis of Fei (now Yutai, Shandong Province)	He joined Liu Bang in Dang as a retinue, entered Hanzhong as an officer in charge of food supply for the army, took part in the war against Xiang Yu as a general under the command of Han Xin, took part in the decisive battle in Gaixia to exterminate Xiang Yu.		January 201 BC

	Marquis of	Description		Date
Chen Xi	Marquis of Yangxia (now Taikang, Henan Province)	He commanded five hundred soldiers to join Liu Bang in the area of Wan, entered Hanzhong, pacified the area of Dai as a general, and took part in the pacification of the rebellion of Zang Tu, the King of the State of Yan.		January 201 BC
Zhou Zao	Marquis of Longlü (now Lin Xian, Henan Province)	He joined Liu Bang's army in Dang as a soldier, followed Liu Bang into Hanzhong as a low ranking officer, established great military contributions in the war against Xiang Yu.		January 201 BC
Ding Fu	Marquis of Yangdu (now in the area of Jiaonan Xian, Shandong Province)	He joined Liu Bang in Ye as a general of the State of Zhao, followed Liu Bang to Bashang, entered Hanzhong, took part in the pacification of Guanzhong, led an army to bring King of the State of Zhai into submission, took part in the war against Xiang Yu, killed Long Ju, the general under Xiang Yu.	7,800	January 201 BC
Lü Qing	Marquis of Xinyang (now Ningxiang, Hunan Province)	He joined Liu Bang as a county governor.	1,000	January 201 BC
Guo Meng	Marquis of Dongwu (in the area of Jiaonan Xian, Shandong Province)	He joined Liu Bang in the area of Xue, was under the command of Lü Ze, entered Hanzhong, took part in the pacification of Guanzhong as a general, defended Aocang, and took part in the war against Xiang Xu as a general.	2,000	January 201 BC

After the creation of the above marquises, an argument as to who should be ranked first place arose. After a heated debate, Liu Bang made the final decision. He said that Xiao He should be ranked first, and Liu Bang allowed Xiao He to come into the palace wearing his sword and to see the Emperor without observing any formalities.

65. The Creation of the Second Batch of Marquises

Having seen the difficulties that arose when he created the above mar-quises, the Emperor wanted to consider the merits of the other generals and ministers very carefully before he granted them any titles. So many generals had not yet been granted any titles at all, and they were unhappy about it. One day, when the Emperor was in the South Palace in Luoyang, he walked up a high bridge with Zhang Liang, from which they could see outside of the palace. When they looked out, they saw some generals sitting on the sandy ground talking to each other where they could not be heard. The Emperor asked Zhang Liang, "What are they talking about?" Zhang Liang said, "Does Your Majesty know that they are plotting a rebellion?" The Emperor said, "Peace and order have just been restored in the whole realm. Why should they rebel?" Zhang Liang said, "Your Majesty rose up as a commoner. These generals followed you through all kinds of hardships and dangers, fight-ing very hard for Your Majesty. With the help of these generals, Your Maj-esty has pacified the whole realm and now Your Majesty holds supreme power over the whole realm. Your Majesty has become the Emperor of the Han Dynasty. Your Majesty has created some marquises, marquises who are relatives and close friends of Your Majesty such as Xiao He and Cao Shen. And Your Majesty has severely punished those whom Your Majesty hates. Now the generals and officials expect that Your Majesty will consider their contributions and grant them some titles. They are afraid that Your Majesty might not grant all of them titles. And during the war period, any general might have made mistakes. Now they are afraid that Your Majesty may find faults with them and punish them. This is the reason why they have gathered together to plot a rebellion." The Emperor asked worriedly, "What shall I do?" Zhang Liang asked, "In the life of Your Majesty, whom does Your Majesty hate the most and whom do the ministers know that Your Majesty hates the most?" The Emperor said, "Everybody knows that I hate Yong Chi the most. Yong Chi joined me when I rose in Pei. When I took the city of Feng, I entrusted the defense of that city to him and I led the main force to take other cities. But later he turned over to the State of Wei and he defended the city of Feng for the State of Wei. When I heard that he had gone over to the State of Wei with the city of Feng, I returned to the city of Feng. I tried my best to persuade him to come back to my side. But he refused and insulted me. I ordered my army to attack the city but could not take it. Then I borrowed an army from Xiang Liang and took back the city. Yong Chi ran away to the State of Wei. But later, during the war against Xiang Yu, he turned to my side again as a general of the State of Zhao. I really wanted to kill him. I did not kill him—only because he made great contributions in the war again Xiang Yu." Then Zhang Liang said, "I would say, Your Majesty should create Yong Chi marquis immediately. When the generals and ministers know that even the person Your Majesty hates the most has been created marquis, all of them will rest assured."

One day in March 201 BC the Emperor held a grand banquet and all the generals and ministers were invited. At the banquet, the Emperor declared that he had decided to create Yong Chi Marquis of Shifang (now Shifang, Sichuan Province), enjoying the tax on 2,500 peasant households in Shifang. And the Emperor declared that he would urge Xiao He, the Premier, to measure the contributions of the generals and ministers and decide the titles to grant them in accordance with the contributions they had made. When the generals and ministers heard this, they all felt at ease. They said, "Since Yong Chi has been made marquis, we don't need to worry anymore."

In the period of March to August 201 BC, and in later years, Liu Bang created 124 marquises. The following table shows some of them:

Name	Title	Merits	Number of peasant households	Time in which the Marquis was created
Yong Chi	Marquis of Shifang (now Shifang, Sichuan Province)	He joined Liu Bang in 204 BC as a general of the State of Zhao, took part in the war against Xiang Yu.	2,500	March 201 BC
Cai Yin	Marquis of Feiru (now Lulong, Hebei Province)	He joined Liu Bang in 204 BC as the premier of the State of Wei, took part in the pacification of the State of Qi, and took part in the battle to defeat Long Ju.	1,000	March 201 BC

Chong Da	Marquis of Qucheng (in Zhuoxian, Hebei Province)	He joined Liu Bang in Dang with 37 followers from Qucheng, followed Liu Bang to Bashang, entered Hanzhong as a general under the command of Lü Ze, took part in the pacification of Guanzhong as the supervisor of the army, took part in the decisive battle in Gaixia to exterminate Xiang Yu.	4,000	March 201 BC
Han Xin	Marquis of Huaiyin (now Huaiyin, Jiangsu Province)	He joined Xiang Liang as a soldier, was under the command of Xiang Yu after Xiang Liang died, followed Xiang Yu to Xianyang, ran away from Xiang Yu's army to Hanzhong to join Liu Bang's army as an officer in charge of food supply, was recommended to Liu Bang by Xiao He and was appointed by Liu Bang commander-in-chief of the Han army, pacified the State of Wei, the State of Zhao and the State of Qi, was made King of the State of Qi, commanded the decisive battle in Gaixia to exterminate Xiang Yu, was made King of the State of Chu later, and was deposed and was made Marquis of Huaiyin.		June 201 BC
Yin Hui	Marquis of Gucheng (now in the area of Peixian, Jiangsu Province)	He joined Liu Bang as a close follower, followed Liu Bang into Hanzhong, and took part in the war against Xiang Yu as a general.	2,000	Mid 201 BC
Wang Ling	Marquis of Anguo (a place in the central part of Hebei Province)	He rose in Feng, carried out military operations in the area of Wan, when Liu Bang began the war against Xiang Yu, he joined Liu Bang with his own army.	5,000	August 201 BC
Ding Li	Marquis of Lecheng	He joined Liu Bang in Dang as a body guard of Liu Bang, entered Hanzhong as a general of the cavalry, took part in the pacification of Guanzhong, took part in the war against Xiang Yu, and took part in the battle against Long Ju in the area of the State of Qi under the command of Guan Ying.	1,000	August 201 BC

Shen Yi Ji	Marquis of Piyang (now in Jixian, Hebei Province)	He joined Liu Bang as a retinue, he took care of Liu Bang's father and wife and son during the war times, was taken prisoner together with Liu Bang's father and wife by Xiang Yu.		August 201 BC
Zhou Xie	Marquis of Kuaicheng (now in Qingyang area, Gansu Province)	He joined Liu Bang as a retinue in Pei, followed Liu Bang to Banshang, entered Hanzhong, and took part in the pacification of Guanzhong. When the army of Xiang Yu destroyed the walled road from Aocang to Xingyang, he followed Liu Bang to Shangguo where Han Xin's army was, was sent by Liu Bang as an envoy to see Xiang Yu to put forward Liu Bang's suggestion to negotiate peace, but Xiang Yu turned down the suggestion.	3,300	August 201 BC
Liu Tuo (original name: Xiang Tuo)	Marquis of Pinggao (a place in the area of Luoyang, Henan Province)	He was a relative of Xiang Yu. After the battle of Gaixia, he turned over to Liu Bang's side as the governor of Dang Prefecture. Liu Bang granted him the family name of Liu.	580	June 200 BC
Lü Sheng	Marquis of Nieyang (a place in the area of Nanyang, Henan Province)	He joined Liu Bang as a cavalry-man, in 203 BC followed Liu Bang to go out of the area of Guanzhong, took part in the war against Xiang Yu as a general of the cavalry, took part in the battle in Gaixia, fought face to face with Xiang Yu in Wujiang; after Xiang Yu killed himself, he got one part of Xiang Yu's dead body.	1,500	Mid 200 BC
Lü Ma Tong	Marquis of Zhongshui (a place in Zhuozhou, Hebei Province)	He joined Liu Bang in 206 BC as a general of the cavalry, took part in the battle in Haozhi, took part in the battle to kill Long Ju in the State of Qi, took part in the battle in Gaixia, fought face to face with Xiang Yu in Wujiang; after Xiang Yu killed himself, he got one part of Xiang Yu's dead body.	1,500	January 200 BC

Wang Yi	Marquis of Duyan (a place in the area of Nanyang, Henan Province)	He joined Liu Bang's army as a cavalryman in 204 BC in Xiapi, was under the command of Guan Ying, took part in the battle in Gaixia, fought face to face with Xiang Yu in Wujiang; after Xiang Yu killed himself, he got the head of Xiang Yu.	1,700	January 200 BC
Yang Xi	Marquis of Chiquan	He joined Liu Bang's army as a cavalryman in 205 BC, was under the command of Guan Ying, took part in the battle in Gaixia, fought face to face with Xiang Yu in Wujiang; after Xiang Yu killed himself, he got one part of Xiang Yu's dead body.	1,900	January 200 BC
Yang Wu	Marquis of Wufang (a place in Shangcai, Henan Province)	He joined Liu Bang's army in 206 BC, took part in the battle to take Xiayang, took part in the battle in Gaixia, fought face to face with Xiang Yu in Wujiang; after Xiang Yu killed himself, he got one part of Xiang Yu's dead body.	700	February 199 BC
Ji Tong (Ji Xin's son)	Marquis of Xiangping (a place near Linhuaiguan, Anhui Province)	Ji Xin joined Liu Bang when Liu Bang rose in Pei, took part in the war against the rule of the Qin Dynasty as a general, followed Liu Bang into Hanzhong, took part in the pacification of Guanzhong, when Xiang Yu laid siege to Xingyang and Xingyang was about to fall, he disguised as Liu Bang to surrender to Xiang Yu so that Liu Bang could escaped from Xingyang. When Xiang Yu found that he was not Liu Bang, Xiang Yu burned him to death. Liu Bang made him a marquis although he had died. Ji Xin's son Ji Tong succeeded the title.		September 199 BC

Zhou Cheng (Zhou Ke's son)	Marquise of Gaojing	Zhou Ke joined Liu Bang when Liu Bang rose in Pei, took part in the war against the rule of the Qin Dynasty, followed Liu Bang into Hanzhong as the Minister of Justice, took part in the war against Xiang Yu, defended Xingyang resolutely, was captured by Xiang Yu and killed by Xiang Yu. Liu Bang made him a marquis although he had died. Zhou Ke's son Zhou Cheng succeeded the title.		April 198 BC
Ren Ao	Marquis of Guang'e (a place in the area of Julu, Hebei Province)	He joined Liu Bang as a close friend of Liu Bang when Liu Bang rose in Pei, during the war against Xiang Yu, he was governor of Shangdang.	1,800	February 196 BC
Jin Jiang	Marquis of Fenyang (a place in Fenyang, Shanxi Province)	He led a thousand cavalrymen to join Liu Bang's army in Yangxia in 208 BC, took part in the war against Xiang Yu, and defeated the Chu army under Zhong Li Mei.		February 196

66. THE RISE OF THE HUNS

The Huns lived in the grasslands of Mongolia. They were nomadic people. They raised livestock such as horses, cattle and sheep. All the people of the Huns, even children, were able horsemen. So the Huns were called "people on horseback." They could all draw strong bows and shoot arrows. The army of the Huns could move very rapidly because they were all on horseback.

During the period of Warring States, they moved into the area of the Great Bend of the Yellow River (including the area of the east part of Ningxia Hui Autonomous Region, south part of Inner Mongolia Autonomous Region). After the First Emperor of the Qin Dynasty unified China, he ordered General Meng Tian to drive the Huns out of the Great Bend of the Yellow River in 215 BC with an army of 300,000 men. The Huns returned to the grasslands of Mongolia. Then the First Emperor of the Qin Dynasty sent more than 100,000 men to garrisons along the frontier to prevent the Huns from coming back to the Great Bend of the Yellow River.

At that time, the name of the king of the Huns was Tumen Luandi. He could not resist the army commanded by General Meng Tian of the Qin Dynasty. He led the Huns to retreat to the north. The situation was not favorable for the Huns. The State of Dong Hu (the Eastern Minority Nationality in the Northeast China) in the east was strong, and the State of Yuzhi (in the area of Gansu Province) was also strong. The Huns were in between these two strong states. Ten years later, General Meng Tian died and China was in great chaos. All the people who were garrisoned at the frontier left. So Tumen Luandi led the Huns back to the area of the Great Bend of the Yellow River.

Tumen's son Modu was the crown prince. Modu's mother died early. Tumen took another wife, and she became queen. Not long later, the queen gave birth to a son. Tumen liked the younger son better than the elder son, and wanted to deprive Modu of the title of crown prince and make his younger son the crown prince. Tumen sent Modu to the State of Yuzhi as a hostage to ensure the peace between the State of Yuzhi and the Huns. And not long after Modu had arrived in the State of Yuzhi, Tumen started a fierce attack on the State of Yuzhi. The King of Yuzhi was in a great rage and issued the order to kill Modu, the hostage. But Modu knew very well that his father's intention was to give the King of the State of Yuzhi an excuse to kill him so that his younger brother could become the successor to the throne. He stole a very good horse from the royal stable of the State of Yuzhi and rode back to his own state.

Modu was a strong man. Tumen appointed him commander of 10,000 men. Modu made some whistling arrows and he ordered that all his men should shoot at the target at which he shot his whistling arrow. He successfully trained these men into an army which absolutely obeyed his order. On a hunting trip with his father Tumen, when they were hunting groups of deer, in the confusion, Modu shot a whistling arrow at his father. All the men under him shot their arrows at the target which the whistling arrow was shooting at. Tumen was struck by many arrows and was killed immediately. Most of Tumen's followers surrendered, but still some of them put up a fight. Very soon those who had put up a fight were killed. Modu went back and dragged his stepmother and his younger brother out of their tents and killed them. Since Tumen, the king of the Huns, had been killed, Modu became the king the Huns. It was 209 BC.

Modu led his army to defeat the State of Dong Hu in the east and the State of Yuzhi in the west. He conquered the State of Loufan (in the areas of Ningwu and Kelan of Shanxi Province) and the State of Baiyang (in the southern area of the Great Bent of the Yellow River). He invaded the areas of the State of Yan and the State of Dai. At that time, Liu Bang was hard at war with Xiang Yu. China was in great chaos. So Modu took this chance to take back all the areas in the Great Bent of the Yellow River.

67. The King of the State of Haan Is Transferred to Defend the Northern Frontier against the Huns

Haan Xin, the King of Haan, was a capable man. The territory he ruled was uncomfortably close to Gong (now Gongyi, Henan Province) and Luoyang (now Luoyang, Henan Province) in the north, and uncomfortably close to Wan (now Nanyang, Henan Province) and Ye (now Yexian, Henan Province) in the south. The territory of the State of Haan also included Huaiyang (now Huaiyang, Henan Province). The whole territory of the State of Haan was of vital military importance. So the Emperor substituted the State of Haan with thirty-one counties in the Prefecture of Taiyuan (now northern part of Shanxi Province). The King of Haan was reinstated in Taiyuan to prevent the Huns from moving south. The Emperor suggested that the capital of the State of Haan should be moved to Jinyang (now in the area of Taiyuan City, Shanxi Province). But the King of the State of Haan pointed out that Jinyang was too far from the frontiers, and he suggested that Mayi (now Shuozhou, Shanxi Province) should be the capital. The Emperor agreed.

68. Haan Xin, the King of the State of Haan, Betrays the Han Dynasty and Defects to the Huns

In the autumn of 201 BC, Modu led any army of the Huns to lay siege to Mayi, the capital of the State of Haan. The King of the State of Haan sent several envoys to the Huns suing for peace. Meanwhile the Emperor sent an army to relieve the King of the State of Haan. When the Emperor found out that the King of the State of Haan had sent several envoys to the Huns, he suspected that he was looking to form an alliance with the Huns. So he sent an envoy to reproach the King of the State of Haan. The King of the State of Haan was afraid of being punished by the Emperor. So in September 201 BC, he surrendered to the Huns and handed Mayi to them. Then Modu led his army through Yanmenguan Pass (now in the north of Daixian, Shanxi Province) to attack Jinyang in the Taiyuan area (now Taiyuan, Shanxi Province).

In October 201 BC, the Emperor personally led an army on an expedition against Haan Xin. Generals Fan Kuai, Zhou Bo, Xiahou Ying and Guan Ying followed. Generals Fan Kuai and Zhou Bo marched their army to Tongti (now Qinxian, Shanxi Province). The army of the King of the State of Haan tried to resist the advancing army of the Han Dynasty and a battle was fought. The army of the King of the State of Haan was defeated and General Wang Xi under the King of the State of Haan was killed. Then Fan Kuai and Zhou Bo moved their army northward to the area of Taiyuan (now the area of Taiyuan, Shanxi Province) and overran six cities of that area.

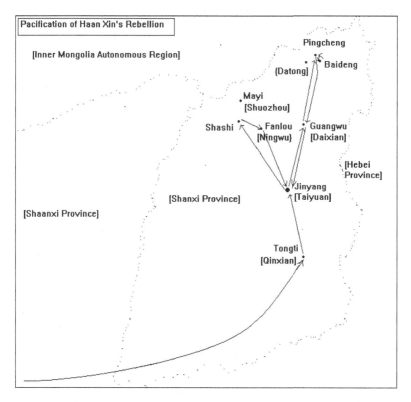

Then the army of the Han Dynasty marched to Jinyang. Haan Xin's army and the Hun cavalrymen were in that city. The Han army fought a battle with the army of the King of the State of Haan and the Huns outside the city of Jinyang. The armies under Generals Fan Kuai, Zhou Bo, Xiahou Ying and Guan Ying were victorious. They took the city of Jinyang. The Emperor and his army entered the city of Jinyang. The King of the State of Haan fled to the area of the state of the Huns.

Generals Fan Kuai, Zhou Bo and Guan Ying moved their army northward to Shashi (in the northwest of Ningwu, Shanxi Province). The Emperor had put the cavalrymen from the States of Yan, Zhao, Qi, Liang and Chu under the command of General Guan Ying. There they met with the army of the King of the State of Haan. The army of the Han Dynasty fiercely attacked the army of the State of Haan and defeated them. The army of the Han Dynasty chased the army of the State of Haan and the Hun cavalrymen for forty miles. Then Fan Kuai and Zhou Bo turned back to attack Fanlou (now Ningwu, Shanxi Province) and took three cities in Fanlou area. Then the Army of the Han Dynasty turned back to Jinyang.

Man Qiu Chen and Wang Huang, under the King of the State of Haan, who remained in the area of the State of Haan, made Zhao Li, a descendant of the former King of the State of Zhao, the king of that area. They collected the scattered soldiers of the State of Haan and organized them into an army. Man Qiu Chen, Wang Huang, Haan Xin and the Huns made a plan to defeat the army of the Emperor. Modu sent two of his generals commanding 10,000 Hun cavalrymen and the army led by Wang Huang to march south to Jinyang. When the Han army attacked them, they were immediately defeated, scattered and ran away. Then they gathered again. The Han army defeated them again and tracked them down. The weather changed suddenly and it became bitterly cold, and it snowed heavily. Most of the Han soldiers were frostbitten.

The Emperor was in Jinyang. He got word that Modu was in Daigu (now northeast to Datong City, Shanxi Province) and he wanted to attack Modu there. He sent several teams of scouts to Daigu to spy on the Huns. Modu hid his strongest warriors and strongest horses, so the scouts only saw the old and weak soldiers and weak horses. More than ten teams of scouts came back and reported to the Emperor what they had seen and said that the Huns could be easily defeated. Then the Emperor sent Liu Jing to spy on the Huns. Before Liu Jing came back, the Emperor sent all his army of 320,000 men north to pursue Modu, and the army had passed Gouzhu Mountain (also called Yanmen Mountain, in the north of Daixian, Shanxi Province). The Emperor had advanced to Guangwu (now southwest of Daixian, Shanxi Province). Liu Jing returned and said to the Emperor, "When the armies of two countries fight, each side shows the other its strength. But this time when I visited Daigu, I only saw old and weak soldiers and weak horses. Modu has shown his weakness to us. He is playing a trick and has laid an ambush to trap the Han army. I don't think that we should attack the Huns." By that time, the Han army had left for Daigu. At Liu Jing's words, the Emperor was in a furious rage. He shouted at Liu Jing, "You have attained your present position just by using your silver tongue. Now you are cursing my army with your wicked words." Then he gave the order to lock up Liu Jing in a prison in Guangwu.

The Emperor reached Pingcheng (now northeast to Datong City, Shanxi Province) ahead of his main force. Modu sent 400,000 select soldiers to surround the Emperor in Baideng, which was situated five kilometers southeast of Pingcheng. The Emperor was surrounded in Baideng for seven days. The Emperor could not get any reinforcements and the food was running out. The Emperor adopted Chen Ping's stratagem. He sent a secret envoy to present precious gifts to Modu's wife. Then Modu's wife said to Modu, "We should not press the Emperor of the Han Dynasty too hard. If you occupy the lands of the Han Dynasty, you will not inhabit these lands. The Heavens protect the Emperor of the Han Dynasty. You'd better think over it carefully." Modu had made an appointment with Wang Huang and Zhao Li to meet in Pingcheng, but they did not show up. This aroused Modu's suspicion that they might have conspired with the Emperor of the Han Dynasty. Then Modu lifted one corner of the encirclement. Incidentally, there was a heavy fog that day. Han soldiers sent out by the Emperor went out and then came back. The Huns did not notice them. Chen Ping suggested that the soldiers line up on both sides of the road leading out of the encirclement using bows with two arrows, ready to shoot in both directions at once. The Emperor made his break-through from the corner of the encirclement. As soon as the Emperor was out of the encirclement, he ordered Xiahou Ying to drive fast, but Xiahou Ying insisted on driving slowly. When they reached Pingcheng, the main force also arrived. So the Huns withdrew and left. The Han army also withdrew.

The Emperor ordered General Fan Kuai to suppress the turmoil in that area. The Emperor went back to Guangwu and released Liu Jing. He said to Liu Jing, "I did not take your advice and fell into the trap in Pingcheng set by Modu. I have already killed the ten teams of scouts who gave the faulty reports." Then he made Liu Jing Marquis of Guannei, entitled to the tax on 2,000 peasant households.

On his way back, the Emperor passed Quni (now Shunping, Hebei Province). The Emperor said, "What a great county this is! Except for Luoyang, I have never seen a greater county like this." Then he made Chen Ping Marquis of Quni, entitled to the tax on all the 30,000 households of that county. Chen Ping often followed the Emperor in expeditions and he presented six stratagems to the Emperor; he gained more tax households with each stratagem.

69. Liu Jing's Advice to Improve Relations with the Huns

Modu led his army to invade the territory in the north of the Han Dynasty many times. The Emperor was worried, and asked Liu Jing for advice. Liu Jing said, "Peace has just been resumed in China. All the soldiers are tired of wars. So it is impossible to bring the Huns to submission by war. Modu killed his own father and made himself king of the Huns. The Huns are not amenable to the doctrine of benevolence and righteousness. The only thing to do is to make a long term plan to make the future generations of Huns your subjects. But I am afraid that Your Majesty will not be willing to carry out this plan." The Emperor asked, "What plan is that?" Liu Jing said, "If Your Majesty is willing to send Your Majesty's eldest daughter to Modu as his wife, Modu will be very happy and make her queen. When she gives birth to a son, he will surely be made crown prince. Every year, Your Majesty can offer Modu gifts of articles that are abundant in China but are scarce in the State of the Huns. Then Modu will be grateful to Your Majesty. At the same time, Your Majesty may send some eloquent persons to the Huns to persuade the Huns to adopt a sense of propriety and righteousness. While Modu is alive, he will be the son-in-law of Your Majesty. After Modu dies, his son, that is, the grandson of Your Majesty, will ascend the throne of the Huns. I have never heard of a grandson who was hostile to his grandfather.

"In this way, the Huns can be brought to submission by and by. But if Your Majesty cannot bring himself to send his own daughter, but just sends any girl of your clan or any girl pretending to be the daughter of Your Majesty, it will be of no use, because when Modu finds out that she is not the daughter of Your Majesty, he will not make her queen." The Emperor said, "Your point is well made."

The Emperor decided to send his first-born daughter Princess Liu Yuan to Modu. But Empress Lü Zhi cried every day, begging the Emperor not to send their only daughter. The Empress said to the Emperor, "We have just this one daughter. Why should we abandon her to the wild area of the Huns?" And Princess Liu Yuan had been married to Zhang Ao, the former King of the State of Zhao. In the end, the Emperor gave up the idea of sending Princess Liu Yuan to Modu. At last, he selected a girl by the family name of Liu and sent her to Modu to be his wife.

70. The Emperor's Intention to Replace the Crown Prince

Liu Bang loved his concubine Qi Ji very much. She gave birth to a son for him. This son was named Liu Ru Yi. The Emperor thought that Crown Prince Liu Ying was soft and incompetent, and would not become a ruler as powerful as he was. He loved this younger son better than his older son. Although Liu Ru Yi had been made King of the State of Zhao, he did not go to the State of Zhao but stayed in Chang'an. Whenever the Emperor went out of Guanzhong to the east, Qi Ji accompanied him. She often cried in front of the Emperor, begging him to let her son to succeed the throne of the Han Dynasty. Empress Lü Zhi was older and stayed in Guanzhong, and never accompanied the Emperor anywhere. So the Emperor and the Empress drifted apart. The Emperor wanted to depose Crown Prince Liu Ying and replace him with Liu Ru Yi. All the ministers tried their best to persuade the Emperor not to do it. Zhou Chang, the vice premier, was resolutely against the Emperor's intention to replace the Crown Prince. The Emperor asked him why. Zhou Chang had a stutter, and he was very angry, so he stammered: "I can't say it well. But I think, think, think that won't, won't, won't do. Your Majesty wants to depose the Crown Prince. I think, think, think I won't, won't, won't take your order." The Emperor laughed heartily. The Empress was standing in the side room, listening. After court was over, the Empress met Zhou Chang. She knelt in front of him and expressed her hearty thanks to him. She said, "Without you, the Crown Prince would have been deposed."

At that time, Liu Ru Yi, the King of the State of Zhao, was only ten years old. The Emperor was afraid that Liu Ru Yi would be murdered after the Emperor died. Zhao Yao, the minister in charge of seals of the government, suggested that a capable minister of whom the Empress stood in awe be appointed as the premier of the State of Zhao. The Emperor asked, "And who do you think should be appointed?" Zhao Yao said, "Zhou Chang." So the Emperor appointed Zhou Chang premier of the State of Zhao.

71. CHEN XI'S REBELLION AND THE END OF HAN XIN

Originally, the Emperor appointed Chen Xi, the Marquis of Yangxia, the premier of the State Zhao. Chen Xi was also commander of the army stationed in the frontiers in Dai area (now north Shanxi Province). Before he went to the State of Zhao to take his position, he visited Han Xin, the Marquis of Huaiyin, to say good-bye to him. Han Xin walked with him into his garden. When they were all alone, Han Xin looked up at the sky, gave a long sigh and said, "Can I talk with you frankly?" Chen Xi said, "I will follow every instruction you give me." Han Xin said, "The place you are going to is of vital military importance. You are a favorite minister of the Emperor. He has great faith in you. When a person comes to inform the Emperor for the first time that you are going to rebel against him, he will not believe it. When he comes the second time, the Emperor will become suspicious. When he comes the third time, the Emperor will become very angry and will personally lead an army against you. Then I will cooperate with you within the capital. Then we may succeed in overthrowing the Emperor." Chen Xi had always believed that Han Xin was a capable man, so he said, "I will follow your instruction."

When he was in the position of the premier of the State of Zhao and the commander of the armies stationed in the frontiers of the area of Dai, Chen Xi had many followers. When he was on leave from the border in the area of Dai, he went past the State of Zhao with a retinue of more than a thousand carriages. The guesthouses in Handan (now Handan, Hebei Province), the capital of the State of Zhao, were all occupied by Chen Xi and his followers. Zhou Chang, the new premier of the State of Zhao, went to see the Emperor. He reported to the Emperor that Chen Xi had a large retinue and that he had exclusive military power in the army stationed in the frontiers of the Area of Dai. Zhou Chang suspected that Chen Xi was plotting a rebellion.

The Emperor sent envoys to investigate Chen Xi's people who were in the area of Dai. The investigations revealed that Chen Xi was involved in many illegal activities. Chen Xi was full of fear.

Haan Xin, the former King of the State of Haan, sent Wang Huang and Man Qiu Chen to persuade Chen Xi to rebel against the Emperor. In May 197 BC, when the Emperor's father died, the Emperor sent an envoy to summon Chen Xi back to Chang'an. In September, Chen Xi and Wang Huang started their rebellion. Chen Xi made himself King of Dai. He occupied the areas of Zhao and Dai. The Emperor personally led an army in an expedition against Chen Xi. When he arrived in Handan, he was very glad and said, "Chen Xi does not occupy Handan and defend it with the Zhang River as its natural barrier. This means that Chen Xi will certainly lose." Zhou Chang reported to the Emperor that of the twenty-five cities in the Changshan area (now Xingtai area in Hebei Province), twenty had been occupied by Chen Xi. He suggested that all of the governors of these twenty cities be severely punished. The Emperor asked, "Are they involved in the rebellion?" Zhou Chang answered, "No." The Emperor said, "They lost their cities because they did not have enough strength to resist the rebels. So they are innocent."

The Emperor asked Zhou Chang to select some strong men to lead the army. One day they saw four men. The Emperor said rudely, "You fools, can you lead an army for me?" The four men were embarrassed. They all knelt down. The Emperor granted each of them the tax on a thousand peasant households and made them generals. The ministers around him said, "Many generals who followed Your Majesty, fighting all the way to the area of Guanzhong, then to Hanzhong, then on the expedition against Xiang Yu, have not yet been rewarded. What services have these four men rendered that they deserve your award?" The Emperor said, "Chen Xi has rebelled. Chen Xi has occupied most of the areas of Zhao and Dai. I have sent out orders to the other states to send armies to take part in the expedition against Chen Xi. But none of kings of the other states has sent any army to help me. Now I have to rely on the soldiers in Handan. It is worthwhile granting the tax on one thousand peasant households to each of these four men so that they will fight bravely for the benefit of the people of Zhao." The ministers around the Emperor agreed with his idea. When the Emperor found out that many of the generals under Chen Xi were originally merchants, he spent a lot of money to buy them over. And many of Chen Xi's generals surrendered.

In the winter of 197 BC, the Emperor was in Handan. Hou Chang, one of Chen Xi's generals, a general who commanded more than 10,000 troops, was moving about threateningly. Wang Huang commanded a thousand cavalrymen who were stationed in Quni (now Shunping, Hebei Province). Zhang Chun sent more than 10,000 men across the Yellow River to attack Liaocheng (now Liaocheng, Shandong Province). General Guo Meng of the Han Dynasty and the generals of the State of Qi commanded by Cao Shen, the premier of the State of Qi, defeated Zhang Chun in Liaocheng. General Zhou Bo, the minister in charge of national military affairs of the Han Dynasty, entered the area of Dai from Taiyuan (now Taiyuan, Shanxi Province). He attacked Mayi (now Shuozhou, Shanxi Province), but the army in Mayi would not surrender. Zhou Bo attacked fiercely and inflicted great damage on the city. The Emperor attacked Dongyuan (now Zhengding, Hebei Province) and took it. The Emperor offered a handsome award for the capture of Wang Huang and Man Qiu Chen. Their own officers captured Wang Huang and Man Qiu Chen and brought them before the Emperor. Chen Xi's army was then totally defeated.

Han Xin did not go with the Emperor to put down Chen Xi's rebellion on the excuse that he was ill. He sent secret agents to Chen Xi to convey a secret plan and pass secret information. Han Xin conspired with his followers to release all the criminals in Chang'an on a false order from the Emperor to pardon them in order to make a surprise attack on the Empress and the Crown Prince. When he was ready to act, he waited for Chen Xi's reply. But at that critical moment, one of his followers committed some offence against Han Xin. Han Xin put that man into prison and was going to kill him. In January 196 BC, that man's brother reported to the Empress that Han Xin was preparing to attack the Empress and the Crown Prince. The Empress wanted to summon Han Xin to the palace, but she was afraid that Han Xin would make an excuse and not come. Then she consulted with Xiao He, and they made a plan. They sent a man out of the capital, and the man came back pretending that he had been sent back by the Emperor. He reported to the Empress that Chen Xi had been killed. All the marquises in the capital and the ministers came to the palace to express their congratulations to the Empress. Xiao He personally went to Han Xin's residence and said to Han Xin, "Although you are ill, you must go to the palace to express your congratulations on the great victory." Han Xin had to go. As soon as he arrived, the Empress ordered the warriors seize him and to tie him up.

Then he was dragged to a room in the palace and executed. Before he was executed, Han Xin said, "I regret that I did not take Kuai Che's advice. That is the reason why I fell into the trap laid by that woman today. This is destiny." All the members of Han Xin's family, all the members of the families of his father, and of his mother, were killed.

72. The End of Haan Xin, the Former King of the State of Haan

In the spring of 196 BC, Haan Xin, the former King of the State of Haan, was staying in Sanhe (now Dingxiang, Shanxi Province) with the Huns, opposing the Han Dynasty. The Emperor sent General Chai Wu with a great army to attack Haan Xin and the Huns in Sanhe. Before he attacked the city, General Chai Wu sent an envoy to Sanhe to see Haan Xin. The envoy entered the city and presented a letter written by General Chai Wu to Haan Xin. The letter read, "The Emperor is lenient and benevolent. When a king betrays him and runs away, if he comes back, the Emperor will forgive him and will put him back to his original position. The Emperor will pardon him and will not kill him. You know this very well from your own experience. You were defeated and had to surrender to the Huns. You have not committed serious crimes. You should come back immediately." Then Haan Xin wrote a letter in reply to the letter written by General Chai Wu. Haan Xin wrote, "The Emperor promoted me from an ordinary person and made me King of the State of Haan. I will never forget his kindness to me. But I have committed many crimes which are not pardonable. In the battle in Xingyang, Zhong Gong, Zhou Ke and I were captured by Xiang Yu. Zhong Gong and Zhou Ke would not surrender and were killed by Xiang Yu. But I was not killed; I was put into prison by Xiang Yu. This is my first crime. When the Huns attacked Mayi, I was not able to stand fast and hold the city. I surrendered to the Huns with the city of Mayi. This is my second crime. Now I am a general commanding an army to fight for the Huns against the army commanded by you who were sent by the Emperor. This is my third crime. In the past, Wen Zhong and Fan Li of the State of Yue, who had not committed any such crimes, were executed by the King of Yue. I have committed all three crimes. It is impossible for me to be pardoned by the Emperor. Now I am hiding in the mountains and valleys. Now I have surrendered to the Huns. I have to try my best to please the Huns. I long to go back home. I miss home as much as a blind man misses the days when he still could see and a disabled man lying in bed misses the days when he still could walk. But I know very well that this cannot be realized in my lifetime." When General Chai Wu got the letter and knew that Haan Xin would not turn over to the Han Dynasty, he started a fierce attack on the city of Sanhe. The army of the Han Dynasty broke into the city. General Chai Wu and Haan Xin met in the battlefield. After several bouts, General Chai Wu killed Haan Xin.

After the area of Dai had been pacified, the Emperor made his son Liu Heng King of the State of Dai. The Capital of the State of Dai was Jinyang (now Taiyuan, Shanxi Province).

73. Kuai Che Is Spared by the Emperor

When the Emperor came back to Luoyang from his expedition to quell Chen Xi's rebellion, he heard the news that Han Xin had been executed. He was glad and at the same time had pity on him. The Emperor asked the Empress whether Han Xin had left any words before he was executed. The Empress said, "Han Xin said that he regretted that he did not take Kuai Che's advice." The Emperor gave the order to arrest Kuai Che from the State of Qi. When Kuai Che was brought before the Emperor, the Emperor asked, "Did you instigate Han Xin to betray me?" Kuai Che answered, "Yes. I really did suggest that he should betray you. But that fool did not take my advice. That is why he ended up like this. If he had taken my advice, Your Majesty would not have been able to kill him."

The Emperor was in a rage and ordered to have Kuai Che boiled to death. Kuai Che said, "It is unjust to kill me." The Emperor said, "You instigated Han Xin to betray me. Why is it unjust to kill you?" Kuai Che said, "The Qin Dynasty lost its power. The power of the Qin Dynasty was like a deer. Everyone in China was running after this deer. Only the most capable person who ran the fastest could catch the deer. The dog of Thief Zhi barked at Yao, the most virtuous emperor in Chinese history. That doesn't mean that Yao was not a virtuous emperor. The dog barked at him only because Yao was not its master. At that time, I only knew Han Xin. I did not know Your Majesty. At that time, China was in great chaos. Many people were doing their best to win the ruling power, just as Your Majesty was doing your best to get it. They failed only because they were not as capable as Your Majesty. Will you cook them all?" The Emperor at last spared him and let him go.

74. The Death of Peng Yue, the King of the State of Liang

When the Emperor started his expedition against Chen Xi, he ordered Peng Yue to command his army to join in the expedition. But Peng Yue did not go personally; he said he was ill. He sent some generals commanding his army to Handan. The Emperor was very angry and sent an envoy to reprimand him. The King of the State of Liang was full of fear and wanted to go personally to apologize to the Emperor. Hu Zhe, a general under Peng Yue, said, "You did not go at the beginning. If you go after the Emperor has reprimanded you, he will arrest you. It would be better for you to rise up against the Emperor." The King of the State of Liang would not listen to him.

The premier of the State of Liang committed some offence against the King of the State of Liang and Peng Yue was going to punish him. He ran away to see the Emperor and reported to the Emperor that the King of the State of Liang and his general Hu Zhe were conspiring to rebel. The Emperor sent some envoys to the State of Liang and arrested Peng Yue by surprise. Then Peng Yue was brought to Luoyang and was imprisoned there. The official in charge of the case found him guilty of conspiracy and the official suggested that Peng Yue be punished according to the law. But the Emperor pardoned him and deposed him as the King of the State of Liang. Peng Yue was sent into exile to Qingyi of Shu (now Mingshan, Sichuan Province). On his way west, he met with the Empress, who was coming from Chang'an. Peng Yue cried and told the Empress that he was innocent and hoped that he would be sent to Changyi (now southeast of Juye, Shandong Province) where he had originally stood up against the rule of the Qin Dynasty. The Empress promised to help him and brought him back to Luoyang. The Empress said to the Emperor, "Peng Yue is a fierce warrior. You have sent him to Shu. That will cause future trouble. It would better to find another excuse to kill him. I have brought him back." Then the Empress secretly asked Peng Yue's followers to accuse Peng Yue of conspiring to rebel again. Wang Tian Kai, the Minister of Justice, presented a memorandum to the Emperor proposing that the entire families of Peng Yue, and of his father and of his mother, be exterminated. The Emperor approved his memorandum and the execution of Peng Yue took place in March 196 BC.

Peng Yue's head was cut off, put in a small cage and hung on a post in front of the gate of Luoyang. The Emperor issued an order to the effect that anyone who paid respects to the head of Peng Yue should be arrested immediately. Luan Bu, a minister of the State of Liang, had been sent by Peng Yue on a mission to the State of Qi. When he came back from the mission, he was told that Peng Yue had been executed. Then he went to Luoyang. When he saw the head of Peng Yue hanging on a post in front of the city gate of Luoyang, he knelt down, wept and paid his respects to Peng Yue. He was immediately arrested and the incident was reported to the Emperor. The Emperor ordered Luan Bu be brought before him. When Luan Bu was brought before the Emperor, the Emperor scolded him and ordered him to be boiled to death. Then Luan Bu was taken in front of the big tripod holding a vat of boiling water. He turned his head and said, "I wish to say something to Your Majesty before I die." The Emperor asked, "What do you want to say?" Luan Bu said, "When Your Majesty was defeated in Pengcheng and retreated to Xingyang and Chenggao, Xiang Yu pursued Your Majesty to that area. Xiang Yu could not advance further west only because Peng Yue occupied the area of Liang and allied with Your Majesty; he cut the supply lines to Xiang Yu's army and attacked the rear of Xiang Yu's army. At that time, if Peng Yue had allied with Xiang Yu, Your Majesty would surely have lost; if he allied with Your Majesty, Xiang Yu was sure to lose. And in the decisive battle of Gaixia, Xiang Yu would not have been destroyed if Peng Yue had not come with his great army. Now the whole realm is quiet, and Your Majesty made Peng Yue King of the State of Liang. He wanted to pass this title on to many generations. But Your Majesty has put him to death only because he could not personally lead his army to join Your Majesty in an expedition. Peng Yue really was ill but Your Majesty suspected that he wanted to rebel. The Minister of Justice could not find any real facts to prove that Peng Yue was going to rebel. He was executed for some trivial offences. I am afraid that from now on, everyone who has rendered outstanding services in the wartime will feel insecure and worry about his own safety. Now that Peng Yue, the King of the State of Liang, is dead, I would rather die than go on living. That is all I have to say. You may cook me now." At these words, the Emperor changed his mind. He released Luan Bu and appointed him commander of the royal guards.

The Emperor made his fifth son Liu Hui King of the State of Liang. Not long later, the Emperor made his sixth son Liu You King of the State of Huaiyang.

75. Zhang Liang's Plan to Stabilize the Position of the Crown Prince

The Emperor still intended to depose Liu Ying as the Crown Prince and make his younger son Liu Ru Yi crown prince. Many ministers spoke out against this intention. But all these efforts had not made the Emperor change his mind. Lü Zhi, the Empress, was worried. She did not know what should be done to preserve her son's position. Someone suggested to the Empress, "Zhang Liang is a very good plan maker. The Emperor has faith in him." Then the Empress sent her brother Lü Ze, the Marquis of Zhoulü, to visit Zhang Liang. He said to Zhang Liang, "You have been the councilor of the Emperor. You have presented many stratagems to the Emperor. Now the Emperor is going to depose Liu Ying as the Crown Prince and make Liu Ru Yi the crown prince. Doesn't this bother you?" Zhang Liang said, "The Emperor adopted my stratagems in desperate situations in wartime. Now the whole realm is in peace. His Majesty wants to replace the Crown Prince with another son he loves. This is a family matter. More than a hundred ministers have expressed their opinions against his intention to replace the Crown Prince. But they were not able to make His Majesty change his mind." Lü Ze said, "Anyway, you must make a plan for me to preserve the Crown Prince."

Zhang Liang said, "It is impossible to persuade His Majesty by words. There are four wise and virtuous old men hiding in the mountains. They are Tang Xuan Ming, Qi Li Ji, Cui Guang and Zhou Shu. The Emperor wanted to summon them to serve His Majesty. But these four men refused to come because the Emperor is rude to people. They have gone into hiding in the Shangshan Mountains. They do not want to serve His Majesty. But the Emperor respects these four old men. If the Crown Prince would write a letter inviting them politely to assist the Crown Prince, and you send an envoy to go to the mountains to visit them with the letter and valuable gifts, they would gladly come. If they come, they should follow the Crown Prince into the court. When the Emperor sees them, His Majesty will ask who they are. When His Majesty learns that the four virtuous old men have come to assist the Crown Prince, it might help to secure his position."

In accordance with the instruction of Zhang Liang, Lü Ze sent an envoy to the Shangshan Mountains to look for the four virtuous old men, with a letter written by the Crown Prince and with valuable gifts. When the envoy found the four old men, he politely expressed the Crown Prince's intention to invite the four old men to assist him. The four old men gladly accepted the invitation and followed the envoy to Chang'an. They stayed in Lü Ze's home for the time being.

76. The Rebellion of Ying Bu, the King of the State of Huainan

When Ying Bu, the King of the State of Huainan, heard that Han Xin, Marquis of Huaiyin, had been executed in Chang'an, he was full of fear. When Peng Yue was killed, the Emperor had Peng Yue's flesh made into chopped salted meat and had it put into pots to present to the other kings. When the envoys came to the State of Huainan with the chopped salted meat made from Peng Yue's dead body, Ying Bu, the King of the State of Huainan, was on a hunting trip. When he saw the pot of meat, he felt sick and was in great fear. He secretly ordered his generals to mobilize his army and sent agents out to other prefectures to watch how things evolved.

Ying Bu's beautiful concubine whom he loved very much felt ill and went to see a doctor. The doctor's house was opposite to the house of Ben He, the minister in charge of the military affairs of the State of Huainan. Ben He brought her precious gifts and he drank wine with the concubine in the doctor's house. Ying Bu suspected that Ben He had committed adultery with his concubine, and he wanted to arrest Ben He. Ben He escaped and went to Chang'an. He reported to the Emperor that Ying Bu was plotting a rebellion. In the report, he told the Emperor that there were signs that showed Ying Bu was intending to rebel, although he had not actually rebelled, and that Ying Bu should be arrested before he could start. The Emperor read his report and discussed this matter with Xiao He, the premier. Premier Xiao He said, "I cannot find any reason why Ying Bu should rebel. I suspect that Ben He has framed Ying Bu out of personal hatred. We'd better keep Ben He in custody while we send an envoy to make a secret investigation on the King of the State of Huainan." The Emperor accepted Xiao He's suggestion.

When the King of the State of Huainan found that Ben He had escaped to Chang'an and reported to the Emperor that he was going to rebel, he knew that the Emperor must be suspicious of him. In July 196 BC, when the envoy was sent to investigate him, Ying Bu did rise in rebellion. He exterminated Ben He's entire family. When the information that Ying Bu had rebelled reached the Emperor, he released Ben He and made him a general. The Emperor called in all the generals and asked them what was the best way to deal with Ying Bu. They all said that an army should be sent to kill that treacherous rat.

Xiahou Ying, the Marquis of Ruyin, consulted with Xue Gong, the former premier of the State of Chu. Xue Gong said, "It is not strange that Ying Bu should rebel." Xiahou Ying asked, "The Emperor treated him very well. His Majesty has made him King of the State of Huainan. Why should he rebel?" Xue Gong said, "Last year, Peng Yue, the King of the State of Liang, was killed. The year before last, Han Xin, the former King of the State of Chu, was killed. Peng Yue, Han Xin and Ying Bu had made almost equal contributions in the war against Xiang Yu. Since Han Xin and Peng Yue have been killed, Ying Bu is afraid that his turn will come sooner or later. That's why he has rebelled. It is not at all strange." Xiahou Ying told the Emperor what Xue Gong had said.

The Emperor summoned Xue Gong to the palace and asked him what should be done. Xue Gong said, "If Ying Bu chooses his best option, Your Majesty will lose the territory to the east of the Xiao Shan Mountain. If he adopts the second best option, it is unclear who will win. If he adopts the worst option, Your Majesty may rest at ease." The Emperor asked, "What is his best option?" Xue Gong Said, "His best option is to send an army east to take the area of Wu, then send an army to occupy the State of Chu, then take the State of Qi and occupy the area of Lu, send an envoy with a letter to the States of Yan and Zhao and let them defend themselves. Then Your Majesty will lose the areas to the east of the Xiao Shan Mountain." The Emperor asked, "What is his second best option?" Xue Gong said, "His second best option is to take the area of Wu, occupy the State of Chu, and take the area of Wei, then take Aocang and use the food stored there; and conquer Chenggao and take advantage of the natural barriers there. In that case, it's not clear who will win." The Emperor asked, "What is his worst option?" Xue Gong said, "His worst option is to take the area of Wu, then take Xiacai; and transport all the army supplies and equipment to Yue. He will end up in Changsha. If he follows that option, Your Majesty may rest easy." The Emperor asked, "Which option do you think he will choose?" Xue Gong answered with great certainty, "He will choose the worst option." The Emperor asked, "Why?" Xue Gong answered, "Ying Bu was a criminal working in Lishan under the Qin Dynasty. Now he is a king. He will only think of his own safety. He will not consider the good of the people. He will not work for the long-term good. That's why he is sure to take the worst option." The

Emperor felt relieved. He granted Xue Gong the tax on a thousand peasant households, and then made his seventh son Liu Chang King of the State of Huainan.

At that time, the Emperor was very ill and did not want to see his ministers and generals. He just stayed in his bedroom in the palace and issued an order that no one should be allowed to go into his bedroom. General Guan Ying and General Zhou Bo came and wanted to see the Emperor urgently, but they were kept away. The Emperor stayed in his bedroom and did not see any of his generals and ministers for more than ten days. Finally, General Fan Kuai ignored the order, pushed away the guards, went through the door and entered the bedroom. Other generals and ministers followed. They found the Emperor sleeping with his head on the thighs of a eunuch. General Fan Kuai said to the Emperor, with tears in his eyes, "In the past, Your Majesty rose up in Pei with us and fought very hard to conquer the whole realm. How powerful and great Your Majesty was at that time! Now the whole realm is at peace. How weary Your Majesty looks! Now Your Majesty is ill. The ministers and generals are all worried about Your Majesty. Your Majesty does not discuss state affairs with the ministers and generals. Your Majesty just stays with a eunuch. Does Your Majesty recall how Zhao Gao, a eunuch of the Qin Dynasty, usurped the power of the Qin Dynasty?" At these words, the Emperor rose up with a smile.

The Emperor wanted the Crown Prince to command the generals in the expedition against Ying Bu. The four virtuous old men who had become the Crown Prince's advisers discussed it among themselves. "We have come to help to protect the position of the Crown Prince. If the Crown Prince should lead an army to attack Ying Bu, he will be in great danger." They said to Lü Ze, "The Emperor has asked the Crown Prince to lead this expedition. If the Crown Prince succeeds in putting down Ying Bu's rebellion and makes great contributions, it will not add anything to his position as Crown Prince. If he fails, he will be in grave danger. The generals the Crown Prince is going to command are all fierce generals who have followed the Emperor in the wars to conquer the whole realm. Asking the Crown Prince to command these fierce generals is like asking a sheep to command a pack of tigers and wolves. They will not obey his orders and will not do their best in the war. It is clear that the Crown Prince will fail in this expedition. Now, Lady Qi Ji stays with the Emperor day and night. She often brings her son Ru Yi to the Emperor and the Emperor likes this son the best. The Emperor

once said, 'I will not allow the son whom I don't like to occupy a higher position than that of the son I like best.' It is clear that the Emperor has made
up his mind to replace the Crown Prince with Ru Yi, the son His Majesty
likes best. How about this: you can suggest to the Empress that she should
find a chance to weep before the Emperor and say to His Majesty, 'Ying Bu
is a fierce general and very capable in fighting in battles. The generals Your
Majesty is going to send are all as fierce as Ying Bu. If the Crown Prince is
asked to command these generals, it would be like asking a sheep to command the tigers and wolves. They will not obey his orders. If Ying Bu knows
that the Crown Prince is in command of the expedition, he will march his
army westward boldly. Although Your Majesty is ill, Your Majesty might
still lead the campaign, lying on a wagon with covers on all sides. Then the
generals will all do their best.' As hard as that would be for the Emperor, it
would be worthwhile for the sake of his wife and children." Lü Ze went to
see the Empress that night. Then the Empress went to see the Emperor and
begged the Emperor, with tears in her eyes, not to send the Crown Prince
to command the expedition and said that the Emperor should command
the expedition for the sake of the children. The Emperor said, "I have been
thinking that the Crown Prince is too weak to take this responsibility. I
will have to go myself." Then the Emperor personally led an army to fight
against Ying Bu.

His ministers stayed in Chang'an. They all saw the Emperor off to
Bashang. Even Zhang Liang, who was seriously ill, got up from his bed to see
the Emperor off. He said to the Emperor, "I should go with Your Majesty.
It is a pity that I am so seriously ill. Ying Bu is fierce. I hope Your Majesty
will not confront Ying Bu personally in a battle of physical strength." Zhang
Liang took this chance to persuade the Emperor to appoint the Crown
Prince Commander-in-chief of the army which remained in the areas of
Guanzhong. The Emperor raised an army of 30,000 men as guards for the
Crown Prince and this army stationed in Bashang.

The Emperor sent an envoy to the State of Qi to order Liu Fei, the King
of the State of Qi, to lead an army to join him in the expedition against Ying
Bu. When the King of the State of Qi got the order, he led an army of a
120,000 men commanded by Cao Shen, the premier of the State of Qi, to
march out of the State of Qi to join force with the Emperor.

When Ying Bu rose in rebellion, he said to the generals under him, "The
Emperor is already old. He is tired of fighting. So he will not come to fight

with me. He will send his generals. Of all his generals, I only feared Han Xin and Peng Yue. Now they are dead, and I am not afraid of any of his generals." As Xue Gong had expected, Ying Bu first attacked the State of Jing (now south part of Jiangsu Province). Liu Jia, the King of the State of Jing, was defeated and was killed in Fuling (now Xuyi, Jiangsu Province). Then Ying Bu crossed the Huai River to attack the State of Chu. Liu Jiao, the King of the State of Chu, sent an army to fight against Ying Bu in the area between Xu and Tong (now the area around Suining, Jiangsu Province). The Chu commander divided his forces into three armies so that when one army was attacked, the other two might come to the rescue. "Don't forget," someone said to the Chu commander, "Ying Bu is skillful in commanding his army. The people all over China are afraid of him. According to the rules of the art of war, if the battle takes place in the area ruled by the king of that area, the local army will easily be scattered because the soldiers can run away to their own homes. Now you have divided your army into three. When one of them is defeated, the other two will simply run away. Why would the other two armies come to the rescue?" The commander paid him no heed.

Ying Bu defeated one of the three Chu armies; the other two scattered and ran away to their own homes as the man had said. Ying Bu marched his army to the west. In October 196 BC, the army of the State of Qi commanded by Liu Fei and Cao Shen joined force with the army of the Han Dynasty under the command of the Emperor in Dan (now Dancheng, Henan Province). The Emperor's army met Ying Bu's army in the west of Dan. The deployment of Ying Bu's army was excellent. The Emperor's army pitched their camps in Yongcheng (within the area of Dancheng). He looked at the formations of Ying Bu's army, which were very much like those deployed by Xiang Yu. This made the Emperor hate Ying Bu all the more. Before the battle started, the Emperor met Ying Bu from afar. The Emperor asked, "Why have you rebelled?" Ying Bu answered, "I want to be Emperor!" The Emperor was very angry and cursed him loudly. A fierce battle started. Ying Bu's army was defeated. They crossed the Huai River and stopped to fight some more. Several battles were fought. Ying Bu lost all these battles and escaped to the south of the Yangtze River with a hundred followers. The Emperor sent some generals to pursue Ying Bu, and he started his journey for home.

The general who was in charge of pursuing Ying Bu fought two battles on the north bank and south bank of Tao River (in Hunan Province). He inflicted a disastrous defeat on Ying Bu's followers. Then the King of Changsha sent someone to lure Ying Bu into following him to a wild, desolate place, pretending that he was taking him to Yue. Ying Bu was brought to a farmhouse where he was killed by the local people of Boyang (in Hunan Province).

77. The Emperor's Visit to Pei, His Hometown

On his way back from the expedition against Ying Bu, the Emperor went past Pei where he had started his career. The Emperor held a grand banquet to entertain all his old friends and the elders of Pei in the palace of Pei. The Emperor was very happy to talk and laugh freely with his old friends and the elders of Pei. They drank a lot of wine. The Emperor sang the following lines in a sorrowful voice:

A powerful wind is rising high,

It blows wild clouds across the sky.

I have won the power to rule the whole realm with great might.

Back in my birthplace which I have missed for so long,

I wish for warriors to defend all the borders, fierce and strong.

One hundred and twenty children sang in company with the Emperor in their sweet voices. The Emperor stood up and danced to the song sung by the children. He felt such a strong mood of sadness that tears ran down his cheeks. He said to the elders of Pei, "I have been away from home for a long time and I have always missed my hometown. I have made Chang'an the capital and I live there, far from home. But after I die, my soul will still always think of Pei. I started my career to overthrow the rule of the Qin Dynasty from Pei and I obtained the power to rule over China. I will exempt all the people in Pei from paying tax forever." All the people of Pei were grateful to the Emperor. The Emperor stayed in Pei for about ten days. When he left, all the people went out to see him off with tears. The Emperor was deeply touched by the strong emotion of the people of Pei. He decided to stay there for three more days. In these three days, the Emperor held banquets to entertain the people of Pei. At one of the banquets, an old man went forward to the Emperor and proposed a toast to his health. Then he said, "We are grateful to Your Majesty for exempting us from tax forever. But the people of Feng have not been exempted from tax. We hope that Your Majesty has pity on the people of Feng and exempts them from paying tax." The Emperor said, "I grew up in the place of Feng. I will never forget this place. I have not exempted the people of Feng from paying tax only because they assisted Yong Chi in holding the city of Feng for the State of Wei against me." But the elders of Pei continued to beg the Emperor to grant the exemption to the people of Feng. At last, the Emperor gave his consent.

78. Liu Bi Is Made King of the State of Wu

When Ying Bu attacked the State of Jing, Liu Jia, the King of the State of Jing, was killed. He did not leave any heir, so the Emperor changed the State of Jing into the State of Wu, and in October 196 BC, the Emperor made Liu Bi, the son of his elder brother Liu Zhong, King of the State of Wu. There were fifty-three cities in three prefectures in the State of Wu.

79. The Areas of Dai Are Pacified

General Zhou Bo was sent to pacify the area of Dai (northeast part of Shanxi Province and northwest part of Hebei Province). He started from Taiyuan (now Taiyuan, Shanxi Province). He pacified seventeen counties of Yanmen Prefecture (around Yuyou in the north of Shanxi Province) and twelve counties of Yunzhong Prefecture (around Tuoketuo, Inner Mongolia). In October 196 BC, Zhou Bo pursued Chen Xi to Lingqiu (now Lingqiu, Shanxi Province). A battle was fought. Chen Xi's army was defeated. Chen Xi was killed in that battle. Chen Xi's Premier Cheng Zong, General Chen Wu and General Gao Si were all captured. Zhou Bo recovered nine counties of the area of Dai Prefecture.

80. Liu Bang's Last Effort to Replace the Crown Prince

After the Emperor came back from his expedition against Ying Bu, his illness worsened. At this point, he felt it was more important to replace the Crown Prince. Zhang Liang tried his best to persuade him to give up the idea, but the Emperor would not listen to him. Zhang Liang got so angry that he stopped attending to state affairs, claiming illness. Shusun Tong, the minister in charge of memorial ceremonies, said to the Emperor, "In the past, when Duke Xian of the State of Jin deposed the crown prince Shen Sheng and replaced him with Xi Qi, the younger son born by Li Ji, the concubine whom the Duke loved very much, it led to chaos in the State of Jin for several decades and became a laughing-stock for the people all over

China. The First Emperor of the Qin Dynasty did not appoint his eldest son Ying Fu Su as his successor while he was alive and this provided the chance for Zhao Gao to make Ying Hu Hai the crown prince by cheating. This led to the fall of the Qin Dynasty. Your Majesty saw this with your own eyes. Now the Crown Prince is benevolent and dutiful. The people all over China love him. The Empress has shared weal and woe with Your Majesty. Your Majesty should not betray her. If Your Majesty is determined to depose the Crown Prince and replace him with the younger son, I am willing to be killed and let the blood from my neck spill all over the ground." The Emperor said, "Okay, okay. I was just joking." Shusun Tong said, "The Crown Prince is the foundation of the whole realm. If the foundation shakes, the whole realm will shake. Why should Your Majesty make a joke with such an important matter?" The Emperor understood that the ministers did not support Liu Ru Yi, so the Emperor pretended that he had given up the idea; but he still wanted to replace the Crown Prince.

The Emperor held a banquet to entertain his ministers and generals. The Crown Prince also attended the banquet. The Emperor found that behind the Crown Prince stood four old men. They were all over eighty years old. The hair and beards of these four old men were white. The four old men were all in grand clothes and they wore grand hats. The Emperor wondered who those four old men were. He asked them, "Who are you?" The four old men went forward to report their names one by one. The first one said, "I am Tang Xuan Ming." The second one said, "I am Zhou Shu." The third one said, "I am Qi Li Ji." The fourth one said, "I am Cui Guang." The Emperor was astonished and asked, "I have been looking for you for many years and have sent envoys to invite you to come to the court. But you refused to come. Instead, you escaped into the mountains. Why have you come to assist my son?" The old men said, "Your Majesty is rude to your subordinates. We did not wish to be insulted by Your Majesty. So we went into hiding in the mountains. And we hear that the Crown Prince is benevolent and dutiful, very polite to people and respectful of virtuous and capable persons. All the people are willing to die for the Crown Prince. This is the reason why we have come to serve the Crown Prince." The Emperor said, "I hope you will do your best to assist the Crown Prince." The four old men went up and proposed a toast to the health of the Emperor. As the four old men were going back to their seats, the Emperor followed them with his eyes.

Then the Emperor pointed at the four old men and said to Qi Ji, "I in-tended to replace the Crown Prince. But these four old men have come to assist him. The Crown Prince has become strong. He is now supported by virtuous and capable persons. It is impossible to remove him from the posi-tion as the Crown Prince. The Empress will be your true master." Qi Ji wept. The Emperor said, "I will sing a song in the style of Chu and you will dance a dance in the style of Chu to my song." Then the Emperor sang in a sorrowful voice the following lines:

The great swan is taking off for the sky,

A thousand miles high will the great swan fly.

The strong wings of the swan are will carry it far and wide;

Far and wide will the great swan fly;

What can we do to a swan that flies high in the sky?

No arrow can harm a swan flying so high.

The Emperor repeated this song many times. Qi Ji wept sadly while she was dancing. Then the Emperor rose from his seat and left.

81. Premier Xiao Is Jailed

When Chen Xi rose in rebellion in 197 BC, we may recall, the Emperor had personally led an army to crush Chen Xi's rebellion. Han Xin planned to take this chance to attack Chang'an. The Empress adopted the stratagem proposed by Xiao He and killed Han Xin. When this was reported to the Emperor, who was at that time still in Handan, the Emperor sent an envoy to convey his greetings and his decision to grant an additional tax on 5,000 peasant households to Xiao He. The Emperor also granted him a party of 500 body guards. This was considered a grand reward. All the ministers and generals who remained in Chang'an came to express their congratulations to him. Only Zhao Ping, a former official of the Qin Dynasty, came to mourn for him. He said to Xiao He, "Trouble will come very soon. The Emperor is now out of Guanzhong and exposed himself in danger fighting a war against the rebels. But you remain in Guanzhong. You are not exposed to arrows and stones. But the Emperor has increased your enjoyment of the tax on the peasant households and granted you a party of body guards. Recently Han Xin rebelled in Guanzhong. The Emperor also suspects that you will betray him. The Emperor is not doing you a favor in granting you a party of five hundred guards. You'd better not accept the additional tax benefits and bodyguards. I suggest that you donate all your properties to the army to support the expedition. In this way, you will please the Emperor." Xiao He agreed with Zhao Ping's suggestion and contributed all his properties to support the expedition. The Emperor was really pleased.

In autumn of 196 BC, Ying Bu rose in rebellion. The Emperor personally commanded the expedition to suppress the rebellion. During the expedition, the Emperor sent several teams of envoys back to Guanzhong to visit Xiao He and convey his greetings to Xiao He. Since the Emperor was out of Guanzhong on an expedition and could not attend to the affairs of Guanzhong, Xiao He did his best to take care of the people in Guanzhong and contributed all he had to the army as he had done during the expedition against Chen Xi. One of his subordinates said to him, "Your clan will be exterminated very soon. As the premier of the Han Dynasty, you are in the highest position of the government. The Emperor once said that you ranked the first among those who had made great contributions in the establishment of the Han Dynasty. Even if you make further contributions, you cannot be promoted to a position higher than the position of the premier. Ten years have passed since you first entered Guanzhong. Most of the time, the Emperor has been fighting outside the area of Guanzhong. You have been in charge of the affairs of this area while the Emperor was not in Guanzhong. You are very popular here and you have earned the support of the people here. The people here live in peace. The reason the Emperor frequently sent envoys to convey his greetings to you is that he is afraid that you will usurp the power to rule the area of Guanzhong. You are already under suspicion. My suggestion is that you should buy a lot of land. You can force the peasants to sell their land to you at low prices. In this way, you will show the Emperor that you are actually a greedy person and have no intention to seize the power to rule the area of Guanzhong. Then the Emperor will be at ease." Xiao He accepted his suggestion and acted as the person had proposed. When the Emperor heard that the premier was busy buying land, his suspicions were allayed.

When the Emperor in his carriage was returning from the expedition against Ying Bu, he came across some people kneeling along the route. They presented to the Emperor written complaints accusing Premier Xiao He of forcing the peasants to sell their land to him at low prices. When the Emperor went back to Chang'an, Premier Xiao He went to the palace to see the Emperor. The Emperor pointed at the thick stack of written complaints, laughed and said, "This is what you are doing to benefit the people!" Then the Emperor ordered Xiao He to take all the written complaints and said, "You should apologize to the people yourself!" Xiao He took the chance and said to the Emperor, "There is not enough cultivated land in Chang'an. But there is a lot of fertile land in Shanglin, the royal hunting ground. I hope Your Majesty will let peasants go into the royal hunting ground to cultivate lands in the openings in the forest. In harvest time the peasants can be allowed to take away the fruits and they should leave the stems and leaves for the animals in the hunting grounds." When the Emperor heard his suggestion, he was furious and said, "You must have taken bribes from the merchants to make this suggestion to me to let them into the royal hunting ground." He ordered Xiao He be put in jail immediately.

像　何　蕭

Portrait of Xiao He

Several days later, Officer Wang, who was in charge of all the Emperor's guards, asked the Emperor, "What serious crime has the premier committed that Your Majesty has put him into jail so urgently?" The Emperor said, "I heard that when Li Si was the premier for the First Emperor of the Qin Dynasty, he assigned all the benefits to the First Emperor of the Qin Dynasty and took all the blame for the emperor's errors upon himself. Now the premier has taken bribes from the merchants to ask me to let the peasants farm on the royal hunting ground, so as to please the people. That's why I have put him in jail." Officer Wang said, "Xiao He is the premier. His job is to see that every measure is taken for the benefit of the people. But Your Majesty suspects that he has taken bribes to do this. When Your Majesty was in a stalemate with Xiang Yu in the area of Xingyang for several years, and when Your Majesty was out of the area of Guanzhong on expeditions against Chen Xi and Ying Bu, the premier stayed in the area of Guanzhong. If the premier ever had any intention of seizing power in Guanzhong, that would have been the best time for him to do it. Then the territory in the area of Guanzhong would not have belonged to Your Majesty. The Premier did not think that it was right to take advantage of the situation at that time; why should he think that it is right to take bribes from other people at a time like this? Do you realize that one of the reasons why the Qin Dynasty fell is that the emperors of the Qin Dynasty never heard any criticism for their own mistakes? Li Si's taking all the blame for the emperor is not a good example to follow." The expression on the Emperor's face showed his regret for what he had done to the premier.

On that day, the Emperor sent an envoy with orders to set Xiao He free. Xiao He was already very old, and he was always cautious. As soon as he was out of jail, Xiao He went to the palace barefooted to express his thanks to the Emperor. The Emperor said, "You don't need to express your thanks to me. You have done what you had to do for the benefit of the people, at the risk of your own life. But I have refused to give the benefit to the people. I am only a very bad ruler, but you are a wise and virtuous premier. By arresting you I only made my mistakes known to the people all over China."

82. Lu Wan's Rebellion

And also Chen Xi rose up in rebellion, Lu Wan, the King of the State of Yan, had sent an army to attack the army of Chen Xi from northeast. At that time, Chen Xi sent Wang Huang into the Huns to ask for help; but Lu Wan sent Zhang Sheng, one of the ministers in the court of the State of Yan, to tell the Huns that Chen Xi's army had been defeated. When Zhang Sheng arrived, he spoke with Zang Yan, the son of Zang Tu, the former King of the State of Yan, who had been exiled to the area of the Huns. Zang Yan said to Zhang Sheng, "You are important to the King of the State of Yan because you are an expert in handling relations with the Huns. The reason why the King of the State of Yan still survives is that the kings have rebelled one after another and wars have broken out one after another, and the wars continue. Now you are working to speed up the fall of Chen Xi and others. If they are all destroyed, soon it will be the King of the State of Yan's turn. The Emperor will capture you very soon. Why don't you try to delay the King of Yan's attack against Chen Xi and make peace with the Huns? If the situation is favorable, Lu Wan can be the King of the State of Yan forever. If the Emperor presses hard, Lu Wan has the Huns to turn to for help." Zhang Sheng agreed with him, and he secretly asked the Huns to help Chen Xi to attack the State of Yan.

Lu Wan suspected that Zhang Sheng had united with the Huns to rebel against the Emperor. So he wrote a statement to the Emperor that Zhang Sheng had rebelled and asked for permission to exterminate all the family members of Zhang Sheng. When Zhang Sheng came back, he explained to the King of the State of Yan why his actions were for his own good. Then the King of the State of Yan wrote another statement to the Emperor, saying that it was a different person who had conspired to rebel. The King of the State of Yan released Zhang Sheng's family members. He sent Zhang Sheng and his family to the Huns and had him stay there as his envoy. He secretly sent Fan Qi to Chen Xi, asking him not to stop fighting against the Emperor.

When the Emperor led an expedition against Ying Bu, Chen Xi often stationed his army in the area of Dai. When Zhou Bo campaigned through the area of Dai and killed Chen Xi, one of Chen Xi's generals who had surrendered revealed that the King of the State of Yan had sent Fan Qi to conspire with Chen Xi. The Emperor sent an envoy to summon Lu Wan to Chang'an. Lu Wan refused to go, saying he was ill. The Emperor sent Shen Yi Ji, the Marquis of Piyang, and Zhao Yao, the Inspector General, to the State of Yan to summon the King of the State of Yan to Chang'an and at the same time made an investigation into the matter among his subordinates.

Lu Wan became more afraid and hid himself and avoided meeting the envoys. He said to his favorite courtiers, "Now the King of Changsha and I are the only kings who do not belong to the Liu family. Last spring, Han Xin, the Marquis of Huaiyin, was killed. Last summer, Peng Yue, King of the State of Liang, was killed. These two persons fell into traps set by Empress Lü Zhi. Now the Emperor is seriously ill, and power is in the hands of the Empress. This woman is wicked and intends to kill all the kings who do not bear the family name of Liu and those who have made great contributions." So Lu Wan made up his mind not to go with the envoys to Chang'an. Most of his retinue fled.

The words Lu Wan had said to his followers were revealed. Shen Yi Ji gathered all such information and reported it to the Emperor. The Emperor was very angry. Later, the Huns who had surrendered to the Han army said that Zhang Sheng was with the Huns as the envoy of the King of the State of Yan. Then the Emperor said, "Lu Wan has really rebelled." In February 195 BC, the Emperor appointed Fan Kuai premier and sent him with an army to attack Lu Wan. And the Emperor made his son Liu Jian King of the State of Yan.

Now, except for the King of Changsha and King of Nanyue, all the kings of the states in China bore the family name of Liu. The following table shows the kings of such states.

Name of the State	Name of the King of the State	Relation with Liu Bang, the Emperor	Capital of the State	Time in Which the King Was Made
The State of Chu	Liu Jiao	Liu Bang's younger brother	Pengcheng	201 BC
The State of Qi	Liu Fei	Liu Bang's eldest son	Linzi	201 BC
The State of Zhao	Liu Ru Yi	Liu Bang's third son	Handan	198 BC
The State of Dai	Liu Heng	Liu Bang's fourth son		196 BC
The State of Huainan	Liu Chang	Liu Bang's seventh son	Shouchun	196 BC
The State of Huaiyang	Liu You	Liu Bang's sixth son	Chen	196 BC

	Liu Bi	The son of Liu Bang's second brother	Wu	196 BC
The State of Wu				
The State of Liang	Liu Hui	Liu Bang's fifth son	Huaiyang	195 B.C
The State of Yan	Liu Jian	Liu Bang's eighth son	Ji	195 BC

General Fan Kuai's wife Lü Xu was Empress Lü Zhi's younger sister, so General Fan Kuai was considered to belong to the clique of Empress Lü Zhi. When General Fan Kuai was leading an army to pacify the rebellion of Lu Wan, some persons who disliked Fan Kuai spread rumors that Fan Kuai would kill Qi Ji and Liu Ru Yi, the King of the State of Zhao, after the Emperor died. When the rumor reached the ears of the Emperor, he was in a great rage. He said, "Fan Kuai thinks that I am very ill and he is looking forward to my death." After he had discussed the matter with Chen Ping, the Emperor summoned Zhou Bo to the palace. He ordered Chen Ping and Zhou Bo, "You two should ride very quickly to the army commanded by Fan Kuai. General Zhou Bo will replace Fan Kuai to command the army to con-tinue the expedition to pacify the rebellion of Lu Wan. Chen Ping should arrest Fan Kuai and execute him on the spot."

After they had got the Emperor's order, Chen Ping and General Zhou Bo dashed off with a party of soldiers to catch up with the army commanded by General Fan Kuai which was marching to the State of Yan. On the way, they discussed the matter. Chen Ping said, "General Fan Kuai is a very good friend of the Emperor. He has made great contributions to the war effort. And he is the husband of Lü Xu, who is Empress Lü Zhi's younger sister. He is a relative of the Emperor and occupies a very high position. The Emperor wants to kill him only because he is in a fit of rage. If Fan Kuai is really killed, the Emperor will regret later. So we'd better arrest him and put him in a carriage and send him back to Chang'an, and let the Emperor decide whether Fan Kuai should be executed." General Zhou Bo agreed with him.

When they were getting close, they stopped and ordered the soldiers to build a platform. They sent an envoy to the army to summoned Fan Kuai with the tally given by the Emperor. When General Fan Kuai found out that Chen Ping had come to convey the order of the Emperor, he immediately rode to see Chen Ping. As soon as Fan Kuai arrived, he was arrested and put into a prisoner carriage. Zhou Bo took over the power to command the army and continued on to the State of Yan. Chen Ping and the party of soldiers escorted General Fan Kuai on their way back to Chang'an. When Chen Ping reached Xingyang, an envoy sent by the Empress conveyed the order of the Emperor that Chen Ping should station his army in Xingyang with the army under the command of General Guan Ying.

After General Zhou Bo took over the command of the army to put down the rebellion of Lu Wan, he marched to the north. At that time, Lu Wan had run away to the foot of the Great Wall with the queen, all his concubines and maids, and several thousand cavalrymen. He stayed there in the hope that the Emperor would get well and would pardon him.

When the army under the command of General Zhou Bo reached Ji (now Beijing), the capital of the State of Yan, Zhou Bo launched an assault on the city. A fierce battle was fought. Di, the commander-in-chief of the army of the State of Yan; Yan, the premier of the State of Yan; Jing, the commander of the army of the prefecture; Shi, the inspector general of the State of Yan; and Ruo, the commander of the garrison of Ji, were all captured. Then Zhou Bo marched his army northwest. He defeated the Yan army in Shanglan (in the northwest part of Hebei Province), then defeated the Yan army in Juyang (in the northwest part of Hebei Province). And all the areas of the State of Yan were brought under control.

83. The Death of Liu Bang, the Emperor of the Han Dynasty

During the expedition against Ying Bu, Liu Bang was wounded by an arrow. The Emperor became seriously ill. The Empress sent for a very good doctor to treat the Emperor. The doctor examined the Emperor and said that he could cure the disease. But the Emperor said, "I started my career as a common person by killing the snake with a sword three feet long, and now I have become the Emperor with the power to rule all over China. This is Heaven's will. Now my life is decided by Heaven's will. Even the best doctor cannot cure me." He had decided not to treat his disease. He paid the doctor handsomely and sent him away.

The Empress asked the Emperor, "After Your Majesty passes away, if Xiao He dies, who can be appointed as premier?" The Emperor said, "Cao Shen can be the premier." The Empress asked, "Who will be next?" The Emperor said, "Wang Ling. But Wang Ling is not very bright. Chen Ping can assist him. Chen Ping is a wise man, but it will be difficult for him to be premier alone. Zhou Bo is honest and kind but not highly literate. But it is Zhou Bo who will save the royal family of Liu. He may be appointed minister in charge of the national military affairs." The Empress asked who could be the next. The Emperor said that he could not tell. In April 195 BC, Liu Bang died in Changle Palace at the age of sixty-one.

The Empress kept the death of the Emperor a secret for four days. The Empress said to Shen Yi Ji, "The generals followed the Emperor when the Emperor rose in Pei as a commoner. They are now subordinate to the Emperor. They are not happy about it. They all think that they are qualified to be emperors themselves. Now the Crown Prince will ascend the throne. They will not be willing to serve the young emperor. If we don't kill them all, the whole realm will break apart." Someone overheard this and told General Li Shang. General Li Shang went to see Shen Yi Ji. General Li Shang said, "I have got information that the Emperor has passed away. But the death of the Emperor has been kept secret for four days and has not been announced to the public. The Empress intends to kill all of the generals. If she does this, the whole realm will be in danger. Chen Ping and General Guan Ying with an army of 100,000 men are now garrisoned in Xingyang. General Fan Kuai and General Zhou Bo are commanding 200,000 men in the expedition to pacify the State of Yan. If they find out that the Emperor is dead and all the generals have been killed, they will unite with each other and march to Guanzhong. The ministers will rebel in Chang'an. The kings will rebel outside Guanzhong. Then the whole realm will be in chaos. The Han Dynasty will fall very soon." Shen Yi Ji immediately conveyed what General Li Shang had said to the Empress. The Empress recognized the danger, and she announced the death of the Emperor.

When Chen Ping got the news, he hurried back to Chang'an. He went into the palace to mourn the death of the Emperor. He cried so sadly that the Empress was deeply moved. He reported to the Empress that he had carried out the order of the Emperor to arrest Fan Kuai but he had not executed him, and that Fan Kuai would be escorted back to Chang'an. The Empress said, "You are very tired now. You may go back to have a rest." But Chen Ping insisted that he should stay in the palace to protect the royal family. So the Empress appointed him commander of the guards of the palace. Later, Fan Kuai was escorted back to Chang'an and was released by the Empress. He was given back the title of Marquis of Wuyang. Lü Xu, Fan Kuai's wife, presented an accusation against Chen Ping to the Empress, but the Empress ignored Lü Xu's accusation because she knew that Chen Ping had actually saved the life of Fan Kuai.

In May the Emperor was buried in Changling (now in the northeast of Xianyang City, Shaanxi Province). In the same month, Liu Ying, the Crown Prince, ascended the throne of the Han Dynasty at the age of sixteen. Lü Zhi, the Empress and mother of Liu Ying, was made Empress Dowager. In accordance with the Chinese customs at that time, a posthumous name was given to emperors when they passed away. Discussing the matter, the ministers said, "The Emperor rose from a commoner. He restored peace out of chaos in China. He is the ancestor of the Han Dynasty. He has made the greatest contribution." So it was decided that his posthumous name should be Han Gaozu, meaning the ancestor of the Han Dynasty who had made the greatest contribution.

84. TROUBLES IN THE PALACE AFTER LIU BANG'S DEATH

Liu Bang had tried several times to replace the Crown Prince Liu Ying
with Liu Ru Yi, so the Empress hated Liu Ru Yi and his mother Qi Ji very
much. She did not do anything to them when Liu Bang was alive. But as
soon as Liu Bang died, and Liu Ying ascended the throne, Lü Zhi, now the
Empress Dowager, took action. She ordered Qi Ji jailed. In jail, Qi Ji wore
the clothes of a prisoner. She had to husk rice with a mortar and pestle. She
would recite the following lines while she was husking rice, "My son is a
king but I am a slave. My son is 3,000 miles away."

The Empress Dowager intended to kill Liu Ru Yi. She first summoned
Liu Ru Yi to Chang'an. But Zhou Chang, the premier of the State of Zhao,
refused to let the young King of the State of Zhao go. He said to the envoys
sent by the Empress Dowager, "Emperor Gaozu entrusted me to protect the
King of the State of Zhao. The King of the State of Zhao is still young. He
is only twelve years old. I hear that the Empress Dowager hates his mother
and has thrown her into jail. She wants to get the King of the State of Zhao
to Chang'an and kill him together with his mother. I do not dare to let the

King of the State of Zhao go to Chang'an. The King is ill. He cannot go to Chang'an."

Then the Empress Dowager summoned Zhou Chang to Chang'an. Zhou Chang had to go. After Zhou Chang had arrived in Chang'an, the Empress Dowager summoned Liu Ru Yi again. Without the protection of Zhou Chang, the young King of the State of Zhao had to go to Chang'an from Handan. Emperor Liu Ying knew that his mother hated Liu Ru Yi, so Liu Ying personally met him in Bashang. Then he put his younger brother in his own palace. He kept his brother beside him and tried in every way to protect him. But one day in December, Emperor Liu Ying had to get up early to practice arrow shooting. The King of the State of Zhao was too young to get up so early, so he stayed in bed. After Emperor Liu Ying left, the Empress Dowager sent a person to the Emperor's palace and forced the young King of the State of Zhao to drink poison. When Emperor Liu Ying came back, he found that the King of the State of Zhao was already dead.

The Empress Dowager then had Qi Ji's hands and legs cut off, her eyes gouged out, and made her deaf and dumb with some poisonous potion. The Empress Dowager put Qi Ji in a toilet and asked Liu Ying, the new Emperor, to see this "human pig." When Emperor Liu Ying saw the "human pig," he did not recognize who she was. When he was told that it was Qi Ji, he burst into tears. He fell very ill and could not attend to the state affairs. He sent a person to tell the Empress Dowager, "This is an inhuman atrocity. Although I am your son, I do not have the ruling power." From then on, he indulged himself in sensual pleasure and did not hold court any more. After Liu Ru Yi, King of the State of Zhao, was killed, the Empress Dowager moved Liu You, King of the State of Huaiyang, to be King of the State of Zhao.

85. Cao Shen Succeeds Xiao He as Premier of the Han Dynasty

In summer 193 BC, Xiao He, the premier of the Han Dynasty, was seriously ill. Emperor Liu Ying went to visit Xiao He. The Emperor asked, "When you pass away, who can succeed you as the premier?" Xiao He said, "Your Majesty knows better than I." The Emperor said, "Cao Shen?" Xiao He nodded and said, "Your Majesty has got the right person." In July 193 BC, Xiao He died.

When Cao Shen, the premier of the State of Qi, learned that Xiao He had died, he told his followers to get ready for the journey to Chang'an because he was sure that he would be appointed the premier of the Han Dynasty. Cao Shen had been the premier of the State of Qi for nine years. During this period, Cao Shen had developed a system to administrate the State of Qi. He adopted the policy of "governing the state by doing nothing against nature." He let the people of the State of Qi live in peace. The government of the State of Qi would do nothing to disturb the peaceful life of the people. So the people of the State of Qi were satisfied with life and all the people said that Cao Shen was a very good premier.

Soon after, the envoy sent by Emperor Liu Ying arrived in Linzi, the capital of the State of Qi, to summon Cao Shen to Chang'an to take up the position of the premier of the Han Dynasty.

Portrait of Cao Shen

When Cao Shen arrived in Chang'an and took up the position of the premier of the Han Dynasty, he strictly followed all the policies laid down by Xiao He and did not make any changes to them. He selected honest people who were not good at talking and writing but who were good at doing practical work to be officials in the office of the premier. Cao Shen's policy of "governing by doing nothing against nature" was adopted by the government of the Han Dynasty.

Cao Shen stayed in the position as the Premier of the Han Dynasty for three years. During this period, the whole realm was in peace. Cao Shen died in August 190 BC. People sang the following lines in praise of Cao Shen, "Xiao He made the laws and policies which are perfect and fair. Cao Shen succeeded Xiao He's position as the premier. He followed the laws and policies made by Xiao He and made no changes. The whole realm is now peaceful. The people now enjoy peace and tranquility."

After Cao Shen died, Wang Ling was appointed first premier, and Chen Ping was appointed second premier.

86. The Death of Zhang Liang, Marquis of Liu

Zhang Liang had made great contributions to the establishment of the Han Dynasty. In his later years, he retired from the political scene. He practiced to be an immortal. He began to practice "breatharianism." He did not eat or drink. But not long later, Emperor Liu Bang died. Empress Dowager Lü Zhi needed his help. So she forced him to eat and drink again. She said, "Life is very short. Why should you treat yourself like that?" Zhang Liang had to eat and drink again. In summer of 189 BC, Zhang Liang died. In his funeral, a yellow stone which he had found in Gucheng Hill in Jibei (now Tai'an, Shandong Province), was buried with him.

87. Empress Dowager Lü Zhi Takes Power

In order to better control Emperor Liu Ying, the Empress Dowager married her daughter's daughter to Emperor Liu Ying. She was the daughter of Zhang Ao and Princess Liu Yuan. That is to say, she was Emperor Liu Ying's niece. The Empress Dowager made her Empress. Since she was Zhang Ao's daughter, she was called Empress Zhang. For several years, Empress Zhang did not have any children. When one of the many concubines of Emperor Liu Ying got pregnant, under the instruction of the Empress Dowager, Empress Zhang pretended to be pregnant. When that concubine gave birth to a boy, Empress Zhang took away the child as her own and the Empress Dowager had that concubine killed. Liu Ying was on the throne for seven years and he died in August 188 BC at the age of twenty-three. Empress Dowager Lü Zhi put that baby on the throne of the Han Dynasty.

At the funeral of Emperor Liu Ying, Empress Dowager Lü Zhi cried very loudly but there were no tears in her eyes. Zhang Pi Qiang, Zhang Liang's son, was an attendant of Emperor Liu Ying. When he saw that the Empress Dowager was crying without tears in her eyes, he said to Premier Wang Ling, "Emperor Liu Ying was the only son of the Empress Dowager. Now he is dead, but the Empress Dowager is not crying sadly. Do you know why?" Wang Ling asked, "Why?" Zhang Pi Qiang said, "Her only son is dead. She has no other powerful son to turn to. She is afraid of the ministers and generals such as you. She means to get rid of you all. If you appoint Lü Tai, Lü Lu and Lü Chan as generals to command the imperial guards in the north and south of the capital and invite the members of the Lü family to take charge of state affairs, the Empress Dowager will be at ease and you will avoid disaster." Premier Wang Ling did what Zhang Pi Qiang had suggested. Then the Empress Dowager was at ease and began to cry sadly.

After Liu Ying died, all the power was in the hands of Empress Dowager Lü Zhi. She wanted very much to make her brothers and her brothers' sons kings. But Liu Bang had made a rule with all the ministers and generals that no one with a family name other than the family name of Liu should be made king. So she summoned all the ministers and generals to court. She asked Premier Wang Ling's opinion. Wang Ling said bluntly, "Emperor Gaozu made all the ministers and generals swear to destroy those kings who are not the descendants of the royal family of Liu. Making members of the Lü family kings goes against the rule." The Empress Dowager did not like that answer. When she asked the opinions of Chen Ping, the second premier, and Zhou Bo, the minister in charge of the national military affairs, they said, "When Emperor Gaozu was on the throne, His Majesty made his brothers and sons kings. Now you are in power. You may do what you like. There is nothing wrong in your making the Lü family members kings." After court, Wang Ling castigated Chen Ping and Zhou Bo angrily. "When Emperor Gaozu made the rule, weren't you there? Now Emperor Gaozu is dead and Empress Dowager Lü Zhi is in power. You two go against the rule to please the Empress Dowager. Won't you feel ashamed when you die and have to meet Emperor Gaozu in heaven?" Chen Ping said, "We are not as good as you are at openly opposing the Empress Dowager's attempt to make the members of the Lü family kings. But as for saving the royal family of Liu, you will not be as good as us."

Empress Dowager Lü Zhi deprived Premier Wang Ling of his power by appointing him tutor to the young emperor. Wang Ling was angry and resigned due to "poor health." Empress Dowager Lü Zhi appointed Chen Ping first premier and Shen Yi Ji second premier. Empress Dowager Lü Zhi made her elder brother Lü Ze, who had already died, King of Dao Wu. This was the first king from the Lü family Empress Dowager Lü Zhi made. In April 187 BC, Lü Zhi made Lü Ze's eldest son Lü Tai King of the State of Lü. Empress Dowager Lü Zhi ordered Liu Shang, the King of the State of Qi, the eldest son of Liu Fei (Liu Fei had died in 189 BC), to cede the territory of Jinan Prefecture (now the area around Jinan, Shandong Province) and made it the territory of the State of Lü. In November 187 BC, Lü Tai, King of Lü, died, and his son Lü Jia succeeded the throne of the State of Lü.

When the baby emperor was a little older, he heard that he was not Empress Dowager Zhang's son. He heard that his mother had been killed. He said angrily, "It is unjust for Empress Dowager Zhang to kill my mother and take me as her own son. I will avenge my mother when I grow up." Lü Zhi kept the little emperor in an abandoned, cold house. She told the ministers and generals that the little emperor was insane and was not suitable to be emperor. The ministers and generals had to agree with her. In February 184 BC, Lü Zhi had the baby emperor killed and made Liu Yi, another son of Liu Ying, emperor.

After Liu Yi was made Emperor, Lü Zhi changed his name into Liu Hong. The Emperor was still very young, and Lü Zhi held the power of the Han Dynasty.

In May 186 BC, Empress Dowager Lü Zhi made Liu Zhang Marquis of Zhuxu (now Langyatai of Jiaonan County, Shandong Province). Liu Zhang was the second son of Liu Fei, the former King of the State of Qi, and was the younger brother of the present King of the State of Qi. Liu Zhang was a strong and brave young man. Empress Dowager summoned him to Chang'an and appointed him commander of the guards of the palace. In order to control him, the Empress Dowager married a girl of the Lü family to him.

In October 183 BC, Empress Dowager Lü Zhi deposed Lü Jia as the King of the State of Lü because Lü Jia had carried out many unlawful activities. In

November 183 BC, she made Lü Chan, the younger brother of Lü Tai, King of the State of Lü.

In April 182 BC, Empress Dowager Lü Zhi made Liu Xing Ju Marquis of Dongmao (now Maoping, Shandong Province). Liu Xing Ju was the younger brother of Liu Shang, the King of the State of Qi, and Liu Zhang, Marquis of Zhuxu. Liu Xing Ju was also a strong and brave man. He was appointed a commander of the guards of the palace.

In December 182 BC, Empress Dowager Lü Zhi summoned Liu You, King of the State of Zhao, to Chang'an. Empress Dowager Lü Zhi had married one of the daughters of her brothers to Liu You. But Liu You did not love that girl at all. He loved other concubines. This girl from the Lü family was angry and lodged a false accusation against him, complaining to Empress Dowager Lü Zhi that Liu You was going to kill her after Empress Dowager Lü Zhi died. Empress Dowager Lü Zhi kept him in a house and did not give him any food. Liu You, King of the State of Zhao, was starved to death.

In February 181 BC, Empress Dowager Lü Zhi moved Liu Hui, the King of the State of Liang, to be King of the State of Zhao. At the same time, she moved Lü Chan, the King of the State of Lü, to be the King of the State of Liang. Lü Chan did not go to the State of Liang to take the throne of the State of Liang. Empress Dowager Lü Zhi asked him to stay in Chang'an to be the tutor of the young emperor. Her purpose was to strengthen the power of the Lü family in the capital. Liu Hui was very unhappy about being moved to be King of the State of Zhao. Empress Dowager Lü Zhi forced him to marry Lü Chan's daughter and made her queen of the State of Zhao. Liu Hui did not like the queen. He loved one of his concubines. The queen sent someone to kill that concubine by forcing her to drink poison. Liu Hui, King of the State of Zhao, could not stand that anymore and committed suicide.

Empress Dowager Lü Zhi sent an envoy to ask Liu Heng, the King of the State of Dai, whether he wanted to be the King of the State of Zhao. Liu Heng politely declined the invitation and said that he would rather stay in the border area. So Empress Dowager Lü Zhi made her brother's son Lü Lu King of the State of Zhao. In September, Liu Jian, King of the State of Yan, died. He had only one son born by one of his concubines. Empress Dowager Lü Zhi sent a person to kill that child. Then, since there was no one to succeed the throne of the State of Yan, Empress Dowager Lü Zhi made Lü Tong, a son of her brother, King of the State of Yan.

Liu Zhang, the Marquis of Zhuxu, was exasperated by Empress Dowager Lü Zhi's action in killing Emperor Gaozu's sons and grandsons. One day in July 181 BC, Empress Dowager Lü Zhi held a banquet to entertain the ministers and generals and the members of the Lü family. Empress Dowager Lü Zhi appointed Liu Zhang to supervise the banquet and see to it that no one would become so drunk as to do anything impolite. Liu Zhang said to the Empress Dowager, "I am a warrior by nature. May I punish those who drink too much in accordance with military law?" Empress Dowager said, "Yes, you may." Then the banquet began and went on happily, and the people were warm with wine. Then Liu Zhang said to the Empress Dowager, "May I sing a song of growing crops?" Empress Dowager Lü Zhi smiled and said, "You grew up in the palace. Do you really know how to grow crops? Anyway, go ahead with your song." Liu Zhang sang the following lines:

I prepare the fields well to grow the species of the crop I choose,
I sow many seeds of the crop and plant the seedlings sparsely
So as to ensure that the seedlings of the crop may grow well.
If I find any seedlings which are not of the species I choose,
I weed them out resolutely.

When Empress Dowager Lü Zhi heard the song, the color of her face changed and she became silent. A moment later, one member of the Lü family was drunk and ran out of the place of the banquet. Liu Zhang ran after him, caught up with him and killed him with a stroke of his sword. Liu Zhang came back, wiping the blood on his sword. He reported to Empress Dowager Lü Zhi, "A drunkard tried to run away. I have executed him in accordance with military law." Empress Dowager Lü Zhi and all the people present were shocked. Since Empress Dowager Lü Zhi had promised that Liu Zhang could punish drunkards in accordance with military law, there was nothing she could say. She had to dismiss the banquet. From then on, the members of the Lü family were afraid of Liu Zhang.

88. The Death of Empress Dowager Lü Zhi

In March 180 BC, Empress Dowager Lü Zhi held a ceremony in the outskirt of Chang'an to offer sacrifices to the Gods for getting rid of disasters and praying for blessings. On her way back to Chang'an city, when her carriage was passing Zhidao, some kind of animal which resembled a big dog rushed up her carriage and thrust its head at Empress Dowager Lü Zhi, by her armpit, but all of a sudden the animal disappeared. She was terribly frightened. When she got back to Chang'an she asked the fortunetellers to explain it. They come to the conclusion that Liu Ru Yi, the former King of the State of Zhao, who had been murdered by Empress Dowager Lü Zhi, had come for revenge. From then on the wound in the armpit of Empress Dowager Lü Zhi began to ulcerate and she became ill.

By July 180 BC, Empress Dowager Lü Zhi was seriously ill. She knew that she was going to die. She had to make arrangements to strengthen the power of the Lü family before she died. She appointed Lü Lu (King of the State of Zhao) commander-in-chief of the army and ordered him to command the army in the north of the capital, and ordered Lü Chan (King of the State of Liang) to command the army in the south of the capital. Empress Dowager Lü Zhi said to Lü Lu and Lü Chan, "All the ministers and the generals are upset with my making the members of the Lü family kings. After I die, they will take action. The emperor is still very young. You must send soldiers to guard the palace. Don't announce the news of my death. Otherwise, you will be helpless." She made Lü Chan premier. She ordered Emperor Liu Hong to marry a daughter of Lü Lu and appointed that girl empress. Not long later, Empress Dowager Lü Zhi died.

89. The Lü Family is Exterminated

The members of the Lü family thought they'd better stage an armed rebellion. But they were afraid of Premier Chen Ping and General Zhou Bo, so they hesitated to put their plan into action.

Liu Zhang, Marquis of Zhuxu, knew the members of the Lü family were plotting, because his wife was Lü Lu's daughter. He secretly sent an envoy with a letter to his brother Liu Shang, the King of the State of Qi. The letter read, "The situation is critical now. The members of the Lü family are going to stage a rebellion to take the power from the royal family of Liu. When you get my letter, you should raise a great army and march your army westward to Chang'an to kill the members of the Lü family. The Marquis of Dongmao and I will operate within Chang'an in coordination with your attack from outside. When the members of the Lü family are done away with, you may declare yourself emperor and take the throne of the Han Dynasty."

When the King of the State of Qi got the letter, he sent out letters to the kings of other states stating the crimes the members of the Lü family had committed and calling on the kings of the other states to send armies to kill the members of the Lü family. Then he raised a great army and marched westward.

When Lü Chan got the information that the King of the State of Qi was marching his army westward, he ordered General Guan Ying to lead an army to attack the King of the State of Qi. General Guan Ying marched his army out of Guanzhong. On the way, he thought over the situation. "Now the members of the Lü family hold the power to command the army in Guanzhong. They are threatening the survival of the royal family of Liu and they are planning to make a member of the Lü family emperor. If I defeat the State of Qi, I will be helping the members of the Lü family in their conspiracy." So when he reached Xingyang, he stationed his army there. He sent out envoys to the State of Qi and other states to express his intention to make peace with the State of Qi and other states and wait till the members of the Lü family carried out their conspiracy, and said he would unite with the State of Qi and other states to exterminate the members of the Lü family. When the King of the State of Qi got the message, he stopped marching his army westward and waited for the situation to change.

The members of the Lü family were keen to stage a rebellion, but they were afraid of Zhou Bo and Liu Zhang in Chang'an. They were also afraid that General Guan Ying would betray them in Xingyang. And they were afraid of the armies of the State of Qi and of the other states. They wanted to delay their rebellion until the time when the army under the command of General Guan Ying and the army of the State of Qi were locked in battle against each other. So Lü Chan and Lü Lu held off. At that time, Lü Lu commanded the army stationed in the north of the capital, and Lü Chan commanded the army stationed in the south of the capital. So the capital was under the control of the members of the Lü family, and there was nothing the ministers could do about it.

When Chen Ping and Zhou Bo got wind that Lü Zhi had died, they decided to take action. Although Zhou Bo was the minister in charge of military affairs for the Han Dynasty, he could not command the army because the tiger-shaped tally was in the hands of Lü Lu. Li Ji, the son of General Li Shang, was a good friend of Lü Lu. Zhou Bo and Chen Ping, after careful discussion with each other, sent some persons to kidnap Li Shang and forced him to ask his son Li Ji to persuade Lü Lu to hand over the tiger-shaped tally to Zhou Bo. Then Li Ji went to see Lü Lu and said to him, "Emperor Gaozu and Empress Dowager Lü Zhi pacified the whole realm together. Emperor Gaozu made nine kings and Empress Dowager Lü Zhi made three kings. All these decisions were discussed among the ministers and were announced to the public. All the ministers and generals think that all these decisions are proper. Now Empress Dowager Lü Zhi is dead. The emperor is young. You are the King of the State of Zhao. You have chosen not to go to the state of which you have been made king. Instead, you are holding military power as the commander-in-chief. All the ministers and generals hate you. Why don't you turn in the tiger-shaped tally and hand over the military power to Zhou Bo, the minister in charge of military affairs, and persuade Lü Chan to turn in the seal of the premier, make peace with the ministers and generals, and go back to your states? Then you and your son and generations to come may enjoy the rights as the kings of your states forever. Believe me, that is your best course." Lü Lu thought that Li Ji was his good friend and would not deceive him. So he gave up the tiger-shaped tally and handed the military power over to Zhou Bo.

When Zhou Bo went into the tent of the commander of the army in the north of the capital with the tiger-shaped tally, Lü Lu had left. Zhou Bo gathered all the soldiers together and issued an order. "Those who are for the Lü family, take off your right sleeves and expose your right arms. Those who are for the Liu family, take off your left sleeves and expose your left arms." All the soldiers took off their left sleeves and exposed their left arms. So Zhou Bo took command of the army in the north of the capital. But the army in the south was not under his command. Premier Chen Ping ordered Liu Zhang to assist Zhou Bo. Zhou Bo ordered Liu Zhang to guard the gate of the camps. Zhou Bo ordered Cao Qu, Cao Shen's son, to go to Weiyang Palace to tell the commander of the guards of the palace to prevent Lü Chan from going into the palace. Lü Chan did not know that Lü Lu had left the army in the north of the capital. He went to Weiyang Palace intending to kill the Emperor and usurp the throne.

But when he arrived at the gate of the palace with a party of soldiers, he was not allowed into the palace. Since he could not enter the palace, Lü Chan walked back and forth in front the gate of the palace. Cao Qu was afraid that Lü Chan would force his way into the palace, so he immediately rode back to tell Zhou Bo that the situation was critical in the palace. Zhou Bo sent Liu Zhang with a thousand soldiers to protect the emperor. By the time Liu Zhang hurried to Weiyang Palace with a thousand men and en-

tered the gate of the palace, Lü Chan had forced his way into the yard of
the palace. Liu Zhang and Lü Chan confronted each other for quite a long
time. At noon, Liu Zhang attacked. And the soldiers of the two sides began
to fight. After a short combat, Lü Chan found that he was no match for Liu
Zhang and tried to run away. At that time a great wind rose and sand and
stones were blown up. The yard of the palace was in great confusion. Lü
Chan took this chance to run into an outhouse. But Liu Zhang saw him and
ran after him into the outhouse, and he killed Lü Chan with one stroke of
his sword.

Liu Zhang rode back to the army in the north of the capital. He reported
to Zhou Bo that he had killed Lü Chan. Zhou Bo rose from his chair, made a
bow to Liu Zhang and said to him, "Congratulations! The only person I worried about was Lü Chan. Now that he has been killed, the whole realm will
be in peace." Then he issued orders to arrest the members of the Lü family.
Shortly, Lü Lu was arrested and executed. Lü Xu was arrested and beaten
to death. All the members of the Lü family, no matter old or young, were all
killed. Zhou Bo sent envoys to the State of Yan to kill Lü Tong, the King of
the State of Yan made by Empress Dowager Lü Zhi.

Zhou Bo sent Liu Zhang to inform the King of the State of Qi that all the
members of the Lü family had been killed and to ask the King of the State of
Qi to lead his army back to the State of Qi. General Guan Ying also led his
army back to Chang'an.

90. Liu Heng, King of the State of Dai, Ascends the Throne of the Han Dynasty

The ministers and generals held a secret meeting to discuss what to do
after the members of the Lü family had been exterminated. They said, "Emperor Liu Hong and his two younger brothers are actually not sons of Emperor Liu Ying. They were the sons of somebody else but Empress Dowager
Lü Zhi took them from their mothers and killed their mothers. Then she
secretly put them in the imperial harem and made Emperor Liu Ying believe
that they were his own sons. Empress Dowager Lü Zhi made Liu Hong emperor for the purpose of strengthening the power of the Lü family. Now the
members of the Lü family have been exterminated. If we let this emperor
stay on the throne, all of us will be killed when he grows up and is empow-

ered. We'd better choose a highly virtuous descendant of Emperor Gaozu and put him on the throne."

One of the ministers said, "Now among the sons of Emperor Gaozu who are still alive, Liu Heng, the King of the State of Dai, is the eldest. He is benevolent and filial, honest and kind. His mother Bo Ji is prudent and kindhearted. He is the most suitable and justifiable person to be the emperor of the Han Dynasty." All of the ministers and generals agreed with this suggestion.

After the ministers and generals had reached an agreement, they sent a secret envoy to the State of Dai to invite Liu Heng to Chang'an to take the throne of the Han Dynasty. When the King of the State of Dai got the invitation, he discussed this matter with his courtiers. After discussion with the courtiers and consultation with his mother Bo Ji, Liu Heng decided to accept the invitation.

Then Liu Heng sent his uncle Bo Zhao to Chang'an to see Zhou Bo. Zhou Bo and Chen Ping said to him, "Of the sons of Emperor Gaozu who still survive, the King of the State of Dai is the eldest. He has the legitimate right to succeed to the throne of the Han Dynasty. We sincerely invite him to Chang'an to ascend the throne of the Han Dynasty." Bo Zhao immediately hurried back to Jinyang (now Taiyuan, Shanxi Province), the capital of the State of Dai, and said to the King of the State of Dai, "Zhou Bo and Chen Ping are very sincere in inviting Your Majesty to Chang'an to ascend the throne of the Han Dynasty. There is no doubt about it."

Then Liu Heng set out for Chang'an with his mother and courtiers. When the procession reached the bridge over the Weishui River which was about two kilometers away from Chang'an, Premier Chen Ping, General Zhou Bo and the ministers and generals were waiting there. As the carriage of the King of the State of Dai reached the bridge, all the ministers and generals knelt down on their knees, touched their heads on the ground, and submitted themselves to the King of the State of Dai. The King of the State of Dai stepped down from his carriage and bowed to them and expressed his heartfelt thanks. General Zhou Bo knelt down in front of the King of the State of Dai and presented him the Seal of the Emperor. The King of the State of Dai accepted the seal, expressed his thanks and said, "We shall discuss this matter when we reach the residence for the King of the State of Dai in Chang'an."

The King of the State of Dai and his entourage arrived in Chang'an in the second September of 180 BC (180 BC was an intercalary year which had two Septembers). They stayed in the residence of the King of the State of Dai. All the ministers and generals went to the residence of the King of the State of Dai. Chen Ping and Zhou Bo knelt down in front of the King of the State of Dai and said, "Liu Hong, the present emperor, and his two younger brothers are not true sons of Emperor Liu Ying. He should not be the emperor any more. Your Majesty is the eldest living son of Emperor Gaozu. Your Majesty has the legitimate right to succeed to the throne of the Han Dynasty. We hope that Your Majesty will ascend the throne of the Han Dynasty." Then the King of the State of Dai ascended the throne of the Han Dynasty.

Portrait of Emperor Wen of the Han Dynasty

Liu Xing Ju and Xiahou Ying with the consent of Emperor Liu Heng went into Weiyang Palace. They force Liu Hong to leave the palace, and kept him in a house near the palace.

In that evening, Xiahou Ying carried Liu Heng, the new Emperor, in the carriage for the emperor from the residence of the King of the State of Dai to Weiyang Palace.

Soon after, the deposed emperor Liu Hong and his two younger brothers were killed in their houses.

Emperor Liu Heng made his mother Bo Ji Empress Dowager. Twenty-five years before, Xu Fu, the fortuneteller, had predicted that Bo Ji would give birth to an emperor. Now Bo Ji's son Liu Heng had become the Emperor of the Han Dynasty. Xu Fu's prediction had at last come true. Liu Heng was wise and virtuous. Under his reign, China entered into a period of peace and prosperity.